Christian Marriage

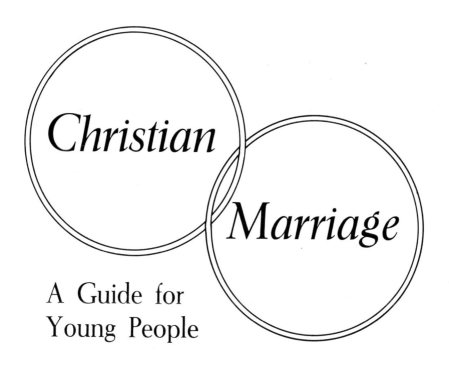

Christian Marriage

A Guide for
Young People

by Rev. Thomas E. Langer, M.A.

SENIOR RELIGION INSTRUCTOR
AQUINAS HIGH SCHOOL, LA CROSSE, WISCONSIN

Milwaukee   THE BRUCE PUBLISHING COMPANY

NIHIL OBSTAT:

> JOHN A. SCHULIEN, S.T.D.
> *Censor deputatus*

IMPRIMATUR:

> ✠ JOHN P. TREACY
> *Bishop of La Crosse*
> June 9, 1962

Library of Congress Catalog Card Number: 62–16837

© 1962 THE BRUCE PUBLISHING COMPANY
MADE IN THE UNITED STATES OF AMERICA

To my parents
from whom I have learned so much
about marriage

FOREWORD

Until the last decade it had been generally assumed that no education for marriage was necessary. This belief has lately been challenged, but there are still many who adhere to the old belief that such knowledge is gained instinctively. They would agree that training is necessary for other vocations. They would certainly agree that those entering religious life should have special training. They would not hire a secretary without special training, but education in the complicated relationships of marriage was considered unnecessary. One has to take an examination to get a driver's license, but as far as I know no examination is required to get a marriage license.

Even among those who urge education for marriage there is disagreement as to what should be taught. Emphasis has until recently been placed on the physical facts of marriage. Lately this has been de-emphasized. Now more accent is given to the psychological interrelationships of the married couple. A knowledge of the sacramental and theological aspects of marriage has been taken for granted because it was considered that these were a part of religious training.

With the increase in mixed marriages, some readily available source of information on these aspects of marriage became necessary. The result has been a rash of books, some good, many bad. Some have emphasized one aspect of marriage, some another. Few have presented a balanced consideration of marriage. Father Langer has attempted to do so in this book. His presentation is a balanced one giving to each aspect of the subject adequate but proportional space. He treats the sacramental, theological, psychological, and physical features of the subject in a lucid, easy-to-understand style. His discussion of vocation is clear and easy to comprehend. The treatment of this subject is equal to the best I have ever read. Overemphasis on the romantic aspects of marriage is avoided.

To the young couple approaching marriage this volume will be most helpful. This is especially true for the non-Catholic member of a mixed marriage who should have a clear understanding of what his prospective spouse believes about marriage in all its aspects. Even though both partners feel that they are adequately informed, a review to systematize their knowledge can be achieved by reading a suitable book together. Suitable books, such as this, will not mislead. A balanced, sound view of marriage is presented in the following pages which will provide a firm foundation for your marriage.

JOHN R. CAVANAGH, M.D.

AUTHOR'S PREFACE

A cynical comedian has defined marriage as a three-ring circus comprising engagement ring, wedding ring, and suffering! It's sad that this 'definition' always draws a laugh from the audience. Even married people seem to agree wryly that this is a realistic picture of the marital situation today. Marriage, however, is not supposed to be an occasion of suffering. It should not be described as one little boy recently did (he confused matrimony with purgatory) that "matrimony is that place between heaven and hell where we are punished for our sins."[1] Perhaps the reason why marriage has been aligned with "misery" is the fact that so many marriages today are failures. At the present time about one out of every four marriages ends in divorce, a total of approximately 400,000 divorces being granted each year.

In 1958, according to figures released from the Bureau of Vital Statistics of Washington, 52 per cent of all divorces granted were to couples married in their teens. From 1938–1958, 3 out of every 4 teen-age marriages ended in the divorce courts; 1 out of every 80 teen-age marriages involved adolescents attempting marriage for the second time.

Lack of Preparation for Matrimony

Every marriage failure discloses somewhat the same tragic picture. Young people are rushing into marriage without knowing what it is all about. They center their attention upon the wedding day and the honeymoon without trying to glimpse at the duties and responsibilities which lie hidden in the background. They are ignorant of the problems — physical, psychological, social, economic, as well as spiritual — which must be solved if the union is to endure and succeed. Preparation for marriage is essential if couples are to make a go of it! Judge Theodore B. Knutson of Minneapolis pointed this up recently. Sixty per cent of the divorces

[1] Rev. Henry V. Sattler, C.Ss.R., "Marriage is a Three-Ring Circus," *Our Sunday Visitor*, October 13, 1957.

granted since his court's family division was established affected those marriages contracted when one or both parties was less than 20 years old. "In almost every case," testified the Judge, "the young people had no premarriage counseling whatsoever."

Unfortunately, the amount of preparation available today appears to be far less than is needed. From his tour of 100 United States dioceses, Msgr. Irving A. DeBlanc, former director of the NCWC Family Life Bureau, found that 50 per cent of the Catholics who marry received no formal premarriage instruction and another 20 per cent got only one talk.[2] Father Edward V. Stanford, O.S.A., author of *Preparing for Marriage,* in a recent Chicago address stated that in the 1957–1958 school year less than 5 per cent of the Catholic high schools in the United States were offering marriage preparation courses. In the 1958–1959 school year, the figure increased to an estimated 20 per cent.[3]

Reasons for Preparing for Marriage

Some individuals may wonder why it is necessary to concern themselves with the details of marriage when marriage for them seems so far away. Let's take a look at the reasons:

1. People are marrying at an earlier age than ever before. In 1890, the average bride was 22 years old; the average groom, 26. Census Bureau figures show that in 1955 the average bride was about 20, the average groom 22½. Today there are more than 1,000,000 husbands and wives in the United States still in their teens. Experts expect this trend to continue for some time.

2. Although some persons are able to take a marriage course in college, the majority must reply on a high school course or their own reading program. Some dioceses do offer Pre-Cana instruction, but circumstances oftentimes arise which prevent you from attending them.

3. Today, you are being bombarded with more mass media about dating, love and sex than ever before. Only a conscientious study of Christian marriage can hope to rectify the distorted viewpoints found among so many people.

4. You are interested in the subject. A brief glance at the number of question and answer columns on dating, love and marriage more than prove your inquisitiveness. But you need more than informa-

---

[2] "Too Young to Marry," editorial, *America,* July 14, 1956, p. 358.
[3] *Catholic Standard,* May 8, 1959.

tion. Proper attitudes to marriage is what is important! This can come about through a systemized course of instructions.

5. The Church has spoken on the need for marriage instructions. Pius XI in his encyclical letter on marriage warns those who approach the sacrament to be "well disposed and well prepared, so that they will be able, as far as they can, to help each other in sustaining the vicissitudes of life, and yet more in attending to their eternal salvation and informing the inner man unto the fullness of the age of Christ."[4]

Reading Is Essential!

If you desire to get the most out of this study of marriage, additional reading is a necessity. At the end of each chapter there is appended a list of pamphlets, books, and articles for this purpose. Read as many of them as you can.

Recently a three-year survey of 600 senior students' reading habits on the subject of marriage in one large Midwestern high school singled out six books as outstanding reading. They are listed here to encourage you to read at least one of them during this course:

SUGGESTIONS FOR READING

Cana Is Forever, Rev. Charles Hugo Doyle (Tarrytown-on-Hudson, N. Y.: Nugent Press, 1949).

The Catholic Youth's Guide to Life and Love, Msgr. George A. Kelly (New York: Random House, 1960).

The Man for Her, Rev. Leo J. Kinsella (Oak Park, Ill.: Valiant Publications, 1957).

The Wife Desired, Rev. Leo J. Kinsella (Techny, Ill.: Divine Word Publications, 1953).

Three to Get Married, Most Rev. Fulton J. Sheen (New York: Appleton-Century-Crofts, 1951).

What They Ask About Marriage, Msgr. J. D. Conway (Chicago: Fides Publishers, 1955).

---

[4] Casti Connubii, Paulist Press, New York, p. 37.

ACKNOWLEDGMENTS

The author expresses his deep gratitude to Mr. and Mrs. Robert
E. Joanis for continued encouragement; Sister M. Judine, F.S.P.A.,
for gratuitous assistance in typing the manuscript and offering
valuable suggestions; and the many writers and photographers who
personally or through their publishers gave gracious permission to
use quotations from their works. To my former instructor, John
R. Cavanagh, M.D., author of *Fundamental Marriage Counseling,*
special thanks for kindly writing the Foreword.

CONTENTS

Chapter I *VOCATIONS AND OCCUPATIONS*

A General Outlook

The Problem of Vocations

One problem which all young men and women eventually have to face is that of vocations. "What should I be when I get out of school?" "What kind of work am I best suited for?" "What are my real interests?" "What fields are overcrowded?" "Is there any future in the business I'm interested in?" These are a few of the questions which crowd teen-agers' minds regarding the future. Throughout high school, boys and girls are ever on the lookout for hints and helps which may aid them in settling this problem. They may enter high school with the feeling of certainty as to what they will do in the future. However, as the years progress, the definiteness of their previous decision frequently gives way to indecision, and with the approach of graduation, the problem for some boys and girls becomes acute.

A vocation is a calling from God to do a part of God's work for the service of God's people.

> The very special work to which God calls a person when He gives a vocation is not merely a call to perform a chore, like a mother calling her daughter to come out to the kitchen and help do the dishes; or a father calling his son to run down to the neighborhood store and pick up a package of tobacco for him.
>
> Neither is a vocation a job or a position in an office or a factory that a teenager might secure after graduation and perhaps retain until re-

1

tirement fifty years later. Nor is it the owning or running of a farm. Nor is it acting on the stage or appearing before the movie cameras. Nor is it even being a big league baseball player or a high level government official. These are all means of livelihood or the expression of artistic or athletic or scientific talent that can fit into the mold or the form of a vocation. But they do not constitute the vocation proper.

A vocation is really the framework of a person's life, that in which his work and his aspirations and his recreations and just about everything he does and thinks about fit, the way a book fits into a box, or better, the way a soul fits into a body. It is a calling to a work that will occupy him the rest of his life, a calling that will permit the doing of very little else outside of the demands of the calling.[1]

Some boys and girls express the attitude many others have with regard to their life's work in the phrase, "My life is mine to do with as I please." Such teen-agers think that they are the masters of their destiny, the captains of their fate. This attitude is, of course, very un-Christian. It is proud and egocentric. It makes man his own beginning and end.

The Christian attitude is that our life is at God's disposal. Since we originate in the divine mind, we are destined for God as our final end. God, therefore, has the master plan of our life. He outlined the broader phases of our life; we will fill in the details, with His assistance.

Have I a Vocation?

When students hear the word "vocation" their minds almost automatically prefix the word "religious" as if this were the only one to be had. Oftentimes the phrases "state in life," "career," and "vocation" are used interchangeably, much to the confusion of those searching for their proper goal. To help students clarify once and for all the question, "What shall I be?" the following information is offered.

Before beginning, however, it is extremely important to keep in mind this fact: short of miraculous grace, as long as you remain in the world it is impossible to know God's will regarding your vocation and/or state in life with **absolute certainty.** Many boys and girls, well qualified and generous, have seriously tortured themselves in seeking to know God's will with **mathematical certainty.** A few saints were favored in this way, e.g., St. Paul, St.

2

Thomas Aquinas, but the vast majority of vocations and/or states in life are determined with only **moral certainty.**

What is **moral certainty?** It is a prudent judgment of oneself, one's abilities, talents, circumstances, opportunities, graces, and the like, to determine what is best for each individual person. It is **reasonable certainty** based upon one's qualities and gifts. Short of divine intervention the most anyone can have regarding one's vocation is **prudent judgment.** Such judgment is based on three things:

1. Prayer;
2. Thought;
3. Counsel.

States in Life

Marriage as a "state in life" is the eventual choice of the great majority of high school graduates. John A. O'Brien in his famous work *Marriage a Vocation*[2] states that "92.7% of men and 93.5% of women marry. . . ." That is why in your senior year emphasis is placed upon marriage as a state in life, established by God, and upon the various elements that contribute to success in fulfilling God's plan for marriage.

Before moving on to the vocation for the majority of mankind, however, it is vitally important that you realize that there are three states in life:

1. The priesthood or religious life (consecrated celibacy);
2. Single life in the world (celibacy);
3. Married life.

Each one of these is sometimes termed as a "calling" or "vocation" in life. To clarify these terms it is always best to think of "vocation" as the lifework or career one has selected, in contrast to the state in life one has chosen. For example, one who follows the career of a doctor may be either a priest or religious (with apostolic indult), a married person or a single person living in the world. Or one could be an engineer, a teacher, or a nurse and still live in any one of the three states in life. Throughout this book the word "vocation" will be used to mean "career" or "occupation."

3

H. Armstrong Roberts

Burroughs Calculator

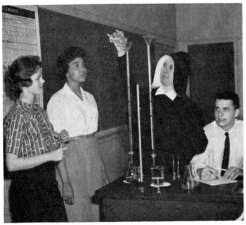

Sisters of Charity

Harris Nowell

The state of life for you is the one to which God calls you. He may call you to become a priest, Sister, or religious Brother; to the married state or to the single state. Whatever your state of life may be, it is the will of God for you, planned for you in His infinite love before the world began. Loyal service to Christ in your state of life is your way of responding to Christ's call in the twentieth century, "Come, follow me" (Mt. 4:19).

Criteria for Choosing or Knowing One's State in Life

"What does God want me to do?" is the question on the minds of many teen-agers as they approach graduation. "Just what state of life shall I choose?" To clarify this problem boys and girls must consider four things better known as the four criteria for choosing or knowing one's state in life. They are:

1. **Intention** — What do I desire to do with my talents, abilities, opportunities, etc.?

2. **Intellectual Fitness** — Am I capable of knowing and performing the duties required in this state in life?

3. **Moral Fitness** — Am I capable of living with God in this state in life?

4. **Physical Fitness** — Do I possess the physical qualities necessary to carry out this state in life?

The failure of so many people to ask themselves such questions as these is one explanation for much of the unhappiness and frustration we see around us. It also explains many of the misfits in our society, many of the square pegs in round holes. The advice of others can help one realize the answers to numbers 2, 3, and 4. As for number 1, *Intention,* the talents, abilities, and aptitudes that are yours have been given to you for a purpose. Before you make your choice it is absolutely necessary that one turn to *prayer.* There has never been a "self-made man."

The Religious Life — the Highest Calling

It has been said that "the grandest privilege and the greatest honor that Christ can confer upon a young man or woman is to give him or her the call to serve Him in religion."[3] Imagine, the Son of God asking you to serve Him. What a privilege! What an honor! Who could refuse such a call? And yet hundreds of boys and girls do just this every year. "How do I know that God wants me; how can I be sure?" That's the question so often asked by boys and girls in their senior year of high school. The answer, of course, is simple: presuming one possesses the signs of a true "calling from God" it can be said that "If you want Him; that is, if you wish to devote your life to Him in the religious state, knowing what it is you seek, then do not hesitate to answer His call. As St. Thomas says, 'It is better to enter religion to give it a trial than not to enter at all, because by so doing one disposes oneself to remain for good.' "[4] In so doing one removes once and for all the fork in the road.

It should be obvious to everybody that without a real "calling from God," it would be impossible for young men and women to undertake the life of a priest, a religious Brother, or a nun. In other words, God's special call and grace are utterly necessary to this form of life, though we do not need miraculous signs.

Signs of a Religious Vocation

No man can become a priest or Brother simply by his own will, nor can a girl become a religious on her own merits. The reason: because the invitation to this state in life is not extended to all. It is a supernatural call to a selected few. Those to whom it does come must accept it readily. Some boys and girls seem to think that there must be an internal invitation from God or even that a vision must be given commanding them to be a religious. Nobody who has read the lives of the saints is unaware that at times the "calling of God" has been miraculously given; but whoever is fit and worthy and aspires to the religious life with a right intention can, with a spirit of charity and courage, easily accept this life.

Some boys and girls know early in life what they want to be. Others go on for quite a while, never quite sure of their vocation until they actually enter the religious life. Both classes have a genuine "calling from God," for, in the last analysis, such a call is determined by answering the call issued by the proper authorities in the Church.

It would be illogical to suppose that no means were available to the Church to determine her choice of those whom God calls. Whenever God calls a boy or a girl to the religious life He must necessarily endow the person He chooses with the aptitudes re-

6

"**For every high priest** taken from among men is appointed for men in the things pertaining to God, that he may offer gifts and sacrifices for sins" (Hebr. 5:1).

John Ahlhauser

quired to fulfill that office worthily. When these aptitudes exist in an individual which renders him fit for the religious life, there is moral certainty that God has set him apart for a special purpose. The sum of all the qualities that render a boy or a girl suitable for the religious life is taken as a sign that God is calling. This is what is meant by signs of a religious vocation.

The qualities which render one suitable for the religious life are moral or spiritual, mental, physical, and the right intention. Let's take a closer look.

Moral Fitness

Undoubtedly, the first requisite for any candidate to the religious life is that he or she be morally and spiritually suited for it. In practice this means that there exists a noticeable desire to excel in the practice of Christian virtues. It is true that "all men are

7

"**And everyone** who has left house, or brothers, or sisters, or father, or mother, or wife, or children, or lands, for my name's sake, shall receive a hundredfold, and shall possess life everlasting" (Mt. 19:29).

Dominican Sisters, Great Bend, Kansas

sinners, and that great sinners have at times changed and become great saints. Therefore, we can conclude that, although unblemished moral purity is desirable, sins in one's past life are not a bar to a religious vocation if there has been a genuine and wholehearted conversion. Remember the early life of St. Paul and of St. Augustine."[5]

Moral suitability covers many angles, which though not individually indicative of a divine calling, yet taken as a whole determine a true estimate of a probable "call from God." One can form a fairly accurate picture of a boy's or girl's divine call or lack of it from watching his conduct.

> For example, a boy who would show a marked preference for girls' company, and whose conversation would run habitually along sex topics, or would frequent the company of boys who are known to indulge in vulgar talk — that boy, without being necessarily immoral, could not be considered fit for the priesthood. If moreover he loves mixed parties where double talk is frequent, and there the physical charms of girls are the chief object of interest, doubtless there is a presumption against that boy's vocation.

8

There are also a number of characteristics which show up in a boy that constitute a serious objection to his acceptance for the priesthood. A boy who is touchy, who nurses grievances, who is socially incompatible, is proud and vengeful, who goes into fits of anger over real or imagined offenses, who is emotionally unstable, moody, easily depressed, is morally unsuitable for the priesthood.

As to what is termed "worldliness" one must be rather careful in judging and estimating its presence in a boy. The mere fact that a boy loves sports, or the movies, or in general is fun-loving is not necessarily a sign of worldliness. These are the natural interests of any normal boy.[6]

There are, of course, some very positive qualities required in every individual who desires to enter the religious life. Some of the basic qualities comprising good moral character include docility, honesty, humility, obedience, and a spirit of reverence. "Reverence for the Church, for priests, for everything that surrounds divine worship and holy things, is a clear proof of moral or spiritual fitness. When a boy is imbued with this respect for the Church and sacred ceremonies, when he loves its devotions and honors the saints with his own private acts of piety, when he feels a true and tender devotion to Mary, Mother of God and his own, he has indications of the action of divine grace calling him to a higher life."[7]

Mental Fitness

When God issues his "call" to the religious life He gives sufficient mental ability to enable one to follow Him. Mental ability, however, is not a question of actual knowledge, but of native ability to learn, since deficiency in learning can be made up by study. The amount needed varies greatly in the different states and levels within the religious life. A person possessing an average to superior intelligence can easily qualify to become a priest or a nursing or teaching religious. Individuals with less than average ability will find plenty of challenges in other avenues of religious life. Needless to say, those who enter the religious life must be mature and mentally healthy. They must be capable of making adjustments and getting along with others.

9

Physical Fitness

Good physical health is necessary for those entering the religious life because the life is not an easy one. Take the life of a priest for example. The ordinary spiritual duties of a parish priest are heavy. Daily celebration of Mass, daily recitation of the Divine Office, daily meditation and Rosary, the ordinary round of private and personal prayers — such duties take a large part of a priest's time. There is no four-day week and eight-hour day for the parish priest. He has to administer the sacraments, care for the sick and aged, look after the instructions of converts, teach and preach, help straighten out the problems of people, manage the affairs of the parish and its school, conduct special religious and civic services and spend every week end on the job. If the parish is small, it is probably burdened with missions that also need constant attention. Young men who dislike responsibility or hard work had better stay out of the priesthood. It is the most wonderful and the happiest life on earth when judged from some aspects, but the life of a priest is far from being "an easy life." The same holds true for other phases of the religious life, namely the Sisterhood and the Brotherhood. The life of a religious requires good health. If you are lacking the health and physical fitness required to live such a life, God evidently does not intend to call you to it.

Right Intention

By right intention is understood the motives or reasons which determine a young person to seek the religious life. This is by all means essential. Each individual must examine his or her motives to determine beyond a doubt that "this is the right life for me." If a boy or girl desires the religious life because of a love of God or because of love for souls, a desire to help others, a love for virginity, a desire for perfection, or a wish to atone for sins, or a longing for his own salvation and that of others, his intention is right. But if a young man would seek to enter the religious life in order to please his parents or for the honor it confers upon him or because it offers security or material comfort,

The early Christians called the priest the **alter Christus** — the "other Christ." The priest is the person of Christ extended through time and space.

or if a girl were to choose the religious life primarily to escape the trials and worries of married life or for some other selfish reason, he or she would be acting from a bad motive and would definitely have the wrong intention.

Impediments to a Religious Vocation

Besides the general signs of a "call" to the religious life, there is another very important one to be considered, namely: freedom from any impediments or irregularities.

Because the vocation to the priesthood is of such importance, the Church sets up certain impediments in order to protect the good name and reputation of her clergy. Those born out of lawful wedlock may not be ordained unless the matter has been rectified or dispensed; neither may a man who has taken another's life or cooperated in such a deed, whether by murder or by causing the death of an unborn child. Here-

11

tics, epileptics, and those who have been insane are also debarred from the priesthood.

There are also certain impediments forbidding entry into the novitiate of a religious community: for instance, age, marriage bond, dependent parents, and so forth.[8]

Neglecting the Divine Call

It must be said here that there are many of today's youth who neglect the divine call of God to serve Him in the religious life. Many teen-agers smother or kill the "call of God" in their hearts by an unwise indulgence in worldly pleasures, as well as a failure to develop in their lives the habit of self-sacrifice. This does not speak too highly of the courage in today's youth. It is true that a "call" to the religious life is an invitation to a higher life and that it does not involve a strict precept. It is likewise true that one who refuses to follow a certain and divinely given vocation to the clerical life does not commit a sin, unless he acts from contempt or other unworthy motives. But it has been noted throughout the years that such persons are frequently far from happy. That is why if you think you may have a desire to serve God in the religious life, foster it and protect it. "Especially train yourself to deliberate acts of sacrifice, regularly denying yourself perfectly lawful pleasures, and avoiding all or at least any excessive indulgence in those things which would make it more difficult for you to follow the religious vocation."[9]

Testing the Divine Call

How does a person find out whether or not God is really calling him to the religious life? The best way to find out is to apply for admission to the seminary or the novitiate. This is one of the purposes of these institutions. They exist not only to train priests and religious, but also to allow individuals to find out whether or not they really have the divine call.

There are some individuals who consider it a terrible disgrace that a boy or girl leave the seminary or the novitiate. These same individuals say very little when a young man or woman

12

quits college and enters some form of business. Such people forget that seminaries and novitiates are training grounds for the religious life. Entering the religious life might be compared with trying out for any school organizations. Those who feel eligible are urged to try. In the last analysis it is the coach or moderator who makes the final decision.

The Priesthood

St. Francis of Assisi once said: "If I met a priest and an angel, I would first salute the priest because of his tremendous powers, and only then the angel." Such is the dignity of the priesthood. Rightfully it can be called the most exalted of all states in life.

The early Christians called the priest the *alter Christus* — the "other Christ." The priest is the person of Christ extended through time and space. As Christ is hidden under the appearances of bread and wine in the Eucharist, He is truly hidden in the priest in such a manner that He uses the lips of the priest to console and to rebuke, to pardon and to castigate. He uses the hands of the priest to bless, to absolve, and to anoint; his feet to carry Him to the sick and the dying. Just think of it. A priest is Christ in our midst. That is why the priesthood has been called the greatest vocation in the world.

John Ahlhauser

The diocesan priest is truly called to be a man among men. He must be spiritual father, counselor, business administrator, educational director, social worker. Diocesan priests serve in hospitals, colleges, high schools, seminaries, edit magazines and papers, and act in many other capacities.

A doctor heals bodies, but a priest heals souls.

A soldier fights for his country against other men, but a priest fights for God and souls against the army of sin and hell.

A teacher trains minds for worldly success, but a priest trains them for eternal happiness.

A judge declares one innocent who has been falsely accused, but a priest in Confession restores innocence even to the guilty.

A policeman guards earthly treasures, but a priest is in charge of the greatest treasures of all — the sacraments.

A warden can open and shut the gates of a prison, but a priest has the power to open and close the gates of heaven and hell.[10]

Two Classes

There are two great general classes of Catholic priests. First, there are those who work in and are permanently bound to a certain diocese. They are therefore called diocesan priests, or secular priests, that is, priests who work out in the world. Secondly, there are priests of the various religious orders. They are subject to the head of their order, and generally remain in monasteries, houses of study, and similar institutions. The priests of the religious orders, which follow the strict religious life, add the three vows of poverty, chastity, and obedience to the other obligations of the priesthood. In this way they vow to lead a life of Christian perfection.[11]

The Diocesan Clergy

Outstanding in number among the clergy of the world are the diocesan priests. These are the priests one most often finds engaged in parish work, in direct contact with souls, although some of them may be in special fields such as hospital or youth work, directing or teaching in high school, college, or seminary. At present, there are over 33,500 diocesan priests in the United States.

All priests take on themselves the obligations of the solemn vow of chastity by which they bind themselves to remain unmarried and to live a life of highest purity. For the diocesan priest this is included implicitly in his acceptance of the obligations of subdiaconate. In addition to this, he makes a solemn promise of reverence and obedience to his bishop at his ordination.[12]

Priests of Religious Orders and Congregations

Engaged principally in the special work for which their order was founded are the priests of religious orders and communities,

Maryknoll Missioners

Father Richard Madden, O.Carm. (above), is known for his work with high school students. Father James Flaherty, M.M., teaching in a Santa Cruz, Bolivia, school.

better known as "order priests." These priests accept the three vows of religion: poverty, chastity, and obedience. Technically speaking, order priests take solemn and perpetual vows while members of religious congregations take simple vows which are either temporal or perpetual. These latter renew their vows from time to time.

Among the 22,000 religious priests in the United States today, there are also religious societies of priests like the Oratorians, the Sulpicians, and the Maryknoll Fathers. Members of these societies bind themselves to the work of their community by a special promise. Technically, however, they remain diocesan priests.

Life in the Seminary

The priest must be equipped with learning suitable to his state; and so the Church insists that before receiving the priesthood a man must study philosophy, theology, sacred scripture, canon law, Church history, and various other ecclesiastical subjects for at least six years. Moreover, this presuppposes that he has completed a high school and junior college course. Clerical studies are usually made in an institution especially adapted to the preparation of candidates for the priesthood, called a seminary. Besides acquiring the suitable knowledge for the clerical state,

15

seminarians are expected to make progress in virtue, and are supervised and directed by prudent and edifying priests. During his years in the seminary a young man can study and test his own character and motives, and find out whether or not he is fitted for the priesthood and whether he is willing to undertake the arduous tasks of the ministry. If he decides that it is better for him not to advance to the clerical state, he is always free to leave the seminary. If he determines to receive Holy Orders, he is given the tonsure and the minor orders during his third or fourth year. Usually the cleric is ordained a subdeacon at the end of his fifth year, a deacon several months later, and a priest at the end of his sixth and final year of study.[13]

What Is a Priest?

Priests are mystery men. They come in assorted sizes, ages, weights and collars. They are found everywhere — speeding along, perspiring over, walking by, kneeling on, praying over, laughing with, preaching to, teaching about, pardoning for, and playing baseball with. Little children run to them; teenagers marvel at them; aged folk turn to them; lay people treasure them; non-Catholics stare at them; and Mary watches over them.

A priest is Prudence in a T-shirt; Fortitude with a breviary in his

Holy Cross seminarians, Notre Dame, Indiana, visit and teach catechism to the children of migrant Mexican workers in South Bend.

Holy Cross Fathers

hand; Justice on a ball diamond, and Temperance at any party. He is Faith with a blueprint; Hope with a sense of humor; and Charity with a golf club in hand.

A priest may be anything from a contemplative monk in a monastery to a magazine editor on Wall Street, from a labor mediator to a TV personality, from a student to a professor. Formerly known as the boy-around-the-corner, he's a member of each family, yet belongs to none. He penetrates secrets, shares sorrows, heals wounds. He has the trust of a child, the kindness of a best friend, the sternness of a top-sergeant, the daring of a tight-rope walker, the authority of an encyclopedia, the versatility of a commando, and the salesmanship of a Fuller-Brush man.

A priest is a humble creature — a mystifying worker at all professions. His hours are the longest; his salary the smallest; his Boss the best! He likes good pastors, the smiles of children, a good sermon, a home-cooked meal, and the name "Father."

A priest is all things to all men in the sight of God. He may be misquoted, mistaken and misunderstood, but he'll always forgive — because he's a mediator; a peacemaker; a go-between heaven and earth. It's no wonder God loves him. He's a man standing at an altar, clothed in Holy clothes, who while being aware of his own nothingness speaks to God for us and to us for God. And although his greatest act is to offer sacrifice, his most consoling one is to say to me, "Go in peace — Your sins are forgiven."[14]

The Brotherhoods

The religious Brothers, along with the priests and the Sisters, form a trinity of workers who have freely given up the attractions of the world to lead mankind to God and to work out their own salvation. Of this group it has been said that the Brothers are the quartermaster corps of the Lord's army, for their vitally important work is auxiliary and supplementary to that of the priesthood.

Religious Brothers are laymen, but in a unique sense. They have dedicated themselves to the service of God in a religious state, which is a fixed form of life approved by the Church, and they bind themselves to this state by vows for their personal sanctification and the salvation of others.

Because of the fraternal love of all men that they profess by their very lives, these dedicated men are given the respectful title "Brother." They give up the distractions of money and ambition by the vows of poverty and obedience. In a selfless life, by a vow of chastity, they even deny themselves the joys of family life so

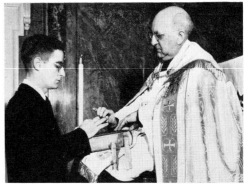

A new member (above) is received into the Society of Mary. The community has both Brothers (left) and priests. Some communities engage in teaching, others nursing. Some Brothers do other kinds of labor.

that they can be the brothers of all men rather than be tied down to looking after one family.

Kinds of Brothers

Brothers do any and all kinds of work for God and for souls. There are three prominent divisions: working brothers, nursing brothers, and teaching brothers. Their name indicates their chief occupations.

As far as the working brothers are concerned, some of them are mechanics, carpenters, gardeners. Others do farming, printing, janitorial work. Some do the cooking, others administer the temporal affairs and property of the community, and so on; but in addition to these pursuits, all of them have their regular daily religious exercises and sanctify themselves and others by observance of their vows.

Nursing brothers, like the Alexian Brothers, are able to do tremendous service to souls in the spiritual as well as the physical care of the sick. The contribution of the teaching brothers to the progress of religion and the welfare of mankind is difficult to estimate, it reaches so far.

There are some communities of brothers like the Christian Brothers or Brothers of the Christian Schools and the Xaverian Brothers who have no priests; while others, like the Society of Mary (Marianists) and the Congregation of the Holy Cross have both priests and brothers. In addition to these, remember, as we said above, nearly every one of the hundred or more religious orders of men in the United States accepts brothers in various capacities.[15]

Need of Brothers

More and more religious Brothers are needed so that the apostolate of the Church can go forward. More hands are needed to gather in the harvest. If any young man is in doubt whether he has a vocation to the Brotherhood or not, he should test it out by becoming a candidate for a period, usually six months. At the end of this time both he and the community are usually able to tell if the candidate should be accepted into the novitiate. At present there are over 11,500 religious Brothers in the United States. The Church could use ten times that number. But God wants volunteers, not draftees. That is why only generous souls need apply.

The Sisterhoods

While our divine Lord did not will women to be recipients of the sacrament of Holy Orders, He has called the so-called "weaker sex" to the state of highest perfection. The most perfect human being is a woman, our Mother, the Blessed Virgin Mary. Girls who enter the religious life do so because they desire to become "other Marys."

Kinds of Sisters

Like their counterparts in the religious life of the priesthood and Brotherhood, the religious orders and congregations of women are divided into definite groups. There are those who are primarily contemplative such as the Carmelites, the Cenacle nuns, the Poor Clares, and others. Cut off completely from the world and its distractions, they pray and work for God and their fellow men throughout the world. "By their great function of public worship of God, and by the severity of the penances they impose upon themselves for the good of others, they devote themselves to the imitation of Christ and thereby contribute more to the welfare of the world than most men realize."[16]

There are many women who are engaged in what is called the active religious life. The majority of these religious women deal in the profession of teaching. At present there are over 97,000 nuns in parochial schools in the United States, out of a total of 173,000 religious Sisters. Of the remaining number, some are to be found working in hospitals, in orphanages, and in institutions for the care of the aged, the crippled, the deaf, the blind, the insane, the wayward, and the delinquent. Still others are in missionary fields at home and abroad, acting as catechists, performing any of the countless other corporal or spiritual acts of mercy that go to make up a Sister's life.

Like the religious Brothers and priests, members of the Sisterhoods take the three vows of religion: poverty, chastity, and obedience. By these vows they renounce for God, worldly possessions, bodily pleasures, and submit their wills to a religious superior whom they obey as the instrument of the will of God. As in religious orders for men, women in the religious life take either solemn or simple vows. Both are binding under pain of mortal sin.

The Great Need

In our ever expanding country as well as in many other countries throughout the world, there is a great need for more girls to enter the religious life. Certainly God is not deficient in issuing His "call" and in giving the necessary graces to today's youth. Could it be that today's youth lack the courage or the self-sacrifice necessary to follow the divine call? As is true for the priesthood or the Brotherhood, the best way to find out whether one has a true desire to become a Sister is to give it a try in the convent. It is here and here alone that one can find the answer to the question: "Does God really want me or not?"

One reason why many girls do not become brides of Christ is because many Catholic mothers think such a life abnormal, that is to say, not a natural one for a girl to choose. The truth of the matter is this: A "call" to the religious life for a girl is as supernatural as that for a boy to the priesthood; what is more, you do not choose God; God chooses you.

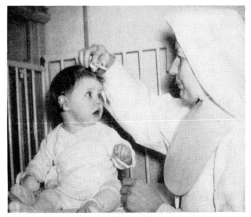

Sisters of St. Joseph of Carondelet

The Sister is called to be a "bride of Christ" and an "other mother of the human race." The harvest is great and more laborers are needed.

School Sisters of St. Francis

Ida Mae Kempel relates an interesting story regarding a mother's interference with a divine call:

Whenever I hear the word "vocation" I think of Kathy. You would have liked Kathy. She was five feet five of vibrant, vivacious femininity. I heard one man say of her — "That girl has more personality in her little finger than most girls have, period."

Besides that, Kathy was smart as a whip. At 17 she led our freshman college class, her blonde hair and broad smile hiding an IQ of high proportions. Yet her "C'mon Pal!" manner let us know she didn't lord it over us. A girl like that can go far. The world would be ready to do her bidding. But the world wasn't Kathy's oyster. She wanted to be a nun. I guess we all knew that. It was something that filled Kathy's whole being. When she knelt before the crucifix in our college chapel, you could have dropped a firecracker behind her and she wouldn't have heard it. When you spoke to her her deep faith popped out all over, carefully camouflaged behind a keen sense of humor.

I remember well the day the new novices took their places at Mass. Kathy and I were outside the chapel when the young girls, dressed in the traditional black dress and small novice's cap, entered the room. For a moment Kathy's eyes filled. Then she grinned back the tears, tossed her poodle-cut hair and followed them in. I wondered about those tears. For a brave girl like Kathy they weren't common gear.

But, as is the way around campuses, gossip fills up the crevices in even the most innocent tales. I soon discovered what was wrong. Kathy was the only child of wealthy parents. Her mother had big plans for her brilliant, pretty daughter that didn't include convent life. After

21

much pleading on Kathy's part she had accepted the only compromise her mother would make — she had entered a college run by Sisters. Because her home-town was 200 miles away she boarded at the school. On holidays and occasional week-ends she commuted by train to her home.

If Kathy had had her way she would have entered the convent that fall instead of the regular college but her mother flatly refused her consent. Even letting Kathy attend a Catholic college was against her better judgment, lest perhaps the good Sisters "persuade" her child to follow in their footsteps. In time she would talk Kathy out of throwing her life away. For the present, the girl was under-age, so there was no problem. She merely stuck to her "No" and that was that.

But plans go astray. Kathy was returning to school after the Christmas holidays when the train in which she was riding crashed. There were other people killed in that crash but Kathy was the youngest and I daresay the loveliest. We were heartbroken. For the rest of the year we gathered in the chapel on our lunch hour to say the rosary for the beloved classmate who had been taken from us. Our tears flowed freely and unashamedly, as did those of the Sisters and the lay teachers who had grown to love her.

Sometimes, as we knelt there, I thought of Kathy's mother and her firm statement — "God can't have her — she's all I have!" and I would feel very sorry for that poor woman. For indeed, God HAD taken her. Not in the way Kathy had planned and hoped for, but in another, more final way. Call it coincidence if you will but surely, in her grief, that mother must have wondered if perhaps she was wrong to flout God's will.

I'm married now and have four little ones of my own. If, when they are grown, they should want to enter God's service, I wouldn't stop them. No matter what my personal reasons for wanting to keep them "in the world" I would be afraid to stand in their way. Afraid of the power of a merciful God Who is nevertheless a just God. I might hesitate. My heart might cry at the thought of "giving them up" so completely. But I know that after a moment my thoughts would race back to that freshman year at college. And Kathy.[17]

What Is a Nun?

Nuns come in assorted sizes, weights and wimples. They are found everywhere — swathed in, seated in back of, kneeling on, speeding down, perspiring over, shopping for, patrolling along, worried about or laughing at. Little children idolize them, teen-agers puzzle them, lay people reverence them, non-Catholics gawk at them and St. Joseph looks after them.

A Nun is Faith with chalk on her hands; Hope, with a patched habit; and Love, with her hair clipped short.

A Nun has the neatness of a pin, the trust of a child, the daring of a paratrooper, the perseverance of a bill collector, the energy of a vest pocket atomic bomb, the authority of an encyclopedia and the versatility of a trouble shooter.

She loves the Blessed Mother, likes a good meditation book, ice cream, Friday afternoons, a letter from home, and free days. She is not too keen on summer school, long sermons, correcting home-work, getting up early, or grumpy pastors.

No one else is so quick to praise, so slow to censure. No one else can give you a licking and cry while she is doing it. No one else can tell stories, or skip rope, or write on the blackboard so well. A Nun is a wonderful creature. You can dirty up her classroom, but her devotion remains unsullied. You can sass her back but her prayers for you are redoubled. You can tax her patience but never deny her influence for good. A Nun is all this and more, for she is God's sweetheart and it is no wonder He loves her.[18]

The Single State

The single state in life is a rare vocation. It has been termed the "forgotten third vocation" because most people get married or join the priesthood or the religious life. Nonetheless, it is a special call from God. So often this state in life has been belittled because of the terms "bachelor," "spinster," or "old maid" which have been associated with a few who live in this state. Not infrequently those who have selected the single state are not helped by those around them. Married friends try their tactful best to conceal their feelings that they did not quite measure up to the demands of catching a wife. If a single person is an outstanding Catholic, religious often cannot hide their insistence that "you should be in the religious life."

Grave injustice can be done by covering with a blanket of reproach all those who have lived and grown old in the single state. For every egotistic, eccentric bachelor or "old maid" there are thousands of very praiseworthy single people who are leading lives of great self-sacrifice, having voluntarily given up marriage or maybe the religious life for some very worthy reason, such as aged parents, educating younger brothers or sisters, or devoting themselves unselfishly to some necessary work for their fellow men. Such persons must not be confused with the self-centered, selfish individuals of whom we rightly complain. In many instances people in the single state are the unsung heroes of self-denial and self-sacrifice.[19]

Advisability of the Single State

Pope Pius XII surprised the entire world on October 21, 1945,

23

Dr. Thomas A. Dooley treating a village child in his hospital in Northern Laos, five miles south of the Chinese border. The late Dr. Dooley was an outstanding example of dedication in the single life.

by calling the single state in life a "vocation."[20] He compared individuals who enter this walk of life with those who willingly renounce matrimony in order to consecrate themselves to a higher life. In 1954, Pius XII once again upheld the pre-eminence of consecrated virginity (celibacy) as a state in life in his encyclical letter, *Sacra Virginitas*. He carefully pointed out that "Virginity is not a Christian virtue unless we embrace it 'for the kingdom of heaven'; that is, unless we take up this way of life precisely to be able to devote ourselves more freely to divine things to attain heaven more surely, and with skillful efforts to lead others more readily to the kingdom of heaven."[21]

Virginity is a higher state than is the married life. Some of the great saints whom the Church has raised to her altars have lived and died in the single state. The single state of celibacy in the world is generally not to be advised. It is a matter that depends upon circumstances and if God really wishes a person to choose this state in life. Fundamentally, the choice of this state is a matter of motives.

A Matter of Motives

Some persons who are in the unmarried state are there because of unworthy motives, such as selfishness, a desire to enjoy greater freedom,

24

an unwillingness to follow an inclination toward the married state and its obligations, or toward the religious life and its abnegations. A person who chooses the unmarried life because of these or other unworthy motives may find it much more difficult to save his soul. It is dangerous to make personal pleasure and comfort the basis for selecting a state in life, when the glory of God and the salvation of one's soul constitute the only safe basis.

There are, however, worthy motives that make the choice of the unmarried state a noble decision, and in some cases perhaps an even greater act of self-sacrifice than the religious life. Such would be a desire to serve and support others, for instance, aged parents and relatives, a desire to allow younger brothers and sisters to enjoy the advantages of a Catholic education, or the conviction that one can best serve God and save his soul by remaining in the unmarried state in the world.

Some, particularly girls, remain unmarried because the opportunity of a suitable marriage never presented itself. Others, however, pass up reasonable opportunities. One suspects that some, stricken with "movie-mirage," determine to wait for a fabulous partner who will be a combination of a movie star, multimillionaire, and saint. They forget that they may be lacking a few perfections themselves.[22]

Difficulties of This State

Like any other state in life, the single state has its peculiar difficulties that should be honestly considered before one attempts to live it. A discussion with a well-qualified counselor or one's confessor is absolutely necessary before one embarks on this walk of life. There are two main difficulties: loneliness and purity.

> There is the danger of loneliness that may end in a very real and very deep discouragement. It is hard to live alone. A man needs the love and warmth of family to help him overcome the normal hardships and disappointments of everyday life. If he does not have this love and warmth and protection, he is inclined to give up when trouble comes. He becomes indifferent, disinterested and uninterested in everything round about him.
>
> The best way to overcome this danger is to be as active as possible in the expenditure of effort and in the dispensing of money for the good of others. Very likely that is why God calls some people to the single life — they can do so much more good that way. To be active in the performance of good deeds for others is a strong method of thwarting feelings of uselessness and discouragement that so easily can come over the single.[23]

The following essay on the unmarried woman brings out the true dedication required of those in the single state.

Of all the women God has created in His image and likeness, one of the most misunderstood, subject of controversy, and unduly pitied, is the single woman. And unfortunately, no one has found a satisfactory substitution for the cruel names: spinster, old maid, etc. The exact day or year when a young girl becomes a spinster is something that no one has yet analyzed and determined.

It was left for the great St. Paul, who loved virginity, to speak words of praise for the unmarried woman who, free from the care of things of the world, is concerned about things of the Lord, how she may please Him.

Many "unsung" heroines are the single women who give unselfishly and lovingly of their talents, energies, and time to worthwhile projects with stability and perseverance. Then we have the splendid daughters who turned their parents' life of poverty into one of comfort, who watched over their long years of sickness, and gave their own bright youth that the old age of their father and mother might know peace and security. Parents in heaven spend long sectors of eternity praying for these saintly ones.

Perhaps one of the most appreciative of the single woman is the Catholic parish priest. To him, these women are the backbone of parish organizations, the dependable ones who can be called on for all emergencies. From the thankless chores of moving chairs to cleaning the altar, they stand ready and eager to do for the Church the lovely, gracious, self-effacing things so Christ-like.

May these saintly women come very close to God — the Catholic teachers, nurses, secretaries, sisters, daughters, and aunts who do, do and do — endlessly without probability of repayment. This is a constant rebuke to the greed and self-indulgence of the world.

The life of a single woman is not an easy one. But having a simple, clear knowledge that this life is but a stepping stone to heaven, the single woman can live from day to day confident of God's love and serene in the fact that this is her vocation in life. Surely our Good Lord must have a special place close to Him for these truly devout Catholic single women who pray daily: "Thy will be done. . . ."[24]

The second most difficult problem for the single is the danger of grave temptation against purity that may end in serious and habitual sin. "There are not the helps to purity afforded the married people. And there are not the special graces that are proper to the priest and to the nun. They must fight their battles, at least as far as special assistance from their state in life is concerned, by themselves. These battles sometimes can be quite serious."[25]

One such battle which takes a terrific toll of single lives is the wishful anxiety complex of a single girl, and her hurried desire to get married before it's too late. This desperate type of girl thinks only in terms of marriage and seldom talks to any man unless there is some future in it, unless he is eligible. Such a person can soon find herself compromising her moral standards, if such a compromise means a wedding ring. Some foolish "last-chance" girls will do almost anything to avoid being single.

A well-balanced single girl, on the other hand, realizes that it is possible to live in this world without sex. Sexual abstinence is not abnormal. It is of the stuff that builds saints. Prudence is required of every girl from fanning the contacts with men into the fires of close relationships. This can only be achieved if she perseveres in daily prayer, God's grace and His sacraments, and learns to sublimate sex into some positive activity, e.g., nursing, teaching, social work, etc. For as St. Paul has written:

> He who is unmarried is concerned about the things of the Lord, how he may please God. Whereas he who is married is concerned about the things of the world, how he may please his wife; and he is divided. And the unmarried woman and the virgin thinks about the things of the Lord, that she may be holy in body and in spirit. Whereas she who is married thinks about the things of this world, how she may please her husband.[26]

Secular Institutes

More and more single people are choosing to stay in the single state in life, some as individuals, others as members of secular institutes. Secular institutes are in the news today and will be heard of more and more. It was Pius XII who recognized this third state of perfection. Unlike the traditionally recognized two states of perfection, namely, the religious state and societies devoted to the common life, members of the secular institutes live in the world, usually as individuals. They take the three vows, but they are not religious. They are "societies of clerics or laity who devote themselves to the life of the evangelical counsels in the world in order to reach Christian perfection there and exercise more fruitfully their apostolate."[27]

> The qualities required for this unique vocation are practically the same as those required for the religious life. Candidates must have an attraction and an aptitude for a life consecrated to evangelical and

27

An **Oblate Missionary** of Mary Immaculate with her second grade pupils. The members of this institute include persons in various careers such as nursing, social work, writing — anything which will serve the Church.

Edward Tenczar

Christian perfection. They must have adequate physical and mental health, intelligence, and physical and moral stability.

And, every candidate must have a true interior attraction for a growing and deepening love of God. In addition, since Secular Institute members live in the world, candidates must be capable of assuming a higher degree of personal responsibility, and of exercising a greater degree of discretion over their actions and decisions, than is necessary for a person entering a religious community.[28]

While each of the present existing nine secular institutes in the United States differs from one another in spirit and in its field of work, today's 400 American men and women who have dedicated themselves to this way of life have one thing in common, "the restoration of all things in Christ," by reaching every strata of society.

Lay Missionaries

Recently, the Bishops of the United States have set up a Lay Missionary Program. This is a new program and has no direct connection with the lay missionaries you may have read about in the past.

Many religious orders have their own lay missionaries to help in their own missions in such places as New Guinea, Africa, and India. Some apostolic men and women have started other private lay missionary organizations.

The Bishops' program is not to be confused with these lay missionaries. Only two areas in the world are involved in this new lay volunteer program — missions right in our own U. S. and missions in Latin America. Lay missionaries going to U. S. home missions are called *Extension Volunteers* because they are being directed by the Extension Society. Latin American lay missionaries are called *Papal Volunteers* and are being directed by the N.C.W.C. Latin America Bureau.

While this new field of missionary work is not yet open to high school students, it is well for you to consider this new enterprise as a possible future field of endeavor.

Careers[29]

While there are only three states in life there are at least 25,000 kinds of careers and many more varied types of jobs or occupations to be had in life.

Some young people choose the path of least resistance in planning their careers. They use little or no judgment in selecting the kind of work they will eventually pursue. When they do enter the occupational world they constantly change jobs without analyzing their interests, abilities, or qualifications. They are known as "drifters."

The Grail is intended for young single women under 30 with some professional or technical skill useful in missions. Its mission areas include Australia, Asia, Africa, South America, Europe, Canada, and the United States.

The Grail

They finally drift into an occupation in which they will have reasonable security and can make a living. Usually they are not happy in their work and have regrets later on, but then it is very often too late or too difficult to make a change because of family obligations. Occasionally they may drift into a suitable occupation and decide to make it their career. They may be successful, but much time and money could have been saved, as well as many disappointments avoided, if they had *planned* for their future vocation.

Know Thyself

An important step in planning is self-analysis. Self-analysis is learning as much as possible about oneself. In order to make an honest study, considerable time and thought must be given to the process. It is only through a careful study — and the jotting down on paper of the facts — that a person is able to make a wise vocational choice. These facts include a comparison of one's vocational assets with the occupation being considered.

The time spent on self-analysis in the planning stage will pay dividends in the future.

Here are a few items to consider in your self-analysis:

1. **Interests** — Examine your interests. In what fields are you interested? Mechanical, scientific, computational, artistic, literary, musical, clerical, social service, religious vocation? Are your interests real or a passing fancy?
2. **Mental Ability** — Check your high school record. Do you have considerable difficulty in mastering certain subjects such as mathematics or science? Your teacher or guidance counselor can provide additional information on the basis of tests, etc.
3. **Personality and Character Traits** — Tact, courtesy, cheerfulness, punctuality, sense of humor, good judgment, initiative, loyalty, cooperativeness, dependability, honesty, perseverance, responsibility, ability to get along with others, ability to adjust to circumstances whether pleasant or unpleasant, emotional control, explosive or even temperament.
4. Consider any special abilities or aptitudes you have discovered from a study of your school records, extra-curricular activities, job experiences, your hobbies, etc.

Some people overestimate their abilities while others underestimate them. Therefore, for a check on your analysis, consult your teacher or school counselor and your parents.

30

E. I. du Pont de Nemours & Co.

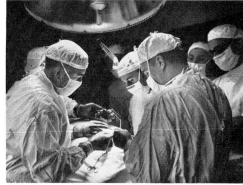

Cornell University

The Mystical Body of Christ is one body having many members. This is to say, it is one body, with Christ as its head, working in and through His various members for the glory of His Father and the salvation of souls. Each one of us is assigned a special task to do. There is no such thing as an unimportant job. It is not what we do but how we do according to our ability. To serve man is to serve God.

Esso Engineering and Research

St. Mary's Hospital, Milwaukee

Common Factors in Many Vocations

In vocational planning it is as impossible as it is unnecessary for the young person to explore in detail the entire vast and complicated world of work. The reading of facts concerning many different occupations sometimes serves to confuse the individual rather than to clarify the immediate issues in vocational planning.

The following factors common to most vocations may suggest others which may be found useful in planning one's vocational goal:

1. The need of personal fitness requirements — personality;
2. The importance of physical fitness;
3. The need for thorough preparation if one is to secure advancement;
4. The necessity in most vocations of in-service training and study;
5. The importance of understanding the fundamentals of modern business practice;
6. The need in almost all occupations of beginning at routine tasks;
7. The importance of adaptability — that is the ability to work in more than one vocational field — particularly during periods when there is a downward trend in employment;
8. The importance of those qualities which enable one to work well with others;
9. The importance of a good general education in this modern age of high specialization and automation. It is well to realize that one's training must be built on a broad background.

When considering a vocational choice, it is desirable to learn something about occupations *related to* that choice. The occupation and its related fields should be carefully considered, particularly the main requirements for entry and success.

Factors Contributing to Vocational Success

The most important factor in success is "attitude." A person's outlook on life, on his work, the firm he works for, his superiors, fellow workers, and associates, will largely determine his place in the world of work. Personality ranks necessarily high here. Your personality to a great extent determines how well you will get along with others and your prospects for promotion.

The following points are useful as a check list in helping one to analyze his personality: (1) ability to get along with others; (2) appearance; (3) respect for those in authority; (4) cheerfulness; (5) sense of humor; (6) adapting yourself to surroundings; (7) honesty; (8) tact; (9) enthusiasm; (10) courtesy; (11) interest in work; (12) dependability; (13) self-confidence;

32

(14) cleanliness; (15) co-operation; (16) manners; (17) emotional control; (18) consideration of others; (19) loyalty.

Achievement — is equally the mark of success; to do is worth as much as to have.

Knowledge — successful people are those who continue to acquire new facts. Successful persons do not close their mind to knowledge when they leave school.

Loyalty — a dominant characteristic of every successful person.

Sound Judgment — the result of a mind well-stocked with accurate information on which to make decisions.

Adjustment — success usually comes to the person who can adapt himself to the varied conditions of work.

Health — you cannot hold an ordinary job today unless you maintain good health.

Ethical Practice — duties as a Catholic to an employer or superiors.

Some important attitudes and achievements for obtaining a promotion are: mastery of detail, industry, mental alertness, initiative, resourcefulness, ability to make decisions, diplomacy, courtesy, technical training.

Preparing for and Participating in Interviews

All too frequently young people are very conscientious about their training and education for a job, only to neglect the planning and preparation necessary to make a successful entry. Many find they have difficulty obtaining a job until they realize that their interview technique is actually serving as their greatest obstacle and needs improvement.

In planning for a job interview one should do the following:

1. Prepare a written (typed) outline or series of statements about yourself, including all items that might have a bearing on the job, such as education and training, special abilities, work experience, personal interests, names and addresses of personal references.
2. Prepare a list of questions that might be asked by the employer and have brief notes as to what your answers might be.
3. Prepare a list of questions you would like to ask of the employer.
4. Inform yourself about the job and the company for which you hope to work.
5. First impressions are important so make sure your personal appearance (dress, make-up, etc.) is first rate, yet not overdone.
6. Make definite arrangements as to time and place of interview and meet the schedule.

During the interview one should:

1. Be kind and courteous throughout the interview and express interest in the company and the job.

2. Be forthright and honest, giving complete information yet keeping your answers brief and to the point.
3. Speak clearly and distinctly, and avoid using slang.
4. Express self-confidence but do not appear "cocky."
5. Be tactful, allowing the interviewer to determine the course of the conversation as well as the time of bringing it to a close.
6. Ask pertinent questions but do not overemphasize topics such as salary or working hours.
7. Never argue or discuss your personal troubles.
8. Never criticize others.
9. Be poised and relaxed. Look directly at the interviewer when talking with him.
10. Express appreciation for the interview.

The above suggestions are by no means all the points to be considered in job interviews.

Avoiding Common Mistakes in Choosing a Career

Just as important, and in some cases extremely vital to the individual involved, are some negative aspects which should not be forgotten. These items, listed below, when not taken into consideration, result in what are known as the most common mistakes made by young people while in the process of choosing a career. Thus, to avoid some common mistakes, the young person deciding upon a career:

1. Should not choose an occupation which would require physical characteristics which he does not possess.
2. Should not choose an occupation that would be beyond his mental capabilities.
3. Should not choose a career which would require training and financing beyond his limitations.
4. Should not choose a career which requires personality characteristics other than he possesses.
5. Should not be swayed by the glamour of the occupation.
6. Should not choose a job in which the openings are too limited.
7. Should not choose a field in which he could not acquire the skills needed for success.
8. Should not choose an occupation to satisfy desires of relatives and friends.

Vocational Scrapbook

A vocational scrapbook offers a basic approach to the problem of investigating the work one wants to do. It cultivates alertness in observing news items about occupations. Material for a scrap-book may be obtained from articles in newspapers, magazines, pamphlets from industry, school catalogues, and other sources. It will be surprising to find the amount of material which can be collected from the daily newspapers alone.

SUGGESTIONS FOR READING

(Starred items are for students and teachers.)

Call to the Laity: Selected Writings on the Lay Apostolate, Most Rev. Richard J. Cushing (Westminster, Md.: The Newman Press, 1956).

*Guide to the Catholic Sisterhoods in the United States, Thomas P. Mc-Carthy, C.S.V. (Washington, D. C.: Catholic University of America).

*Guide to the Diocesan Priesthood in the United States, Thomas P. Mc-Carthy (Washington, D. C.: Catholic University of America, 1956).

*On Holy Virginity, encyclical letter of Pope Pius XII (Washington, D. C.: National Catholic Welfare Conference, 1312 Massachusetts Ave., N.W., 1954), 28 pp.

*The Lay Apostolate, an address of Pope Pius XII to the World Congress of the Lay Apostolate, October 14, N.C.W.C., Washington 5, D. C., 1951.

Men in Sandals, Richard Madden, O.C.D. (Milwaukee: The Bruce Publishing Co., 1954).

*The Mystery of Love for the Single, Dominic J. Unger, O.F.M.Cap. (Chicago: Franciscan Herald Press, 1958), 192 pp.

A Seal Upon My Heart: Autobiographies of 20 Sisters, edited by George L. Kane (Milwaukee: The Bruce Publishing Co., 1957).

The Silent Life, Thomas Merton (New York: Farrar, Straus and Cudahy, 1957).

Spinsters Are Wonderful People, D. A. Lord, S.J. (St. Louis, Mo.: The Queen's Work, 3115 South Grand Blvd., 1947).

Why I Become a Brother, edited by Rev. George L. Kane (Westminster, Md.: The Newman Press, 1954).

Why I Became a Priest, edited by Rev. George L. Kane (Westminster, Md.: The Newman Press, 1954).

Why a Religious Brother?, Rev. M. D. Forrest, M.S.C. (St. Paul, Minn.: Radio Replies Press Society, 500 Robert Street), 32 pp.

You Can Change the World: the Christopher Approach, James Keller, M.M. (New York: Longmans, 1948).

Chapter II MAKING MARRIAGE A SUCCESS

On February 10, 1939, Pope Pius XI issued his last written document. It was a letter to the bishops of the Philippine Islands. In it he forcibly stated that "the first and most important form of Catholic lay action is the restoration of Catholic family living." Since that time considerable attention has been focused upon family problems in our midst. Schools are increasingly reorienting themselves; the liturgy is slowly being revitalized in family circles; Cana Conferences, the Christian Family Movement, and lectures on marriage and family living are becoming more familiar. High school seniors in particular are becoming more and more interested in success in love and marriage. In high schools throughout the country marriage courses are being introduced. The purpose: to stem the tide of too early and ill-prepared marriages.

Marriage is the most important act in the life of the majority of men and women. When it is a good marriage, it brings men and women to the fullness of the life God intended for them. When it fails, it leaves behind a trail of faded hopes and dreams and broken lives. For those who are planning marriage, therefore, it is vitally important that they know what marriage really is. Certainly no one can find the secret of successful marriage without first having a clear understanding of what marriage is. Is it merely a civil contract, entered into by a man and woman mainly for companionship and social and material security? Is it the result of a purely physical attraction, thoughtlessly embarked upon in the full bloom of youthful ardor? Is it only a pleasant companionship which may not survive the trials and tribulations of family life? No one can hope to realize the full fruits of a good marriage without first understanding what marriage is.

Many erroneous notions regarding marriage are still being circulated these days, particularly in reference to its permanence and its obligations. The reason for these errors is the failure to recognize the sacredness of marriage. Marriage is not, as some seem to think, a legalizing of sexual relationships between a man and a woman. It is, instead, a relationship established by God Himself primarily for the generation and education of children. The very name "Matrimony" signifies this: it comes from two Latin words, *matris munus,* meaning "the office of motherhood" or "the duty of the mother," which duty is the generation and education of new life.

What Is Marriage?

Marriage is an institution as old as the human race itself. It started in the Garden of Eden with our first parents. God blessed Adam and Eve: "Increase and multiply and fill the earth" (Gen. 1:28); and God's fundamental laws with regard to marriage are well expressed by Adam: "Wherefore, a man shall leave father and mother, and shall cleave to his wife: and they shall be two in one flesh" (Gen. 2:24). Thus, marriage can be defined as a life-long union between a man and a woman who are lawfully capable of giving irrevocably to each other the right to acts necessary for the generation and education of children, mutually obliging themselves to a common way of life in order to work out their eternal salvation. Among the baptized, every true marriage is, in itself and by itself, a sacrament instituted by Christ to produce grace.

The most essential factor in marriage, of course, is the contract. A contract is an agreement between two parties, each assenting to give something to the other or to do something for the other for a definite length of time. There cannot be a contract without the free consent of both parties.

There are six obstacles to consent.

1. **Lack of the use of reason.** Infants, the seriously mentally ill, the intoxicated, the drugged, the hypnotized cannot give true consent.
2. **Defective knowledge.** In order to give consent, the person must know the essentials — that marriage is a permanent union of a man and a woman for the purpose of procreating children. He must know that this requires bodily cooperation of husband and wife. After puberty, it

37

is presumed that the person knows these basic facts. It is not necessary that he know all the biological mechanisms involved in the sex act, conception, pregnancy, and birth.

3. **Mistaken identity.** If you "marry" one person but thought that you were marrying another (his twin, for example) there is no true consent.

4. **Pretense.** People who say "I will" while acting out a marriage on the stage or in a movie are, of course, not married. There is no intention of getting married and, hence, no true consent. But if a person is a bride or groom in a real wedding ceremony, his external consent by saying "I will" is taken as evidence of true internal consent. He would have great difficulty trying to prove later that he said "I will" but did not really mean it.

5. **Force or fear.** Canon Law is specific on this matter, saying that "invalid is a marriage entered into through force or grave fear unjustly inspired from without, such that in order to escape from it, a party is compelled to choose marriage. No other fear, even if it furnish the cause for the contract, entails the nullity of marriage" (Canon 1087).

If you are forced into a marriage by a force that cannot be resisted, you have not given true consent. There is no marriage in such a case.

What about fear? Notice the conditions. It must be grave or serious fear. It must come from without, that is, from some other person. It must be unjust. Finally, it must be fear of such a nature that the only way to escape it is to marry. If fear fulfills *all* these conditions, it results in forced consent and there is no marriage.

6. **Intention contrary to the essence of marriage.** If one or both parties would deny that marriage really is a contract binding on both parties, or that marriage gives the right to sexual intercourse, the marriage would be invalid, because denial would indicate a failure to understand what marriage really is. You certainly are not making a contract when you do not believe there is a contract. And you are not making a contract involving sexual intercourse as one of the things promised if you do not believe that sexual intercourse is one of the things promised. But, as we have defined, marriage is a contract involving promise of sexual intercourse.

However, if one or both have the intention of not having children, or of refusing sexual intercourse, or of not fulfilling other duties, the marriage is valid. It is considered that they freely accept and consent to the married state but are not willing to fulfill its duties.

The difference is this: in the first case, the existence of any contract is denied; in the second case, the existence of a contract is admitted, and the contract is made, even though at the very moment of making the contract one has every intention of violating it.[1]

Marriage is a lawful contract between a man and a woman by which they give to each other the perpetual and exclusive right to those bodily functions which are naturally apt to generate offspring. Just what does this mean? Since the bearing and rearing

38

A Catholic wedding is both a religious and social event. It is religious because it is a sacrament and is governed by Church Law. It is social because the partners are obliged to have children, if God permits, and to raise them as good members of society.

Jeanne Taggett

and education of children involve a certain amount of sacrifice on the part of parents, God made the attraction between the sexes a delightful experience. In marriage, "the sex act is one of intense pleasure. Many people would not have entered the married state if they thought only of the trouble it involves. But they 'fall in love' and desire to fulfill that love in the sex act with the beloved. To do this, they get married, have sex relations, a child is conceived and — after nine months — born."[2]

Marriage Is Both a Contract and a Sacrament

A marriage contract cannot be entered into unless both parties freely express their marriage consent in words or equivalent signs. It must be definite and visible. In marriage this consent is ordinarily the "I will" pronounced separately by both the groom and bride. It is precisely this expression of mutual consent which Christ uses

39

to produce grace in the sacrament of matrimony. A sacrament, as you know, is an outward sign instituted by Christ to give grace. The saying of "I will" by both the bride and the groom is not only the consent of the contract; it is also the outward sign or the sacrament. It not only signifies, but also actually produces in the souls of the newly married couple an increase of sanctifying grace and the special grace of the sacrament of matrimony. These special graces enable the couple to live up to all the responsibilities of married life.

Just when Christ instituted the sacrament of matrimony we do not know. Some think that it was at the wedding feast of Cana, which He blessed with His presence. Others say that He did so when He stated that marriage could not be dissolved. Still others maintain that marriage was made a sacrament when He spoke to His Apostles about matters pertaining to the kingdom of God, between His resurrection and His ascension. This latter is the more commonly accepted teaching. The exact time when matrimony was instituted is, of course, unimportant. The fact that Christ actually did institute it is perfectly clear from the earliest traditions of the Church.

Matrimony is a sacrament of the living. To get the graces attached to it, both parties must be properly baptized and in the state of grace at the time of receiving it. Unlike other sacraments, which are usually performed by a priest, the groom and the bride themselves are the ministers of the sacrament of matrimony. The priest has no part in the giving of the external sign. He merely acts as the Church's official witness of the contract. The Church requires his presence, so that without him the marriage of a Catholic would not be valid. The marriage of two Catholics before a justice of the peace or a minister of some other religion is, of course, an invalid marriage. A mixed marriage performed by a Protestant minister is not only invalid but also entails excommunication for the Catholic party. In some dioceses, this is also a "reserved sin," that is, it cannot be removed by an ordinary confessor, but recourse must be had to the bishop. In some dioceses, marriage before a justice of the peace also incurs a similar penalty. The severity of the punishment indicates the evil of the sin; one is cut off from the sacraments by excommunication until he repents.

40

The child may be considered an extension of the personality of his father and mother. At the same time, he compels them to look beyond the pursuit of their own contentment to the well-being of others.

© 1961 Clairol Incorporated

Non-Catholics who are properly (sacramentally) baptized likewise receive the sacrament of matrimony whether they realize it or not. The Church recognizes such marriages as truly sacramental and valid. On the other hand, in a marriage between a baptized and a nonbaptized person (disparity of cult), it is doubtful whether even the baptized one receives the sacrament. This is something to keep in mind if you should ever think of taking a nonbaptized spouse. A dispensation will be required to make such a marriage lawful and valid, but it will never make it a sacrament.

The Purposes of Marriage

Everything in this world exists for a definite purpose, and marriage exists for a very definite purpose. In fact, the purposes of marriage are three, and they can be divided into primary and secondary. An easy way to remember these purposes is the mnemonic word: **car:**

C — Children	(Primary)
A — Affection	(Secondary)
R — Relief of Concupiscence	(Secondary)

Primary Purpose

The primary purpose is clear from the definition of marriage

41

given above. The reason for marriage in the divine plan is the begetting and education of children. God's original blessing "increase and multiply" makes of man and woman in wedlock His co-creators of new life. It is for this reason that God gave man his sexual powers. Children are the fruit of the union, and the essential stamp of unity of the husband and wife in marriage. For the child is a single being and he bears in himself the personality of his father and his mother. He is "flesh of their flesh": something of themselves which detaches itself from them for the purpose of forming a new being. What comes from the father cannot be separated in him, nor can it scarcely be distinguished from that which comes from his mother. In the child, the married couple's unity is realized in an absolute fashion. The child is the couple's unity realized and projected outside themselves. Each spouse rediscovers the other in the child, and also finds himself anew. The child at the same time gives greater depth and breadth to married love, because he compels the husband and wife to reach beyond themselves, to rise above the sole pursuit of their own contentment by orientating their life toward other beings — toward other beings who at the same time are in a sense themselves, the prolongation of themselves. The child imparts a purpose to life since, thanks to the child, a parent has something that goes on after he is dead. Through the child, then, the love found in marriage takes on its full value.

Secondary Purposes

The secondary purposes of marriage are mutual help and affection, companionship, and the allaying of concupiscence. The most intimate companionship of husband and wife demands sincere love. It is not that love based on pleasing words only, but on the deep attachment of the heart which is expressed in action. Mutual love and self-sacrifice are the virtues upon which marriage succeeds. Besides the begetting of children, therefore, marriage exists for the mutual help the partners can give each other in living the good life, for their mutual love and devotion, and for the protection they afford each other against temptation. To paraphrase the instruction in the ritual for the marriage ceremony: the couple begin their married life by the voluntary and complete surrender of their individual lives in the interest of that deeper and wider life which they are to have in common. From then on they are to belong entirely to each other. They will be one in mind, one in heart, and one in affections. This is marriage — that wonderful contract which Christ raised to a sacrament to sanctify those who pledge themselves to it.

Qualities of Marriage

In addition to sanctity, marriage has two chief qualities or characteristics:

Unity

Unity of marriage means that husband and wife equally do not give to any third party what by marriage they pledge to give to one another; nor do they grant to one another whatever is forbidden by God's law. It is between one man and one woman, "What God hath joined together let no man put asunder" (Mt. 19:6) until death. Although relaxed to an extent for a time, unity of marriage was restored by the teaching of Christ: "Therefore they are no longer two but one flesh." Not only did He condemn polygamy in all of its forms, but He even forbade as sinful the willful desire of such things.

Marriage of an individual person of one sex to an individual person of the other sex is called monogamy. Opposed to monogamy is polygamy in all of its forms: polygamy (marriage of one man to many women) and polyandry (marriage of one woman to many men). Monogamy is the recognized form of marriage among civilized people. The experience of mankind, the voice of nature, and the institution of Jesus Christ proclaim that monogamy is the proper and only form for man and woman.

Indissolubility

Along with the unity of marriage, Christ taught the second great quality of marriage: indissolubility, which implies perpetuity and permanence. When God gave Adam the command to "cleave unto his wife" He did not say such a union should last only until a more attractive woman came along; it was until death. Today's world seems to think that marriage can be broken because the wife doesn't measure up to the husband's expectations, or the wife may pack up and leave because her husband's income is too small to fulfill her desires. Successful marriage, a truly Christian marriage, demands love and loyalty, a spirit of tolerance, the willingness to make sacrifices, large and small. It calls for understanding and co-operation, and above all for faith in God and trust in one another. It admits, moreover, of no divorce, for it recognizes the fact that marriage is a permanent union until death, indissoluble regardless of the difficulties of married life and/or the fact that many are being divorced. "What God hath joined together let *no man* put asunder" makes it abundantly clear that no one has absolutely any power to dissolve a valid Christian marriage in which two baptized persons have been united, and which has been consummated.

Divorce does not remedy marriage ills but aggravates and multiplies them. When a man divorces his wife and marries another he persuades himself that he has found an angel and that his new life will be a path of roses. But before long he finds the thorns as before. Divorce leads to divorce. Many people live more miserably with their second mate than with their first, and yet more miserably

Milwaukee Journal Photo

This man and wife are celebrating their golden anniversary. Successful marriages are built on love, loyalty, and willingness to make sacrifices. For this Christ also rewards one hundredfold.

with the third. Why? Because true happiness can never come to one who is in sin, and to remarry after a divorce while your first lawful mate is still alive is just that . . . a sin of adultery. "Whoever shall put away his wife and marry another, committeth adultery against her. And if the wife shall put away her husband, and be married to another, she committeth adultery" (Mk. 10:6–12).

Marriages Are Made Not Born

A successful and happy marriage is no accident. It must be prepared for very carefully and it must be founded on mutual love and self-sacrifice. There are all sorts of practical everyday problems associated with the combination of a man and a woman, and many special and most difficult problems which are not foreseeable.

The husband must have both the will and the competence to provide for the material needs of his wife and children. The wife must be able to fulfill the practical obligations of motherhood — maintaining the home, caring for the children, and acting in general as a helpmate to her husband in every phase of family life.

> The husband who wants to make a success of his marriage must realize that he will be called upon to do many things that would not have been expected of him as a single man. The wife must realize the same. And both must recognize that they may have to give up certain of the privileges and liberties they formerly enjoyed.
> The husband will have to be industrious to supply the family's daily needs by his labors. He will have to be ambitious to improve his earning capacity to meet the increasing requirements of clothing, education and pleasure of the children as they grow up and costs increase. If his income is not sufficient to provide adequately for his family and still enjoy little pleasures of his own, he must sacrifice his own enjoyment for the welfare of his dependents. . . .
> The responsibilities of a woman are no less, but in a different direction. She cannot fairly or properly expect her husband to perform the labors and services which are in the proper sphere of the wife. If the husband's income is not sufficient to indulge her wishes for the kind of dresses, hats and shoes she would like to have, she must reconcile herself to the reality and not destroy the peace of the home by her unreasonable and impossible demands.[3]

More is required of marriage than lipstick for the girl and broad shoulders and a cute grin for the boy. The modern woman, for

45

example, must be at least an amateur psychologist, public-relations expert, dietitian, shopping and efficiency expert, accountant, interior decorator, housekeeper, cook, and chauffeur, to mention just a few of the directions in which she may be called upon to render vital service to her husband and family. Such talents aren't acquired overnight. It doesn't take intelligence to fall in love, but it takes real intelligence to stay in love.

It Takes Love and Faith

Fruitful and lasting marriage is largely a matter of true love and faith.

When there is genuine love and a consecrated Faith the practical problems of life are not too difficult to meet and conquer. When these qualities are lacking, even the smallest personality differences will often bring discord and destruction to a marriage and family life.

There are times when even the most devoted husband and wife have their differences. Maybe the baby cried all night and the parents were worried and short-tempered. A petty spat follows. Perhaps the husband is down in the dumps when he sees the next door neighbor's new car and he can't afford one. Or the wife sees Mrs. Jones with a smart new dress and would like one but can't have it. . . .

The husband may be slow, quiet, easy-going and the wife volatile, exuberant, and impetuous — and these personality differences may at times be provoking to one or the other. One may have a livelier sense of humor and overdo it now and then at the other's expense. One may be patient, the other just the opposite. . . .

These and countless other big and little differences can cause pain and discord in the family life. But where love and Faith prevail . . . where there is a proper understanding of the mutual character of the marriage relationship . . . where husband and wife are truly "two in one flesh" — these differences never lead to the divorce court.[4]

The fact that the husband is the recognized head of the home does not mean that he may act like a dictator imposing his every whim, opinion, and will upon the entire household. A true husband regards the rights, interest, and welfare of his wife as well as himself and any children that may be born.

Under God's specific direction, therefore, marriage is a mutual relationship founded upon love, faith, and the physical attraction of a man and a woman for each other. Its success depends upon the willingness and the ability of *both* parties to fulfill their respective obligations. It takes a good man and a good woman to make a good marriage.

Marriage is a mutual relationship founded on love. "Sharing" describes this partnership well — sharing of joys, of sorrows; of success, of failure; of responsibility, of blessings.

Pittsburgh Plate Glass Company

The Catholic Church and Marriage

Because marriage is a sacrament as well as a contract, it is absolutely necessary to consider the laws (canons) of the Church regarding marriage. The Church is the guardian of the sacrament and must set up safeguards. The chief protections against unholy or unhappy marriages are impediments — obstacles, you might call them — that block the marriage. They make the union either invalid or at least unlawful. Such impediments are of two kinds: prohibitive and invalidating.

Prohibitive Impediments

A prohibitive impediment is one that forbids a marriage under pain of mortal sin unless a dispensation from the impediment is obtained. A marriage contracted without a dispensation from a prohibitive impediment would be unlawful but nevertheless valid. There are three of them:

1. **A Simple Vow of Chastity** (Canon 1058) as distinguished from a solemn vow is a prohibitive impediment. Someone who has made a private vow of chastity or who is a member of a religious congregation of Sisters or Brothers could validly marry but it would be a serious sin to do so unless a dispensation from the vow had been granted.
2. **Legal Relationship** (Canon 1059) is that which occurs between one who legally adopts another and the adopted. The Church follows the

47

laws of the particular State in interpreting whether the relationship thus set up is a prohibitive or an invalidating impediment. While this impediment does not apply in the United States, if a country declares that, for example, a brother-sister relationship produced by adoption renders any attempted marriage by these two null and void, the Church in that jurisdiction accepts legal adoption as an annulling impediment. If, however, the State forbids such a marriage but does not declare it null and void, the Church in that jurisdiction considers legal adoption as merely a prohibitive impediment.

3. **Mixed Religion** (Canon 1060) means that one party is a Catholic and the other a validly baptized non-Catholic. Unless a dispensation is granted, such a marriage would be valid but sinful. In granting a dispensation in a mixed marriage the Church does so with great reluctance, and then only when she has made certain that there is no danger of the Catholic party or the offspring losing the Faith. This impediment will be considered in greater detail later in this book.

Invalidating Impediments

An invalidating impediment is one under which a proposed marriage is not only forbidden but rendered null and void from the beginning unless, where possible, a dispensation had been obtained. An invalidating impediment is sometimes termed as a diriment or annulling impediment. There are thirteen of them:

1. **Age** (Canon 1067) required for marriage under ecclesiastical law is 16 for the man, 14 for the woman. While such ages may appear very young in this land of ours, one has to remember that the Church legislates laws applicable to all countries and climates. Actually, young people should not marry as soon as they are 16 or 14. Canon Law is careful to add that pastors should try to deter young people from marrying before the ages customary in their country. For the United States, the average age at marriage is about 22 for the man, 20 for the woman.

2. **Impotency** (Canon 1068) means the inability to perform the marital act. If one is impotent he is incapable of making a valid marriage contract. This impotence can be temporary or perpetual. If it is perpetual and if it *precedes* the wedding ceremony, the marriage is null and void. If perpetual, and occurs *after* the marriage has been contracted, it does not change the validity of the marriage. If the impotency is curable or temporary the marriage is valid. Oftentimes such a condition occurs because of nervousness during the first few days or weeks of marriage.

Impotency is not the same as sterility. A sterile person can perform the sexual act. In a sterile man, however, the sperm cells are too few or too feeble to fertilize the ovum. In a sterile woman, ova may not be produced or passages may be blocked, thus preventing fertilization and conception. Sterility never voids a marriage, providing both parties are capable of the sexual act.

3. **Bond of Previous Marriage** (Canon 1069) renders invalid the attempted marriage of a person already validly married. Since marriage is entered into "until death do us part" a married person whose spouse dies is free to marry again. The death of a spouse may never be presumed. It must be proven. The Church is very exact in this matter. Mere lapse of time or the presumption of death which civil law sometimes sets up, is not sufficient.

   This impediment is binding also upon Protestants and the unbaptized; ordinarily there is no freedom to remarry. Exceptional cases will be considered later under the heading "Dissolution of the Marriage Contract."

4. **Disparity of Worship** (Canons 1071–1072) applies to the attempted marriage of a nonbaptized person and a baptized Catholic. Unless the Church removes this impediment, oftentimes called "disparity of cult," the marriage is null and void. Typical examples of nonbaptized persons are Mormons, Jews, Moslems, Hindus, and the various pagan peoples of Asiatic countries. Included with these are those who may be generally classified as "Protestants" but who have never been baptized, or have been baptized invalidly. Like the prohibitive impediment of mixed religion, a dispensation of disparity of worship is reluctantly granted by the Church.

5. **Sacred Orders** (Canon 1072) renders an attempted marriage null and void. This applies only to those with major orders, never to those with minor orders. Major orders are subdiaconate, diaconate, and priesthood. This impediment is of ecclesiastical law, dating from the year 1139. Hence the Church can, but rarely does, grant dispensation from this impediment. Roman Catholic priests of the Byzantine rite are permitted to marry before receiving the subdiaconate and are allowed to continue their married life after ordination.

6. **Solemn Vows** (Canon 1073) likewise render attempted marriage null and void. Solemn vows, you will remember, are taken by those in religious orders; religious congregations have simple vows which are merely a prohibitive impediment to marriage.

7. **Kidnapping** (Canon 1074) means that a man detains a woman in a place without her consent and attempts to force marriage upon her. There can be no marriage as long as she remains in his power. He must first set her free. After this is done, should she consent to marriage, the impediment ceases.

   When one reads of an elopement in the newspapers, it is not to be confused with abduction or kidnapping which is an invalidating impediment. In an elopement, the woman freely runs away for the purpose of marriage; in kidnapping, the woman is not capable of making a free choice.

8. **Crime** (Canon 1075) is an invalidating impediment which refers to a certain kind of crime: adultery with promise of or attempt at marriage; adultery and murder without conspiracy; and murder by conspiracy. The primary purpose of this impediment is to protect the

innocent spouse of an adulterer by depriving the guilty party of the hope of marrying his accomplice and thus profiting by his sin.

9. **Consanguinity** (Canon 1076) or blood relationship renders invalid the marriage of all blood relatives in the direct line, and to the third degree inclusive in the collateral line. Thus, a man cannot marry his mother, his daughter, granddaughter and so on. Nor can a woman ever marry her father, her son, or her grandson. Along the collateral line, a man cannot marry his sister, or vice versa. In the second degree (first cousins) and third degree (second cousins) the Church may grant a dispensation if there is a good reason.

10. **Relationship by Marriage or Affinity** (Canon 1077) sets up an impediment between a married person and the blood relatives of the spouse. A man cannot marry his deceased wife's sister or mother or daughter (by another marriage). Neither can a widow marry her former husband's brother, father, or son. No impediment exists, however, when two brothers of one family marry two sisters of another. Likewise, a stepson may marry his stepmother's mother, sister, or her daughter by a former marriage. This impediment is entirely of Church Law.

11. **Public Decency** (Canon 1078) is an impediment arising from an invalid marriage or from public concubinage; it annuls marriage between one party and the blood relations of the other in the first and second degrees of the direct line. This means that if a man and woman openly live together as husband and wife, even though not validly married, the man may not later marry the woman's mother or daughter. The impediment does not prevent the marriage of the parties themselves who are involved in the invalid marriage or concubinage.

12. **Spiritual Relationship** (Canon 1079) invalidates marriage between those who have contracted spiritual relationship through Baptism. This means a person cannot validly marry one's sponsor in baptism or the person who baptized him.

13. **Legal Relationship** (Canon 1080) or adoption renders invalid the marriage of those whose marriage is invalid by civil law. While this law may exist in some countries, it does not exist in the United States. Therefore, a person may validly marry his adopted sister.

Dissolution of the Marriage Contract

While it is true, as stated previously, that a man and a woman once having entered a valid marriage contract have no power to dissolve that contract, it is also true that under some circumstances a valid marriage contract can be dissolved by the Holy Father. At first glance this may sound like a contradiction. The general principle to remember is this: no person or institution on earth, whether in the Church or in the State, has the power to dissolve a ratified (sacramental) marriage after it has been consummated by sexual intercourse. Once the contract has been rightfully fulfilled, death alone ends the bond. There are times, however, when certain circumstances enter in to give a dissolution of the marriage contract. There are three occasions:

1. **Dissolution of a Ratified and Nonconsummated Marriage.** In a sacramental marriage (both parties baptized) yet one in which the husband and wife have not become "two in one flesh," the Pope may dissolve: when one partner enters a religious order in which solemn vows are taken. This may be done without the consent of the other spouse, but, of course, permission must be granted by the Holy See and acceptance made by the order involved. When one spouse pronounces the solemn vows, the other spouse is then free to marry.

   The unconsummated marriage can be dissolved by papal dispensation after the worthiness of the parties and the public good have been investigated and considered, leaving both parties free to marry. As to the justice of the cause, this is for the Holy See to decide.

2. **The Pauline Privilege.** This dissolution of the bond of matrimony takes its name from St. Paul who explains it in 1 Corinthians 7:12–16. Though a consummated sacramental marriage can never be broken, yet St. Paul says that a contract can be broken in favor of a sacrament. This is true when two unbaptized persons contract marriage and afterward one of them becomes a Catholic and the non-Catholic will not continue to live with the convert, or at least will not do so without danger to the convert's Faith. Then the convert may enter into a sacrament of matrimony with another Catholic and the sacrament automatically dissolves the contract.

3. **The Privilege of the Faith (Petrine Privilege).** When a baptized and a nonbaptized marry they receive no sacrament. If one becomes a Catholic, he or she may petition the Roman Court to be permitted to enter into a sacrament of marriage with another Catholic. Then the sacrament dissolves the previous contract.

The Dignity of Marriage

Marriage is a state in life in which husband and wife love God by loving each other, by serving each other, and by building a family life with children according to the will of Him whom they serve in serving each other. This has always been the teaching of the Church regarding the dignity of marriage. It is indeed strange that the world has not paid greater attention to her teaching. But whether the world will ever do this or not, determine here and now that you will accept the Church's teaching on marriage.

Determine here and now that you will accept the happiness that marriage itself provides, together with the duties which will build that happiness! Determine to do this whether you fully understand what marriage is or not! Only in using a thing according to the purpose of the Maker can you use it prudently. You can only use a watch wisely to keep time. You cannot utilize it as a hammer. You can only use marriage efficaciously according to its nature. You cannot determine your own objective since you did not invent marriage. Resolve to live marriage as it is in the mind of the Maker. Otherwise, you will soon discover that you can only proceed from friendship to courtship to battleship.[5]

SUGGESTIONS FOR READING

Cana Is Forever, Charles H. Doyle (Tarryton-on-Hudson, N. Y.: Nugent Press, 1949).

*Christian Marriage, Edgar Schmiedler, O.S.B., an analysis and commentary on the encyclical letter *Christian Marriage* of Pope Pius XI (Huntington, Ind.: Our Sunday Visitor Press), 88 pp.

Christian Marriage, encyclical of Pope Pius XI (Washington, D. C.: National Catholic Welfare Conference, 1312 Massachusetts Ave., N.W., 1931).

To God Through Marriage, Brother Gerald J. Schnepp, S.M., and Rev. Alfred F. Schnepp, S.M. (Milwaukee, The Bruce Publishing Co., 1958).

Grow Up and Marry, Raphael C. McCarthy, S.J. (St. Louis, Mo.: The Queen's Work, 3115 South Grand Blvd., 1945), 32 pp.

*A Guide to Catholic Marriage, John L. Thomas, S.J. (Milwaukee: The Bruce Publishing Co., 1955).

Happy Marriage, John A. O'Brien (Garden City, N. Y.: Hanover House, 1956).

Is Marriage Your Vocation?, M. J. Huber, C.SS.R., Liguorian Pamphlets (Liguori, Mo.: Redemptorist Fathers, 1956), 29 pp.

Man, Woman and God, James A. McCowan, S.J. (St. Louis, Mo.: The Queen's Work, 3115 South Grand Blvd., 1948), 37 pp.

Marriage, Martin J. Scott, S.J. (New York: The Paulist Press, 401 West 59th Street, 1941), 122 pp.

Marriage and the Family, Alphonse H. Clemens (New York: Prentice-Hall, Inc., 1957).

Marriage and the Family, Edwin O'Rourke (Champaign, Ill.: Newman Foundation at the University of Illinois, 1957).

*No Longer Two: A Commentary on the Encyclical "Casti Connubii" of Pius XI, Walter J. Handren, S.J. (Westminster, Md.: Newman, 1955).

Parenthood, D. A. Lord, S.J. (St. Louis, Mo.: The Queen's Work, 3115 South Grand Blvd., 1946), 38 pp.

Preparing for Marriage, Edward V. Standord, O.S.A. (Chicago: Mentzer, Bush & Co., 1958).

Teenagers and Marriage, E. F. Miller, C.SS.R., Liguorian Pamphlets (Liguori, Mo.: Redemptorist Fathers, 1956), 23 pp.

Toward Happiness and Holiness in Marriage (Washington, D. C.: Family Life Bureau, N.C.W.C., 1955), 12 booklets in spiral binder.

*What They Ask About Marriage, James D. Conway (Chicago: Fides, 1955).

Chapter III THE BASIS OF HAPPY
MARRIAGE

"I want a girl just like the girl that married dear old Dad," so go the words of a popular old song. Whether the song writer knew it or not, he was absolutely correct. Every boy seeks in a girl those qualities he has known in his mother, and every girl chooses a man that reflects her father. "This human process explains why happy marriages repeat themselves from generation to generation and why also, in some families, there is a continuity of unhappy marriages."[1] The basis of a happy marriage, and ruin of an unhappy marriage, is prepared and set in the souls of boys and girls during the period of adolescence by their parents.

Parents' Role

Dr. Karl Stern, noted psychiatrist, states the logic of the situation in this manner: "Man needs preparation for marriage as he needs it for any other vocation or sacrament. The basic and essential preparation consists of the entire development of the personality beginning in earliest infancy. More formal preparation, of course, such as marriage courses, is good and necessary. But the person is basically formed in his attitudes and inclinations through his school years to early adulthood. His degree of maturity and prerequisites for marriage are determined by his parents."[2]

Because of this, parents must recognize their own personal responsibility in the matter of giving premarital education to their children. "Parents are the primary educators of their child

Parents are the primary educators of their child and have the responsibility for his total development.

The Chemstrand Corp.

and incur the basic responsibility for the total development of the child to maturity of person. This responsibility stems from their physical parenthood and is implicit in it. It is coextensive with the total preparation of the child for adult life. Preparation of the child for marriage is then but a special part of the general education parents are obliged to give their child in the effort to bring the child to the Christian perfection of person necessary for natural and supernatural living in later life."[3]

> True parental love aided by intelligence, tactfulness, patience, and a generous measure of common sense can do much to give a child a good start in life. The child is such a complicated little creature that he needs development in his emotional, mental, moral, religious, and physical life. Fortunate is the child with parents who are both able and willing to do their job, who set a good example for their child, and who provide a happy home life where the child has a feeling of security in knowing that he is loved by both father and mother. Under such favorable conditions an excellent foundation is laid for the child to build upon when he reaches the age of discretion.[4]

Many a young man lacks strong character and manliness because of the lack of companionship with a good father, from whom he could learn how good men think, feel, and act. Many a young woman lacks essential womanly qualities because her mother has

54

never displayed them. Children experiencing the loving and giving of parents learn to love and give of themselves even against the desires of their own selfish natures. Example speaks louder than words. That is why it is true to say: "Happy marriages come from happy marriages."

A true father helps his daughter know what to expect in a husband. Any lack of fatherhood on his part will leave a lasting impression upon her choice of a life mate. A true mother gives her son an ideal of womanhood and a formation in spiritual love that will both help him to respect all women and aid him in the selection of a wife. Attitudes of children are for the most part acquired from their parents. Only unselfish parents, therefore, can guarantee the right foundation of a happy marriage for their children.

Youth's Role

When boys and girls are growing up, they go through various stages in their relationship, just as they do in their physical growth. Small children play together without much thought of whether one is a boy or another a girl. Their games are very much the same.

However, after children enter school, differences begin to appear. Most of them come about because of what is customary for boys and girls. Clothes are different. Games begin to be played separately. Boys become "Cub Scouts" and girls join the "Brownies." There develops a period when there are boy-boy gangs and girl-girl groups. Each sex seems to find its recreation together and its interests in common. "To a boy a girl is a delicate, troublesome, mysterious package, made up of curls and dresses, and uninterested in doing the only things in life that matter, such as playing baseball, basketball, fishing in the river and kicking a football. To a girl a boy is a boisterous noisy thing who gets his chief fun out of pulling a girl's hair, playing with bugs and going around with an unwashed face on hikes."[5]

Alan Beck has immortalized this age with his writings which follow:

WHAT IS A BOY?

Between the innocence of babyhood and the dignity of manhood we find a delightful creature called a boy. Boys come in assorted sizes, but

55

Small children play together without much thought as to whether one is a boy or a girl. After children enter school, however there is a period when there are boy-boy gangs and girl-girl groups.

A. Devaney, Inc., N. Y.

all boys have the same creed: to enjoy every second of every minute of every hour of every day and to protest with noise (their only weapon) when their last minute is finished and the adult males pack them off to bed at night.

Boys are found everywhere — on top of, beneath, inside of, climbing on, swinging from, running around, or jumping to. Mothers love them, little girls hate them, older sisters and brothers tolerate them, adults ignore them, and heaven protects them. A boy is Truth with dirt on its face, Beauty with a cut on its finger, Wisdom with bubble gum in its hair, and the Hope of the future with a frog in its pocket.

When you are busy, a boy is an inconsiderate, bothersome, intruding jangle of noise. When you want him to make a good impression, his brain turns to jelly or else he becomes a savage, sadistic, jungle creature bent on destroying the world and himself with it.

A boy is a composite — he has the appetite of a horse, the digestion of a sword swallower, the energy of a pocket size atomic bomb, the curiosity of a cat, the lungs of a dictator, the imagination of a Paul Bunyan, the shyness of a violet, the audacity of a steel trap, the enthusiasm of a firecracker, and when he makes something, he has five thumbs on each hand.

He likes ice cream, knives, saws, Christmas, comic books, the boy across the street, woods, water (in its natural habitat), large animals, Dad, trains, Saturday mornings, and fire engines. He is not much for Sunday school, company, schools, books without pictures, music lessons, neckties, barbers, girls, overcoats, adults, or bed time.

56

Nobody else is so early to rise, or so late to supper. Nobody else gets so much fun out of trees, dogs, and breezes. Nobody else can cram into one pocket a rusty knife, a half-eaten apple, 3 feet of string, an empty Bull Durham sack, two gumdrops, six cents, a slingshot, a chunk of unknown substance, and a genuine supersonic code ring with a secret compartment.

A boy is a magical creature — you can lock him out of your workshop, but you can't lock him out of your heart. You can get him out of your study, but you can't get him out of your mind. Might as well give up — he is your captor, your jailer, your boss, and your master — a freckle faced, pint size, cat-chasing bundle of noise. But when you come home at night with only the shattered pieces of your hopes and dreams, he can mend them like new with the two magic words — "Hi, Dad!"[6]

WHAT IS A GIRL?

Little girls are the nicest things that happen to people. They are born with a little bit of angelshine about them and tho it wears thin sometimes, there is always enough left to lasso your heart — even when they are sitting in the mud, or crying temperamental tears, or parading up the street in mother's best clothes.

A little girl can be sweeter (and badder) oftener than anyone else in the world. She can jitter around, and stomp, and make funny noises that frazzle your nerves; yet just when you open your mouth, she stands there demure with that special look in her eyes. A girl is Innocence playing in the mud, Beauty standing on its head, and Motherhood dragging a doll by the foot.

At this age, girls are no more interested in playing with boys than boys are interested in playing with them.

Girl Scouts of the Milwaukee Area, Inc.

Girls are available in black, white, red, yellow, or brown, yet Mother Nature always manages to select your favorite color when you place your order. They disprove the law of supply and demand — there are millions of little girls, but each is as precious as rubies.

God borrows from many creatures to make a little girl. He uses the song of a bird, the squeal of a pig, the stubbornness of a mule, the antics of a monkey, the spryness of a grasshopper, the curiosity of a cat, the speed of a gazelle, the slyness of a fox, the softness of a kitten, and to top it all off, He adds the mysterious mind of a woman.

A little girl likes new shoes, party dresses, small animals, first grade, noise makers, the girl next door, dolls, make-believe, cans of water, going visiting, tea parties, and one boy. She doesn't care so much for visitors, boys in general, large dogs, hand-me-downs, straight chairs, vegetables, snow suits, or staying in the front yard. She is loudest when you are thinking, the prettiest when she has provoked you, the busiest at bed time, the quietest when you want to show her off, and the most flirtatious when she absolutely must not get the best of you again.

Who else can cause you more grief, joy, irritation, satisfaction, embarrassment, and genuine delight than this combination of Eve, Salome, and Florence Nightingale? She can muss up your home, your hair, and your dignity — spend your money, your time, and your temper — then just when your patience is ready to crack, her sunshine peeks thru and you've lost again.

Yes, she is a nerve-racking nuisance, just a noisy bundle of mischief. But when your dreams tumble down and the world is a mess — when it seems you are pretty much of a fool after all — she can make you a king when she climbs on your knee and whispers, "I love you best of all!"[7]

The Big Switch

During the early teen years, the big switch occurs. Girls become interested in boys. Boys begin to see girls in a new light. Boy-boy gangs and girl-girl groups take on a coed appearance. More and more activities are now involved with members of the opposite sex. A boy finds it pleasant to associate with girls of his own age without fear of being called "sissy." A girl finds it pleasant to associate with boys of her own age without fear of being tagged "tomboy." Mixed groups become great fun. They afford a chance for both sexes to begin to round out their personalities.

Dating Begins

The next stage in social development is the date. Dating isn't just running around with the crowd. There's something personal

The big switch occurs during the early teens. More and more activities of boys and girls are involved with members of the opposite sex.

American Oil Co.

about it. It means a particular boy has asked a particular girl to go to a movie or dance or some place with him. It isn't the crowd any more.

In the United States, dating has become a highly social interrelationship. Emphasis is placed on fun, but it is well to understand that dating is more meaningful than just having a good time. Dating or the association of boy and girl is a long-term preparation for marriage. It can be divided into two types: social and serious.

Social Dating

Social dating, sometimes called casual or circulating dating, is very common among high school and college young people who delay serious consideration of marriage for the sake of an education. It may begin as early as junior high school days and sometimes lasts until the individual is ready to marry.[8] Usually, however, this type of dating begins about the first or second year of high school and continues throughout the college course. This type of dating is the result of the natural instinct in boys and girls for companionship. Each party desires the company of a pleasant, congenial, sympathetic, interesting person for a brief period of entertainment and recreation. "One week the young man may

59

date a girl because of her dancing ability; the second week another girl, because with her he can enjoy an interesting game of tennis. The young girl will accept dates with several young men because she and they have common social and recreational interests and also because she enjoys the companionship of virile and generous friends."[9] Casual dating is not intended to have any special reference to marriage.

Serious Dating

The period of casual dating gradually gives way to more serious dating. Choice of companions and dating partners now becomes more careful and is made with an eye to the selection of a marriage partner. "This is, then, 'the looking around' kind of dating. Since dates during this time have implications of courtship and of steady company keeping, the young man will date only a girl whom he would like to marry and whom he would be happy to have as the mother of his children. The young lady will accept dates with young men likely to prove themselves excellent husbands and fathers."[10] Noting these distinctions, it can be said that for the majority of boys and girls in high school, social dating is the ordinary pattern with an increase of more serious dating the nearer students approach graduation.

The Importance of Dating

Dating is a healthy educational experience. Much can be learned from this activity in preparing boys and girls for adulthood and the intelligent selection of a marriage partner. During a dating situation a young man and girl can learn to get along with people, and through their association with different types of personalities they will be able to make a more intelligent selection in the narrowing-down process. "They will be able to notice that some have a nice disposition and are congenial, some are loud and extroverted, others are more retiring and introverted, some are selfish and egotistical while some others are most considerate and more altruistic. The dating relationship, therefore, has definite meaning in addition to wholesome fun and recreation."[11] It helps develop

60

Dating is a healthy educational experience which helps to prepare boys and girls for adulthood and the intelligent selection of a marriage partner.

Philip Gendreau, N. Y.

one's personality. But personality development is nothing if unaccompanied by spiritual growth. "And prominent authorities tell us that dating does help the boy and girl mature spiritually. Urban Fleege, a noted Catholic psychologist, remarks: 'A moderate association between the sexes during the adolescent period is beneficial to the boy's spiritual life.' Father Gerald Kelly, S.J., writing in his booklet *Modern Youth and Chastity,* supports this position: 'Ordinarily speaking a wholesome social life between the sexes should be helpful rather than harmful to chastity, as it prevents the unnecessary repression of sex attraction and should develop in each sex a fine respect for the other.'"[12] Dating's ultimate purpose, of course, is eventually to find a suitable partner for marriage.

Thus, dating provides the teen-age boy or girl an invaluable, threefold opportunity: to develop his personality, to gain the adequate background experience essential for an intelligent marriage choice, and to foster his spiritual growth.

Going Steady

Like any other human activity, dating is not without its problems. Anyone who reads today's newspapers and magazines can verify this. It is seldom that one does not find a column or article directed at teens regarding dates and dating.

One dating habit that has assumed the proportions of a major problem within the past fifteen years, is the practice of "going

61

steady" among teen-agers. "What was once a trend, and then a pattern, has more recently developed into one of the most dangerous crises ever to confront our youth."[13] Few have had the courage to rise above it.

So that there will be no misunderstanding as to what this problem is, it is important that we define what we mean by going steady in the sense of a dangerous teen-age problem. All authorities agree that going steady consists of three elements. It must be a

1. Frequent association — a teen-age boy and girl may see each other two or three times a week;
2. Exclusive — There is an understanding between the two that she is his "girl friend" and he is her "boy friend," even though they may "occasionally" date someone else;
3. Association motivated by some measure of affection — frequent kissing, etc.

What has brought about this vogue of going steady among today's teens? The reasons are almost as many as the boys and girls engaged in the practice.

The biggest argument in favor of going steady is that it assures the boy and girl of a date for every social function, and greatly reduces the worries and heartaches over not having a date that plague so many teen-agers. "Nearly everybody is doing it, so unless you get yourself a steady girl, you are out of luck when it comes to dates and dances." "A steady takes away all the uncertainty about dates. In this way I am always sure of my date for dances or parties or for an evening at the movies." "You belong to someone who belongs to you." "It gives you a feeling of security when you have a steady girl." "You have a very close friend with whom you can relax, and share ideas and activities." "It's the custom in our community." "It's cheaper than dating someone different every week end." "My girl is a good Catholic girl and she's a help to me religiously. I don't want to take chances with a person whose moral standards are not clearly known."

These and similar reasons pour in from those going steady. At first glance they may appear quite valid and noble. A closer inspection, however, finds that they are all based on the assumption that exclusive dating is a "must." This, of course, is not true. Wide

62

experience in dating is still considered favorable to intelligent mate selection. Young people who have dated several different fellows or girls are less likely to rush into marriage. But let's take a closer look.

> Social dating for teen-agers implies that a teen-age boy, for instance, dates a number of girls during the course of a year, the more diversity the better. This serves the very desirable purpose of enabling a young man to become acquainted with many girls of different types and dispositions. He can get to know girls better, can understand them better, and can make comparisons between their good and bad points.
>
> As a young man grows older he begins to think of the possibility of marriage. He is then inclined to be more serious about his dating of girls because he is definitely looking for the girl that he would like to choose for a life partner. When he finds, or thinks he has found, this girl, he becomes more exclusive in his dating and starts going steady. This is the beginning of the courtship period which is intended to lead to engagement and then to marriage.
>
> Now when a teen-ager jumps these two steps and begins to keep exclusive company with one girl, it is like jumping from grade school into college and completely bypassing high school. No one would seriously consider doing this because the chance of succeeding in college would be very unlikely without the necessary preparation of high school.[14]

Because of the psychological differences in the make-up of the two sexes it is not an easy thing to understand the opposite sex. It takes a good bit of acquaintanceship and study to achieve sufficient understanding for a successful working relationship. This cannot come about by dating exclusively too soon just one individual. Variety is the spice of life for the young. Going steady should be postponed until such a time when marriage can be reasonably assured.

This is not the Church's teaching alone. Marriage counselors, educators, judges, psychiatrists, and parents all testify to the disadvantages of going steady. Recently even the United States Navy expressed itself on the subject:

> Officers and faculty members at the United States Naval Academy look at this phenomenon (going steady) with grave misgivings. After all, a midshipman's contacts during the week are with his shipmates, his professors and various officers — all male. Then, when the weekend arrives, he supposedly has the opportunity to broaden his social development with delightful feminine contacts. But what has been happening under the going-steady rule that modern youth has imposed on itself? He takes his date to the dance and spends the entire evening con-

stantly at her side. His outlook and experience are enhanced by the thoughts, opinions and personality of just one female. What should be a lighthearted change of pace from the midshipman's demanding routine and an opportunity to learn some social graces, all too often becomes a serious, headlong, almost frantic search for a lifetime mate! The disinclination of today's young men to play the field means that many of them are electing their future wives before they have developed much judgment in such matters — before they have had a chance to appraise a representative cross-section of the marital market. This, we think, is not the ideal way to choose Navy wives.[15]

The Moral Problem

Besides losing the social advantages and contacts that have a great influence upon a person in later life, going steady frequently exposes one to serious moral dangers. Of course, when a couple first starts going steady, sin is usually the farthest thing from their thoughts, and so they are naturally very resentful of anyone's suggesting that they may be placing themselves in an occasion of sin. But with the darkness of the intellect and the weakness of the will (the result of original sin) moral problems are going to arise sooner or later.

It's natural for boys and girls to want to be together . . . but to be together exclusively long before there is any prospect of marriage is quite another thing. The natural tendency for a couple going steady is to show affection to one another. At first this show of affection will probably be very innocent and well meant. After a short period of going with the same girl, the boy often finds that simple signs of affection, like holding her hand or a decent kiss, become rather tame, so that he has to go a little further to re-experience the thrill of that first kiss. And while she still may desire only affection, he may well desire something more. Once this takes place one of two things happens: either they will give in to the temptation they feel or they will fight the temptation. If they give in, they commit a mortal sin; if they don't, they often become so irritable just from the struggle that one or the other or both oftentimes give in sooner or later (if they continue to go steady) just to soothe the other's irritated feelings.

Now when it comes to temptations, it is not enough alone to pray. A boy and a girl cannot place themselves in a deliberate occasion of sin and then turn to God and complain about how badly they are tempted. God expects them to know enough to realize that they have no right to complain about temptations if they did everything to bring them on themselves. Steps have to be taken to remove themselves from the proximate occasion of sin. This means, of course, breaking up . . . circulating instead of steady dating. Of course, there are a lot of teen-agers who are too far "gone" to admit this fact. When counselors point out the fact that this going steady could be an occasion of sin, many of these young people become very resentful. They try to forget two things: that they might actually be in an occasion of sin and, second, that it is a further sin to place themselves deliberately in circumstances where they almost invariably sin. Boys and girls going steady close their minds to such reasoning. Stubborn stupidity is their weapon against God's command.

To show to what degree these teen-agers are both stubborn and stupid . . . soon they begin asking the question (the unbelievably stupid and revealing question): "How far can we go without sinning?" If they continue to date exclusively, standards fall and like Lucifer they commit the sin of pride; their idea that they are going to be the exceptions to falling is soon smothered beneath the barrage of lust. They soon come to realize that they can no longer say, "We never sinned together."

Once this happens, consciences often awaken, thanks to God's grace . . . and when they look back at how they got into the sinful situation, they realize a lot of things: that they were leading up to sin for a long time, that there were sins of thought and desire scattered all along the way, that many of the times they sinned alone it was because of their going steady. Discouragement or a mild form of despair enters the soul. . . . This, of course, can only be removed by going to confession and promising to avoid that occasion of sin in the future . . . which means, breaking up.[16]

The Only Solution

The only reason justifying going steady is marriage within the very near future. "Some teenagers think that this rule applies only to their set; the truth is of another color. Even with persons of marriageable age steady and exclusive company-keeping between a man and a woman cannot be justified on moral grounds unless they have serious intentions of marriage. This means in effect that even though a man be 30, 40 or 50 years old he has no right to go steady with any woman unless there is both the freedom of and the possibility for marriage in the foreseeable future (within 2 years)."[17] With so many going steady, however, the above words may sound puritanical if not prudish, but they are far from that. They are well thought out and prudent. For remember, dating is a prelude to courtship and steady dating is a form of courtship intended only for those who will definitely marry in the near future. In general the high school boy or girl is not ready for immediate marriage. Authorities say that only one out of every seven couples who go steady eventually wed one another. Therefore, going steady is morally wrong for the vast majority. There are many high school students who realize this. Among them are the boys and girls at McNicholas High School in Cincinnati who have formed a new club called the "Polywogs." According to *Co-Ed*, the school paper, the purpose of this club is to accommodate fellows and girls who aren't going steady, but who want to have fun anyway.

Their club is appropriately named. *Poly* is a Greek word for "many." Then we have

W — We
O — Oppose
G — Going
S — Steady

Add it up and you get POLYWOGS. (For further information write to McNicholas High School, 6532 Beechmont Avenue, Cincinnati, Ohio.)

An Unwed Mother Tells Her Story

Most likely there will be some high school students who will scoff at the above words of wisdom. Should you be one of them let me conclude this instruction on going steady by inviting you to visit a home for unwed mothers in your area. There you will see the tragic results of going steady before one is ready for marriage.

To illustrate what you would discover and learn in such an institution read the words of a particular unwed mother who arrived at St. Joseph's Hospital, Scranton, Pennsylvania, some years ago to have a baby out of wedlock. Her words are printed here in hopes that teen-agers now keeping steady company will realize that weakness, sin, and tragedy play no favorites.

> I still can't believe it. I can't believe that a few short days ago I became a mother, an unwed mother. I can't get used to the idea that I had an illegitimate baby.
> It's like a dream. A bad dream. I have no one to blame but myself. . . .
> I can't blame the nuns who taught me or the priests who gave our high school retreats. They did speak to us about the dangers of steady company keeping, about dating, petting, parking and things like that.
> But frankly it never rang a bell. In fact, we thought it was a great

66

joke and referred to the nuns as "Holy Hags" and the priests as the "Holy Joes with the loose habits." We accused them of having evil minds, of being suspicious, out of date, behind the times. We even said they were bitter and frustrated.

I was especially critical because the priest in charge of our high school took me aside one day and lectured me on the dangers of keeping steady company in high school.

I was furious. It was none of his business if I walked to school with my boy friend, if I was with him between classes, walked home with him after school and dated him three times a week.

The more Father talked, the more I clammed up, and the more I determined that no matter what Father said, there was nothing dangerous about company keeping. Bob and I loved each other and that was enough. Even my mother agreed that it was enough.

Well, it wasn't. And not long after Father's talk, things started to get out of hand. I don't know how it is with other couples, but we slipped into sin gradually, with our falls becoming more frequent and more shameful as time went on. We were both sorry, we both went to confession and promised, never again.

But our promises didn't last. How could they? We were seeing each other constantly, indulging in long embraces, permitting more and more serious liberties.

A lot had already happened to me, but I simply couldn't see it. I couldn't see that now no one, not my parents, my confessor, or my teachers could tell me a thing. I knew more than them all — more than the priests, more than the Church, more than God Himself.

I was really on the skids, but I was too blind, or too dumb, or too proud to admit it.

Things went on like that for months until one night, boom, it happened. Just like that. For once I let myself go too far, and nothing, neither thoughts of my parents, my education, my background or my religion, was enough to stop me.

All of these things crossed my mind during that first experience and those that followed. One thing never occurred to me: That I might become pregnant. It didn't happen the first time, so why worry! Anyway, I thought, it can't happen to me.

I kept repeating this to myself even when I knew beyond a shadow of a doubt that it had happened. I invented a dozen explanations. I was sick, upset. I had a cold. I was run down. I was everything, but I was not pregnant.

One month passed, a second and then a third. Now there was no mistake. I was pregnant. I was going to have a baby. It had happened to me.

I wonder if there's any use trying to describe how a girl feels when she finally faces this fact. Actually, only those who have known the shock — the panic — the shame — the fear and the hell of such a discovery can even remotely understand what it's like.

You can't eat. You can't sleep — you can't even think straight. Your world has collapsed. You are trapped, ruined, disgraced.

67

I wanted so much to tell Mother and Dad but I couldn't. I hated the idea of hurting them after all they had done for me. And I was ashamed to face them — ashamed of letting them down.

One by one I thought of possible solutions. I thought of suicide and abortion. I thought of running away — but desperate as I was I knew these would settle nothing.

I finally decided on marriage. This was an easy out. No one would be surprised and with the marriage announcement predated, no one would be the wiser.

So off I went to tell Bob. I was so sure of what he'd say that I almost told my parents before I went out that we were already married.

It's a good thing I didn't because Bob flatly refused to marry me. Sure he loved me — but he had his career to think of. Another thing, he couldn't disappoint his parents.

Oh, he'd help with the expenses. He'd foot the bills if I went away and had the baby, but as for marriage, it was no dice.

I couldn't believe it. This was the boy I loved. The one who loved me; the boy for whom I had endangered my reputation, my future, my eternal salvation.

I thought he was joking when he drove up to the house, opened the car door and said, "I'm awfully sorry, Kit." I knew the joke was on me.

Now the real hell set in. And it was a hell that lasted for five long endless months. A hell that was made all the more unbearable because no one knew the terrible secret I was carrying around. Not even my parents.

How did I conceal it so long? By wearing a girdle all the time, by pulling myself in constantly and by living in dungarees and a large, loose shirt.

People did remark that I was putting on weight — but since no one suspected that a girl like me would be pregnant, nothing was said.

Finally, mother took me by surprise. She came into my room one night unexpectedly and knew immediately that something was wrong.

In an instant I was in her arms and before I knew it, both of us were crying. I, tears of relief. She tears of unbelief and bewilderment.

Later that night my father came in. He, too, was kind, sympathetic, and forgiving. But his eyes were red from crying, and I could feel him tremble as he held me close. . . .

If I only listened to my parents, my teachers, and my priests. If I only watched the beginning of things. If I only believed that it could happen to me.

What's the use! It did happen. And you know something more amazing? IT CAN HAPPEN EVEN TO YOU.[18]

Sensible Dating

The only sensible dating pattern for high school youth who have no intentions of immediate marriage is social dating. Going steady

The **development** of healthful, creative, and challenging interests and skills is important for sensible dating and a successful marriage.

involves very serious responsibilities which should not be undertaken lightly or hastily. It should be preceded by wide and friendly mingling with others. Marriage, remember, means not just going out together and having fun and loving one another. It means a secure and paying job for the boy, and it means work in the home for the girl — doing housework, caring for the children, and being a helpful citizen in the community. It takes grown-up people to do these things, people who are happy and grown-up enough to keep God's laws in marriage.

Those who have studied successful marriages know that a marriage can be no better than the two personalities that enter into it. People who have undesirable traits before marriage will not suddenly lose these traits. Marriage does not change basic personality structure. That is why it is all important during your dating days to pay careful consideration to the qualities of your dating partner. According to 12,500 high school students polled on this question there are four chief qualities the perfect dating partner should possess. They are: (1) dependability, (2) maturity, (3) cleanliness in thought and action, and (4) considerateness. According to

69

this same survey, the girls listed some undesirable traits in boys, while boys did not hesitate to list the undesirable traits in girls. They are listed below only to serve as a checklist for yourself. Remember you are in marriage what you are before.

Undesirable Traits in Boys	Undesirable Traits in Girls
(*According to girls*)	(*According to boys*)
1. Vulgarity in speech and actions	1. Overdependent
2. Withholding compliments	2. Too serious
3. Disrespectful	3. Flighty
4. Demanding of necking and petting	4. Complaining
5. Being overtalkative about themselves	5. Money-minded
6. Dishonest flattery	6. Sensitive

Sound Rules for Teen-Age Dating

Like any other human activity, dating has its rules. The basic rule is prudence. This virtue will determine details of activities and conduct, but it cannot be effective without an honest good intention to do what is right on the part of both parties. Thus for successful dating the following rules should be observed.

1. Dating can be fun without resorting to sex and cheap conduct. Plan your dates. Have something to do: movies, dances, parties, games, concerts, TV.
2. Group dating is sometimes wise; "there is safety in numbers" but only if the couples are all highly principled.
3. Drinking and dating don't mix well. Liquor has a double-edged effect — it excites the emotions and passions at the same time that it weakens the will.
4. A safe pathway to success is to blend harmoniously "living modern" with old-fashioned virtues and traits. The Ten Commandments do not change for lovers.
5. Know your date! Don't go out on "blind dates" unless another couple is along — and then be cautious.
6. Stay out of "Lovers' Lanes." Don't place yourself in an occasion of sin. (An automobile is a vehicle for locomotion, not parking.)
7. Don't ask for trouble — girls should dress sensibly; boys should drive with both hands on the wheel.
8. At the first moment, turn away from unclean thinking. The struggle for purity is won or lost in thought.
9. There is a tendency because of late dating hours and preoccupation with the pleasures of dating to lessen religious living. The great dangers of dating demand more grace, not less. Wise boys and girls participate at Mass and receive Communion more regularly than previously.
10. At the close of every date, both are honestly able to say to God: "Thank You, I've had a wonderful time."

Prayer Before a Date

O Mary, Mother of us all, you have taught us the meaning of true friendship by your constant concern for helping and pleasing others, primarily your own divine Son. Your life is a perfect example of genuine interest, generosity, courtesy, warmth, and unselfishness.

Mary, help us to make this date strengthen true friendship in our hearts. Only then will it be worthy to be offered to your Son as a pledge of our respect for Him and for each other. Help us to be an occasion of grace to each other and to all who share these hours with us. Protect us body and soul. Make us aware of the presence of God in one another.

Keep us chaste, O Virgin most pure.

Make us wise, O Virgin most prudent.

Brighten our date with laughter, O Cause of our Joy.

We will then be richer in mind and heart for having shared each other's company. We will be strengthened in true friendship for you, for your Son, and for each other, through Christ our Lord. Amen.[19]

SUGGESTIONS FOR READING

Blame No One but Yourself, Charles H. Doyle (Tarrytown-on-Hudson, N. Y.: Nugent Press, 1955).

Child Behavior, Frances L. Ilg, M.D., and Louise Bates Ames, Ph.D. (New York: Dell Publishing Co., Inc., 1958).

"The Going Steady Crisis," Roma R. Turkel, *Information,* Vol. 71, March, 1957, pp. 12–19.

*"Juvenile Courtships," Francis J. Connell, C.SS.R., *The American Ecclesiastical Review,* March, 1955, pp. 181–191.

"Looking Forward to Marriage," Ed Willock, *Today,* Vol. 13, November, 1957, pp. 10–12.

So You Want to Get Married, Dorothy Fremont Grant (Milwaukee: The Bruce Publishing Co., 1947).

Teen-Age Dating, Lawrence G. Lovasik, S.V.D. (Techny, Ill.: Divine Word Publications, 1958).

Teen-Agers and Dating, Donald F. Miller, C.SS.R. (Liguori, Mo.: The Liguorian Press, 1956), 23 pp.

Tips for Teens, Alvena Burnite (Milwaukee: The Bruce Publishing Co., 1955).

Training the Adolescent, R. C. McCarthy, S.J. (Milwaukee: The Bruce Publishing Co., 1934).

When They Start Going Steady, Father Conroy (St. Paul: Catholic Guild Education Society, 1954).

Your Adolescent, Lawrence K. Frank and Mary Frank (New York: New American Library, 1956).

**Your Dating Days,* Paul H. Landis (New York: Whittlesey House, 1954).

You Should Be Going Steady, Joseph T. McGloin, S.J. (St. Louis: The Queen's Work, 1957).

Chapter IV APPROACHING THE SACRAMENT

Without a doubt, the saddest refrain in all the world is the one so often spoken by the unhappily married: "Oh, if I had only known what kind of a person I was marrying, I would never have gotten married!" After one is married, however, it's too late to do anything about this factor. It's do or die. That is why courtship is such an important period. It is during this time that a young man and a young woman determine what they consider most suitable for an ideal life mate.

Courtship Important

Pope Pius XI stressed the importance of the careful selecting of a life mate during courtship: "To the proximate preparation of a good married life belongs very specially the care of choosing a partner; on that depends a great deal whether the forthcoming marriage will be happy or not, since one may be to the other either a great help in leading a Christian life, or a great danger and hindrance."

Courtship, therefore, represents a very important step leading to marriage.

It is more advanced and serious than dating and implies that both parties are now thinking about marriage and its responsibilities, its societal expectations and its objectives. Serious courtship for most young men and women begins after graduation from high school. If they are contemplating college, courtship is delayed for a few years, although approximately 25% of the college and university population is now married.

72

Courtship affords a testing period to see if a couple is ready for marriage. True love wants to prove itself.

H. Armstrong Roberts

As two people make the transition from dating to courtship, they become more and more involved with each other and less and less involved and concerned with outsiders. To a certain degree they live in a world all their own and the whole basis of this unique experience is to please one another, each seeking to satisfy the emotional needs of the other. They prefer one another's company to that of anyone else. The feeling of belonging and knowing that she is loved brings great happiness to the young lady. To be considered worthy of love adds to the young man's self-esteem. This experience gives rise to intense feelings of happiness.[1]

That is why courtship is such a serious period in one's approach to the sacrament of matrimony. Hasty decisions during this time lead eventually to divorce courts. Infatuation and exaggerated romanticism may make one momentarily happy, but they certainly will not make an enduring marriage. Courtship affords a testing period to determine whether or not the couple is really ready for marriage, whether they really love one another. It constitutes a discussion period to test each other's disposition and personality.

73

It is during this period that a couple should be able to determine whether or not it is wise for them to marry.

> Consequently, a young man should have definite ideas as to the qualifications he expects in the girl he hopes to marry, and at the same time he must have an understanding of the qualifications he himself can offer. A popular writer on marriage has expressed this thought in a very positive way. "The young man who starts out on his matrimonial adventure by looking around for a girl good enough to be his bride is making a false start. The first thing for him to do is to make certain that he is good enough to be a fine girl's husband."[2]

Narrowing Down the Choice

There is no foolproof way in which one can assure himself of the right mate for marriage. However, a number of studies have been made which could easily serve as guides in a more careful and less haphazard way of selecting a husband or wife. The first of these guides or norms is personality.

Personality

Marriage is never better or worse than the two personalities that go into it. The kind of personality one brings into marriage, therefore, is of utmost importance. It determines or conditions to a great degree one's success or failure in marriage.

Personality is one's inner self. It is *you*. It is you with all your powers, abilities, habits, and virtues. Very evidently, husband and wife can be happy together if each has a pleasing personality. Thus it is important to know the answers to the questions: What kind of person am I? And when you can answer that, you are ready to ask: What kind of person must I have in order to meet my emotional and other needs? How well one has learned to acquire and practice the seven great virtues of: (1) Faith, (2) Hope, (3) Charity, (4) Prudence, (5) Justice, (6) Fortitude, (7) Temperance; as well as the seven little natural moral virtues of (1) tact, (2) order, (3) courtesy, (4) punctuality, (5) sincerity, (6) loyalty, (7) caution in speech, will determine the quality of one's personality and its strengths, and will assure you of a happy and successful marriage.

According to the late Lewis T. Terman, a noted psychologist, the personality traits to look for in a woman are the following:

1. Kindly attitudes toward others.
2. Expects kindly attitudes from others.
3. Does not easily take offense.
4. Is not unduly concerned about the impressions she makes upon others.
5. Does not look upon social relations as rivalry situations.
6. Is cooperative.
7. Does not object to subordinate roles.
8. Is not annoyed by advice from others.
9. Enjoys activities that bring educational and pleasurable opportunities to others.
10. Likes to do things for the dependent and underprivileged.
11. Is methodical and painstaking in her work.
12. Is careful in regard to money.
13. Is conservative and conventional in religion, morals, and politics.
14. Has an optimistic outlook on life.

The personality traits to look for in a man are the following:
1. Emotionally, he is even and stable.
2. He is cooperative.
3. Has benevolent attitude toward inferiors and the underprivileged.
4. Respects womanhood.
5. Tends not to be self-conscious and somewhat extroverted.
6. Shows superior initiative.
7. Shows great willingness to give close attention to details.
8. Is willing to assume responsibility.
9. He likes to do things methodically and he likes methodical people.
10. Is saving and cautious in money matters.
11. Holds conservative attitudes.
12. Has a favorable attitude toward religion.
13. Strongly upholds the sex code and other social conventions.[3]

In other words, the first thing that you look for in a mate is to find out if he or she is well adjusted, emotionally mature, a possessor and user of common sense. Pure, ordinary, unadulterated common sense is an essential ingredient in marriage.

For example, common sense would indicate that women who nag, are not affectionate, are selfish, inconsiderate, complaining, interfering, slovenly and quick-tempered are great risks in marriage. And men who are selfish, inconsiderate, unsuccessful at their jobs, untruthful, complaining, not affectionate and harsh are poor risks in marriage.[4]

Desire for Children

Since marriage is primarily meant for the rearing and education

75

of children, the desire to have children is definitely related to marital happiness. Both parties should have a strong desire to be cocreators with God. The exact number of children need not be arrived at before marriage; but having children, if it is God's will, must be desired by both parties. Couples who want children are more successful in their marriage than couples who do not want children.

Home Life

A close study of a girl's home life will help a young man arrive at an exact picture of his partner. As stated in the last chapter, good marriages come from good homes. That is why it is all important for a young man to meet his partner's parents far enough in advance of marriage to determine whether or not she is a "house devil" or a real "home-loving girl." The more desirable qualities a family has, the greater the chance that marriage with a member of that family will be successful. In looking at the family background of a prospective life mate, the following ten circumstances should be considered:
1. Superior happiness of parents,
2. Childhood happiness,
3. Lack of conflict with mother,
4. Firm but not harsh home discipline,
5. Strong attachment to mother,
6. Strong attachment to father,
7. Lack of conflict with father,
8. Parental frankness about sex,
9. Infrequency and mildness of childhood punishment,
10. An attitude free from disgust or aversion toward sex.

Occupation and Finances

Believe it or not, occupations have something to do with stability of marriage. A young man considering marriage should be settled in his work and have some money saved. Precisely how much depends on the economic standard which he and his girl set for themselves. This, of course, will be based on the kind of lives they are in the habit of living. The prospective husband should have a steady source of income — one which can support a wife and a family.

Health

In your picture of the ideal mate, there should certainly be an element of normally robust health. Marriage and family life can take a great toll of one's physical resources. Bearing a child, though it is a normal physiological fact and by no means a sickness, is nevertheless not something to be undertaken lightly. Good physical condition is necessary to support a family, to keep a home in good order, to bear the strain and worry of sleepless nights with sick children, to get up at two in the morning for a feeding or to give a child a "drink of water" is not easy for even the most robust. It becomes almost impossible for those who are in poor health. Common sense, then, demands that you choose as your partner in marriage someone reasonably healthy, and that you give yourself to that partner with the health necessary for the performance of your functions as husband or wife, father or mother.[5]

Education

Education is essential in making a success of marriage. Just how much depends on the individuals entering into the union. It is hoped in this day and age that both partners possess at least a high school education. According to the leading marriage counselors, it is far better that the young man have more education than the young lady. The reason is obvious. It is man's role in marriage to be the head of the home.

Age

Although, in general, rural people marry at an earlier age than urban people, the uneducated earlier than the educated, the unskilled earlier than the skilled, and lower classes earlier than the upper classes, all studies show that the chances for happiness in marriage are much less when men marry before the age of 20 and when women marry before the age of 18.[6]

Rosalind Russell of Hollywood and Broadway fame places great emphasis on the proper age in marriage.

My theory has always been that the girl who shops carefully for a husband or a dress, generally gets better value than one who picks the first article which strikes her fancy. I was 29 when I said, "I do," that's ten years later than most girls wed nowadays. From my own

77

The unique companionship of courtship is made complete by companionship with Christ.

John Ahlhauser

experience, and from all I see, I am convinced that today's boys and girls who are so anxious to set up housekeeping will have much more real happiness if they marry later. To begin with, young people who grow up first and marry later are far more likely to pick the right partners for the right reasons. Too-young brides and grooms expect the prince to be charming forever and the princess to be a dream girl always. But when the romantic haze lifts, a man and a woman stand revealed with their faults showing. To young people this may come as a rude shock. Older people are wiser and more ready to adjust.[7]

Moral Character

If there is anything that constantly appears on the top of the list of qualifications expected in a life mate, it is moral character. By moral character we mean not only personal goodness, but also the ability to maintain personal goodness as a way of life. There are few things more pathetic than the perpetual adolescent who enters marriage unable to realize that he owes obedience to God, to society, and to all those who are lawfully placed above him in life. A person with good moral character will show his maturity before marriage. It will be evident in his attitude toward sincerity, honor,

78

purity, duty, and religion. It will be revealed in his taste in recreations, amusements, reading, and everything which he performs.

A person of good moral character has the proper attitude toward sex. Today, many young people are being misled to believe that it is perfectly all right to have sexual relations before marriage. A person of good moral character knows that such conduct is morally wrong. Furthermore, he realizes that individuals who indulge in this conduct make extremely poor risks in marriage.

Religion

While this subject will be considered at greater length in a future chapter, let it be said that all reputable studies of marriage counselors show that mixed marriages in which both husband and wife hold their separate faiths have a much higher rate of failure, separation, and divorce than other marriages. These same studies reveal that when both partners are Catholic the divorce rate is the lowest of all marriages mixed and nonmixed.

Use Your Head as Well as Your Heart

The above qualifications indicate that finding the ideal life mate is far from easy, but it is not impossible. If one uses his head as well as his heart in "falling in love," marriage can be a success. Keep in mind, however, that it is not so much to find the right partner as it is to be the right one. Before venturing forward in search for a partner in marriage, make doubly sure that you measure up to your own standards.

Marriage Is Not a Reform School

In considering a life partner, one has to bear in mind many things. Among the important items is this basic fact: marriage is not a reform school. A person is in marriage what he was before. That is why it is all important to constantly bear in mind that sympathy for a person will never make a successful marriage. It takes true love, and true love consists in using one's head as well as one's heart.

There are some individuals in this grand world of ours that just

79

aren't ready for marriage. They should be avoided at all costs. Father Charles Hugo Doyle in an excellent book for teen-agers and all those contemplating wedlock, *Blame No One but Yourself,* gives a list of individuals who just aren't set for marriage.[8]

Girls Should Beware of the Following Type of Suitors

1. **The Sugar-Daddy Type.** He is a real pain in the neck. He is getting on in years and wants to kid himself and you, if you are that stupid, into believing that he can give you security where a younger man can offer you only love.
2. **The Job-Hopping Type.** Be awfully careful of marrying a man who in the past two years has not been able to hold a job for more than a month or two at a time. Try to find out the "why" of the numerous moves. Is it because your boy friend is not capable of holding a job, is untrustworthy, is lazy, or cannot get along with his superiors or his fellow workers? Only the desperate marry this type.
3. **The Accident-Prone Type.** A good deal of care ought to be exercised before you consider marriage to a man who is always having accidents. Usually accident-prone persons have unstable work records, change jobs frequently, are spontaneous and casual in their social relationships, but are irresponsible toward their families.
4. **The Dominant Type.** Most girls like the masterful type, but not the dictatorial type. He may say, "Honey, after we're married, we will be as one," but *he'll* be that one.
5. **The Patriarchal Type.** This man will boast more of being the father of your children than he will of being your husband. He'll be a good father, but a vacuous sort of husband.
6. **The Stock-Market Plunger, or the Gambler Type.** Caution must be exercised before a girl considers marriage with a person who has an idea that he can beat the horses, the numbers, or the stock market. This type usually turns out to be the wrong one on which to bet a marriage.
7. **The Parasitical Type.** This is the fellow who wants to marry a girl with money, so that he can enjoy the finer things of life, to which he is unaccustomed. The milder form of this type is the *sponger,* but he is just as bad as other types. He usually calls just before meal-time, and hangs around all day or evening looking at TV. He is the proverbial *free-loader.* You could do nicely without this type of character.
8. **The Jealous Type.** Jealousy lives upon doubt, and comes either to an end or becomes fury as soon as it passes from doubt to certainty. Watch out for the nosy, inquisitive beau. There is more self-love than love in this individual.
9. **The Alibi Type.** In good, plain old English, this type is made up frequently of chronic liars. How can you live long or happily with a person you cannot trust or depend upon?

80

10. **The Escapist Type.** This type is usually emotionally unstable or immature. He will never face up to problems. He will, in fact, run away from problems. Marriage, remember, is no reform school.

There are also a few types of women young men ought to avoid in selecting a partner for life. According to Father Doyle the following types of women can make a man's life pretty miserable.[9]

Boys Should Beware of the Following Type of Girls

1. **The Maternal Type.** This type of girl, while essentially wholesome, can be a pain in the neck. She will straighten your tie, offer to sew on a button, will worry about your not getting enough rest, etc. She is a good type for a person who feels the need of mothering, but most fellows get away from home to avoid just such dependence.
2. **The Baby-Doll Type.** This type is quite familiar — dreamy eyes, dimples, round face, and a little on the plump side, employs baby talk, and is frequently noticeably selfish. Marriage is no game for either babies or dolls.
3. **The Competitive Type.** The competitive gal is one who delights in setting her net for the young man her best girl friend has been dating regularly. She gets more of a kick out of landing the fish on some other girl's line than in doing her own fishing. This type is a bit of a risk in marriage since, if the competitive spirit is deep-rooted, she may work as deftly on someone else's husband.
4. **The Possessive Type.** This type can be a real headache, for such a woman often holds her husband so closely that she stifles him. The possessive type dominates every waking moment of her husband's life. She resents his friends, she wants him solely for herself. Be cautious of the girl who wants you to give up all your friends for her.
5. **The Romantic Type.** When this "dreamer" is tied down to talk about a home, finances, budgets, housekeeping, or children, she naïvely remarks that "All that matters is love." Be more than a little cautious of the gal who keeps saying: "Do it because you love me."
6. **The Matriarchial Type.** This is the "Lady MacBeth" type. She will scold if your shoes are dirty or if your hair is not combed or not recently cut. Some men need such a wife, and they could go places under her domination and pushing; but for one who can take such a deal, there are 99 whose ulcers would have ulcers in no time at all.
7. **The Huntress Type.** Here we have the boy-crazy individual who gets more kick out of the chase than in the capture. The older she gets, the more desperate she may become. She giggles, flirts, wears daring gowns and outlandish hats, and takes keen delight in knowing that she is fancy bait. The trouble in marrying such a girl is that she may not be easily domesticated.
8. **The Fragile, Helpless Type.** This type is so helpless that she cannot cook, manage a house, or clean a window. Such a wife certainly won't make a "helpmate"!

81

9. **The Masculine Type.** This type can change a tire with one hand tied behind her back, shingle a roof, face a mouse or a moose with equal calm; and she wears men's clothes at the drop of a hat. . . . But a girl should definitely possess some feminine traits.

10. **The Extravagant Type.** Every young man contemplating marriage and faced with the choice of a suitable mate ought to consider well the girl who, among other qualities, is careful, thrifty, and economical. Boys, be especially careful, of a clothes horse — that is, the girl who spends all her wages on clothes. Be careful, too, of the girl who goes on spending sprees, one who buys things not because they are needed but because there is a sale going on somewhere. If such a one hasn't learned to save any of her own money . . . she won't save yours.

11. **The Career Type.** This type would rather sacrifice her husband than her career. Such a wife doesn't make for a happy home.

12. **The Nagging Type.** One of the most common reasons given for broken marriages is that one or the other of the mates indulged in the miserable habit of nagging. Unless you have the nerves of steel and a hide as tough as a rhinoceros, don't marry this type.

From the above lists of individuals to avoid as a life partner, one can readily see how necessary it is to prepare for marriage. Because of this, it is essential to the outcome of marriage that both parties make use of prayer in their individual lives. It takes three to get married, the lover (man), the beloved (woman), and God, who is Love. To stay in tune with the will of Love requires regular habits of prayer, because without God man can do nothing. A true spiritual life does not admit of a "self-made man."

Importance of Prayer

In his great encyclical *On Christian Marriage,* Pope Pius XI stressed the importance of prayer during this period. "Let them diligently pray for Divine help, so that they will make their choice in accordance with Christian prudence, not indeed led by the blind and unrestrained impulse of lust, nor by any desire of riches or other base influence, but by a true and noble love and by a sincere affection for the future partner. . . ." As in the other states in life which we have considered, prayer is essential toward achieving a successful marriage. An old Russian proverb testifies to this:

> Before embarking on a journey, pray once.
> Before leaving for war, pray twice.
> Before you marry, pray three times.

Love and Marriage

Happiness in marriage does not result automatically from the mere act of getting married. It is achieved only by mutual striving, endless patience, and persistent effort. The happiness a couple gets out of marriage must be earned. This means supreme effort on the part of both must be maintained before marriage ever takes place. A lofty unselfish love in marriage is prepared for beforehand by a lofty unselfish love during courtship. This implies, of course, that both parties understand what love really means.

It is amazing and even tragic how prevalent is the false idea of the meaning of love in the minds of many high school students. "Love is falling for someone," a boy writes, "it'll strike like a thunderbolt." A girl states: "Every time I look at him I have a wonderful feeling inside." "Butterfly-in-stomach feeling," ventures another.

It's almost as if someone cooked up a gigantic conspiracy to produce this fuzzy thinking. In many instances it is produced. The plot is extreme romanticism. It reaches us daily through songs, the advertisements for soap and cosmetics, the radio, the movies, television, and the books and magazines we read. You know the typical story. It goes something like this:

She was sweet sixteen and a doll. Nothing much had ever happened to her. She had been living a life of innocent waiting, doing her schoolwork, helping her mother around the house. Suddenly, one night at a school dance he appeared. This was it! Right away they knew that they were made for each other. They had "that ol' feeling." Suddenly nothing else in the world mattered. They were in love. Completely, utterly, suddenly, madly in love. From the very first kiss they realized that fate had thrown them into each other's arms. There was nothing else to do but get married for this was the real thing. And so they eloped and got married and lived happily ever after.

This romantic fairy tale has deceived many teen-agers into thinking that they are really in love when in reality it is nothing more than mere infatuation. How many more happy marriages there would be if this false idea of love were not so widespread. True love is not infatuation, everyone knows that. But how to tell the one from the other? Monsignor J. D. Conway, the famous question-and-answer priest, makes some very definite distinctions between love and infatuation in his book: *What They Ask About Marriage*.

> Love grows and growth takes time. It has to sink its roots firmly into the deep soil of the soul. It is a perennial plant, and these grow slowly. You fall into infatuation. Falling is fast, with acceleration. Falling is uncontrollable. It comes as a whirlwind sweeping one off his feet . . . but it seldom lasts long, and is often disastrous. It provides only thrills.
>
> True love is based on knowledge. It knows well the one it loves and why it loves. It observes. It appraises. It is held firmly by many ties. It can enumerate in detail the points of beauty of the loved-one, the flights of spirit, the qualities of soul, the walk, voice, words, interests and mannerisms. Infatuation is apt to be swept up in the strong attraction of a few compelling traits. It sees blonde hair, fine face and fancy figure and forgets all the rest. In other words, true love stresses the internals, infatuation stresses the externals.
>
> True love is realistic. It embraces the entire personality. This includes virtues as well as shortcomings and defects. Infatuation thrives on fancy and fantasy, ignoring the entire personality. This sort of "love" is really blind.
>
> True love has as much giving in it as of seeking. It is centered on the loved one, not on self. It seeks a real union of two partners. Infatuation would dominate unknowingly, seeing the loved one as a source of personal joy, pleasure and satisfaction.
>
> True love is honest. It does not express what it does not feel and believe. Expressions of love come slowly, sincerely, naturally. They are never forced or faked. Physical expressions, when they do come, have real deep meaning. Infatuation reverses the process. It is born of expression, thrives on it for hasty growth and may as quickly wither. The meaning is lacking; it is just fun, thrilling but not lasting.
>
> Love is constant, enduring, even patient when it must be. Infatuation is as changeable as it is hasty. Love tends to be faithful. Infatuation is apt to flitter. Love gives calmness, security, peace, trust and happiness. Infatuation gives thrills, joys, sorrows, jealousies and uncertainties. Love has ideals but never idealizes without looking squarely at realities.[10]

As one can rightfully see, therefore, true love is something noble, dignified, and precious. It is something natural, but it is also very spiritual. If it seeks to unite two beings of opposite sex into one; if it seeks to bring together two intellects, two free wills into one life, it is because the Creator "made them male and female," and because Christ consecrated this union in the Sacrament of Matrimony.

84

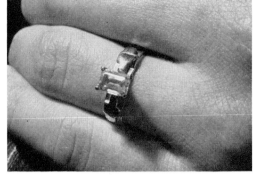

Liturgical engagement and wedding rings symbolize the sacramental character of marriage.

Milwaukee Journal Photo

How important it is for both parties to know whether or not they are really in love. To enable a person to do this, the following set of questions has been devised. Positive answers to these questions should be arrived at before a couple pledge themselves "for richer, for poorer, in sickness and in health, until death."

1. Do you think that your love is morally helpful, respectful to God's laws and self-sacrificing?
2. Do you really respect each other deeply in addition to the physical attraction you feel for each other?
3. Do you have similar ideas about children? about money? about right and wrong? about give and take in getting along together? about God's laws governing dating, courtship, and marriage? about sticking it out through thick and thin?
4. Can you get along with the other's family?
5. Do you find much to say and do together, in addition to expressing love?
6. When disagreements arise, is your thought to strengthen the relationship rather than to win a victory?
7. Are you proud to have your partner meet your friends and relatives?
8. Do you love him (her) just as he (she) is, faults and all, without a desire to reform or improve him (her)?
9. Do you do your thinking and planning in terms of "we" and "what we will do," rather than of "I" and "what I want"?
10. Are you inclined to give much consideration to his (her) ideas, wishes, and judgments, even when they conflict with your own?
11. Do you feel that among all those you know, he (she) is the one you would select as the father (mother) of your children?
12. Do you feel that there is room in you for a good deal of growth and improvement, which association with him (her) will produce?
13. Do you think of yourselves not merely as delightful or thrilling companions, but as partners in an enterprise that is great enough to demand your best talents, and efforts all the rest of your life?
14. Have you stopped to listen to your head . . . as well as your heart? Have you asked Christ of Cana about your love?

85

Love Has Its Hazards

Two people who have discovered that they are in love want to do more than merely tell each other about it. They want to manifest their love. This is natural. But demonstrations of affection must be held within the bounds of the moral law and the accepted standards of social propriety. True love tends toward union, a union of hearts, not necessarily of bodies, certainly not before marriage. All marriage counselors agree to this. They realize that a chaste courtship is necessary for happiness and success in marriage. The non-Catholic director of the American Institute of Family Relations, Paul Popenoe, expresses this fact very strongly in his book, *Modern Marriage:* "Continence is not only important but absolutely necessary, during the years preceding marriage. . . . It is not only a desirable but an indispensable means to an important end, namely, a successful marriage."[11]

Sex attraction, therefore, is intended to lead to marriage, but *only after marriage* to its joys and privileges. God has made man, male and female. Each is possessed of a different nature. Those differences are both physical and psychological. These two natures, each incomplete in itself, find their completion in that sacred fusion which is achieved in matrimony only. It is sufficient for young people to know this without seeking to explore the physical basis of these differences. The physical element of sex has been limited by God to marriage only. Outside of marriage inordinate physical enjoyment is lust, not love.[12] That is why young people in love have to be on their guard lest too much physical contact degenerate their love into sordid and selfish passion. Because of this, a clear understanding of the morality of lovemaking before marriage is essential to assure a chaste courtship and a happy marriage.

The Morality of Kissing

There are kisses and kisses, but the general rule of morality is this: kissing or embracing is a serious sin against chastity for those unmarried to each other when it is done with the intention of stimulating or promoting the sexual appetite or sexual desire, or when one thereby is freely and knowingly exposed to the proximate danger of unlawful sexual activity or of consent to sexual pleasure. This means that necking (prolonged and passionate kissing) and petting (allowing a person to place his hands upon the intimate parts of the body) are seriously sinful for those unmarried to each other. They are deliberate assumptions of privileges and rights which have no place outside of marriage. They are preludes to procreation. The same holds true for the "French kiss," or whatever name it goes by (it has several). Such actions are mortally sinful because of what they normally do to the passions of the persons involved.

> Even in cases where there is no evil intention or no proximate danger of sin, kissing or embracing without a relatively sufficient reason would not be free from venial sin. In the beginning of courtship (dating) there might appear to be no danger at all in kissing or embracing because neither party has immodest intentions. Nevertheless, the couple are emotionally thrilled just to be together, and this emotional state is heightened by caresses even when modest. In this heightened emotional state, physical passion is easily aroused. Even modest signs of affection must be avoided if they are frequent, prolonged, and ardent, because these things invariably arouse physical passion and this cannot be the aim of unmarried people in expressing their affection.[13]

This does not mean, however, that every kiss is seriously immoral. An occasional kiss given with genuine affection and purity of thought is too lovely and good to be that. It's just that young people have to bear in mind constantly that kissing can very easily get out of hand, because of different attitudes of the two sexes regarding kissing.

The attitude of a girl toward a kiss is quite different from the attitude of a boy. A girl loves affection and is little afraid of passion. She enjoys being admired. And she may maintain that she is not tempted in her body no matter how prolonged the kissing. So to her the kiss may simply indicate that she is attractive to some boy who shows his affection for her with a kiss.

With a boy the attitude is different. He may first kiss a girl calmly and peacefully when he says good night, and the whole experience may seem quite harmless. But if he continues to kiss her, the warmth and intensity grow. In no time at all he is likely to find himself excited and strange, with unmistakable yearnings manifesting themselves in his body and his soul.

Very few individuals realize this when they embark on dating and give the first kiss. They forget or overlook the fact that because of the sin of Adam, the animal is strong in man . . . so strong that if one carelessly exposes oneself to the danger of arousing it, it can easily brush aside all considerations of honor and self-respect and the promptings of virtue in order to gratify its eager desires.

This has been pointed out again and again. A high school senior wrote:

> Remember that first kiss? He was your one and only and he kissed you. Your heart gave a big thump and you sighed softly. The first kiss satisfied you for a whole week. Then another date, another kiss. This time one kiss wasn't enough . . . so you stayed out a few minutes later saying goodnight. A few dates later found you spending more and more time trying to achieve the same thrill you got out of that first kiss. Every time you were together you'd "scrounge" a little longer and go a little further. Then the answer to "When will I be satisfied?" got a little vague. Maybe you could have stopped when you wanted to, but it's hard to control emotions. You might not be able to stop until it's too late . . . so think it over.[14]

Are there any rules or guides regarding the question of kissing? Perhaps the best rule of thumb to go by in the matter of kissing is this: The *FEAR* guide.

When kissing is F — *Frequent,* repeated often in a comparatively short time;

E — *Enduring,* the kisses are prolonged (How often do you kiss your sister or mother that way?);

A — *Ardent,* going beyond the warmth of the friendly or affectionate limits;
Then it is PASSIONATE AND CANNOT BE JUSTIFIED before the court of . . .

R — *Reason* or *Religion* for those unmarried.[15]

Self-Respect and Sex

A young man who is seriously interested in a girl does not want their friendship spoiled by too much physical contact. The girl who finds her date overly eager for physical intimacies has a right to doubt his respect and sincerity. Boys who are worth dating respect a girl for drawing the line and are more likely to love and respect her and to want to marry her if she keeps control of the situation. This does not mean that she must be cold and unfeeling or fail to act as if she appreciates and is interested in the affection of her date. Neither boys nor girls have serious problems in courtship if they have *self-respect* and confidence in their ability to win and keep friends without using sex as a lure.

The way the world treats the matter of kissing and lovemaking today is one of the chief causes that leads many young people to indulge in impure liberties with each other. Teen-agers must not forget that God has constructed them so that they cannot indulge in intimate physical contact with one of the opposite sex toward whom they have a liking without arousing deep responses . . . sex impulses over which they have difficulties of self-control. **This does not mean that boys and girls can't control themselves.** It simply means that when boys and girls play with the fire of sex, their reason boils and is blocked solidly by the enflamed passions. Boys and girls must remember that they are playing with dynamite when they place one another in occasions of unnecessary and immoral "lovemaking."

Well, some people ask, "What's wrong with premarital relations anyway?" Besides being a serious sin against the Sixth Commandment of God, it is against the entire courtship code itself. One might compare marriage to a cake composed of three layers: (1) children, (2) mutual fidelity — this includes mutual respect and confidence, (3) indissolubility — marriage bond cannot be severed except by death. Sex relations are the frosting which, after all, should not be put on the cake until after it is baked. Too many have wrecked their lives by experimenting with "love." Remember, God's courtship code was created not to annoy and frustrate you or to keep you from having a good time, but to assure you of rightful living and a more happy marriage. You will expect your partner to bring to the altar on your wedding day three gifts: a clean mind, a clean heart, and a clean body. Your partner also has a perfect right to expect the same from you.

To quote Paul Popenoe once again:

> There is no scientific basis for the idea that previous sexual experience is a good, much less a necessary preparation for marriage. This is sufficiently proved by statistical finding . . . that the happiest marriages, and those with the best sexual adjustment between the partners, are those in which neither husband nor wife has had any previous sexual experience. They have nothing to unlearn, nothing to try to forget, nothing to regret.[16]

89

College Marriages

If there is anything increasing on college campuses throughout the United States it is the appearance of married college students. Prospective life mates planning college should keep in mind that marriage while in college means more than having a congenial roommate. It requires tremendous sacrifice to make a success of marriage under such circumstances. And although some colleges have good-naturedly granted wives of married students an honorary degree known as PHT (Putting Hubby Through), the hazards of combining marriage and education should not be taken lightly.

The Engagement

After a considerable time of courtship an engagement is established. An engagement is a mutual promise to enter into marriage in the near future. The young man frequently gives the girl an engagement ring which she wears on the third finger of her left hand. There are two types of engagements: informal and formal.

Informal

The informal engagement can occur almost anywhere. This is the one that has been described in romance literature time and time again. The young man proposes to the girl in the moonlight and she says "Yes." He then places the ring on her finger and they are engaged. They then proceed to announce the fact to their relatives and friends.

Formal

On the increase in this country is the formal engagement, better known as the "solemn engagement." This is the only kind of an engagement officially recognized by the Church (Canon 1017). The ritual for the ceremony of solemn engagement is simple but meaningful, foreshadowing the day when the couple will be united sacramentally in Christ. While there is no standard formula for the ceremony itself, in most instances the ceremony is conducted in the following manner either in conjunction with a Mass or as a candle-light ceremony in the evening.

Milwaukee Journal Photo

The ritual for the ceremony of solemn engagement fore-shadows the day when the couple will be united sacramentally in Christ.

Kneeling at the Communion rail, the couple join their right hands, and, before the priest and witnesses, promise to marry one day "according to the ordinances of God and Holy Church."

"I will keep faith and loyalty to thee, and so in thy necessities aid and comfort thee," promises the prospective bridegroom, "which things and all that a man ought to do unto his espoused I promise to do unto thee and to keep by the faith that is in me."

A similar pledge is recited by the young woman.

After the priest has blessed the engagement ring, the man places it on his fiancée's finger, invoking the blessing of the Father, and of the Son, and of the Holy Spirit. The priest opens the Missal to the beginning of the Canon, and presents the page imprinted with the crucifix, which is kissed first by the man, and then by the woman.

The ceremony ends as the couple sign a document asserting that they "have this day promised the eventual consecration of one

91

another in the sacrament of Matrimony." The priest and witnesses also sign the paper.

Motivation for the ceremony may be discovered in the prayer of the young people themselves, which is included in the document recording their solemn engagement. It reads:

> May the Divine Spirit with His grace and manifold gifts enlighten our minds and move our wills to spend the days of our engagement soberly, piously, and justly, awaiting the blessed consummation of that union to which we have been called and to which we are solemnly pledged. In Thee, O Lord, do we put our trust. Let us nevermore be confounded.

It should be noted here that no engagement, not even a formal one, can compel a marriage if one of the parties decides not to marry. Engagement leads to marriage, but it is considerably removed from marriage because it does not bind with the same force as does marriage itself.

Because engagements are not marriages, it must be constantly noted that any display or manifestation of love between the engaged that involves the arousing of sensual desire or feeling and the danger of consenting thereto is as wrong and sinful in the engaged as for the unengaged. In other words, there are no sexual privileges for the engaged.

> While engaged couples may kiss each other on meeting and parting in a decent and chaste way, in a way that would not be considered shameful and improper in the presence of others, it is obvious that there are some kinds of kissing and embracing that by their very nature lead to intense sexual desires and feelings. Such would be close, prolonged, passionate kissing and embracing. Without a doubt there will be severe temptations to indulge in these things for a couple who are deeply in love and looking forward to marriage. But if they truly want their marriage to be good and holy and blessed in the eyes of God, they will resist the temptation to cheat by taking in advance that which God can make lawful and virtuous for them only after they will have married. Moreover the virtue of prudence will suggest that they do not spend too much time alone and in secret together, when the very circumstances would make more acute the yearning for passionate and sinful love-making. They must deeply convince themselves that the right to such things is given by God only to the married.[17]

Length of Engagement

How long should an engagement last? How often this question

92

is asked. The answer depends, of course, on the circumstances in each individual instance. The general rule is that an engagement should not be so short as to give them insufficient time to decide about their mutual compatibility; also the engagement should not be so long as to permit matters to drag on needlessly, especially if the couple sees a lot of each other. The emotional strain under which lovers exist should not be prolonged more than necessary. As a general rule, except in special circumstances, an engagement should not last longer than a year.

Paul Popenoe, whom we have quoted before in this chapter, says:

> Ordinarily it [an engagement] should not last many months — certainly no longer than a year, if the two see a good deal of each other. The emotional strain under which lovers exist is damaging and should be ended as soon as possible. Long acquaintanceship preceding marriage is desirable; long betrothal is injurious. . . . Many exceptions will occur, but not enough to vitiate the general rule that if a man and woman are deeply in love, and if they had any right to become betrothed, they should and will marry without letting things drag indefinitely.[18]

How long your engagement will be remains to be seen. But make certain that it is long enough so that you and your partner have time to change your minds about getting married before it's too late. By scheduling the wedding too soon after proposal and acceptance, a young couple may discover all too late that they just don't get along with each other.

So Much to Do

The period of engagement is truly a serious one. It should not be wasted on a hectic round of parties, dances, and dates. The engaged couple should seriously consider the sacrament they are soon to enter. The questions of religion, money, choice of friends, ways of dealing with parents and other family members, tastes in recreation, way of bringing up children are but a few of the practical things which must be resolved before tying the knot. Certainly the time of engagement should be a time of intense prayer and frequent reception of the Sacraments.

> An engaged couple should not feel embarrassed to begin and end each date with a simple little prayer for their happiness and success in marriage. After all, in a brief time, they will be kneeling together

93

each night to say their night prayers. This should not be a strange experience. It is very heartening to see so many engaged couples in the United States going to Mass and Communion together. Such spiritual unity is a good indication that they will continue to strive together for the sanctity of their state of matrimony.[19]

During the months of engagement both parties should avail themselves of some good Catholic reading on the subject of marriage. A representative selection of available books and pamphlets is found at the end of each chapter in this book. Perhaps your parish priest will suggest a few. Whatever the case, an engaged couple should do some serious reading on the sacrament they are about to enter.

If Pre-Cana talks are available, the engaged couple should take advantage of this opportunity and attend them faithfully. At such conferences, they will learn the ins and outs of marriage from experts. It also affords a couple the chance of meeting other couples with similar problems and the sharing of solutions.

In areas where Pre-Cana talks are not available, a correspondence course, "Together in Christ," is now being offered from the St. Paul Seminary, St. Paul 1, Minnesota, and St. Mary's Seminary, Baltimore 10, Maryland. Directed by Father Henry V. Sattler, C.SS.R., of the N.C.W.C. Family Life Bureau, this course of instructions consists of eleven instructions and questionnaires at a fee of $7.50. Upon the completion of this course the student receives a diploma and notice is sent to the sponsoring parish priest.

Gradually increasing in popularity are week-end retreats for engaged couples or engaged men or engaged women. If aspirants for religious life conclude their novitiate with a closed retreat before vowing themselves to God, how natural it should seem for the engaged to close their engagement "novitiate" with a retreat before pronouncing their vows to each other in God. If there is no retreat house in your area, at least spend a weekly Holy Hour together for the few weeks before your marriage. Make sure that the last minute preparations on the evening and morning before your wedding are not so full of scurry that you do not have time to pause for a moment in the presence of God to take stock in prayerful awareness of the great religious step you are taking.[20]

Breaking the Engagement

Since an engagement is a promise of a contract of marriage but not yet the real thing, it can and does happen that engagements are broken. This may appear at first glance to be a distressing fact. Not at all. Broken engagements prevent marriages which almost certainly would end in unhappiness, and possibly divorce. A considerable number of young people become engaged for reasons having very little to do with marriage. Typical is the case reported by the young man who explained, after breaking his engagement: "We were both the most popular in our school for two years. I played football. She was vice-president of our class. We were leaders in our respective groups. My fraternity and her class had our marriage all planned." It was only after their engagement that they realized they were not suited for one another.

Somewhere between one third and one half of all young people experience at least one broken engagement before entering the one that ultimately leads to marriage. The reasons for breaking the engagement are many. Authorities list the following as the chief reasons:

1. An undesired and protracted long engagement
2. Unfaithfulness
3. One party decides to consecrate his or her life to God
4. Serious illness or accident
5. Immaturity
6. Personality differences
7. Economic incompetence
8. Fear of marriage
9. Cultural contrasts
10. Mutual consent

In breaking an engagement both parties should make sure that they make a complete break with each other. This means that the engagement ring must be returned. If other gifts were given in an anticipation of marriage (as wedding gifts), these, too, must be returned. There should be no self-pity. One should set about developing new friends and interests and getting back into the swing of things. And stay clear of marrying on the rebound. All that has been mentioned in this chapter about selecting a life mate should once again be looked over, so that a future engagement ring doesn't end up in one's nose.

SUGGESTIONS FOR READING

The Art of Happy Marriage, James A. Magner (Milwaukee: The Bruce Publishing Co., 1947).

*The Family Clinic, John L. Thomas, S.J. (Westminster, Md.: The Newman Press, 1958).

Getting Along With People, Milton Wright (New York: McGraw-Hill Book Co., 1955).

The Girl Worth Choosing, Daniel A. Lord, S.J. (St. Louis, Mo.: The Queen's Work, 1953).

Happy Marriage, John A. O'Brien (New York: Hanover House, 1956).

Kissing, Winfrid Herbst, S.D.S. (St. Louis: The Queen's Work, 1952).

Love, Sex, and the Teenagers, Daniel A. Lord, S.J. (St. Louis: The Queen's Work, 1947).

The Man of Your Choice, Daniel A. Lord, S.J. (St. Louis, Mo.: The Queen's Work, 1952).

Marriage Guide for Engaged Catholics, William F. F. McManus, S.T.L. (New York: Paulist Press, 1961).

*Marriage and the Family, Alphonse H. Clemens (Englewood Cliffs, N. J.: Prentice-Hall, Inc., 1957).

*Modern Youth and Chastity, Gerald Kelly, S.J. (St. Louis: The Queen's Work, 1943).

Modesty, Rev. Vincent Fecher, S.V.D. (Techny, Ill.: Divine Word Publications, 1960).

*"Petting and Courtship," Max J. Exner, *Sex-Character Education,* edited by John A. O'Brien (New York: The Macmillan Co., 1953).

Pucker Up, Taylor Klose (New York: Paulist Press, 1960).

Purity and Power, Vincent Fecher, S.V.D. (Techny, Ill.: Divine Word Publications, 1960).

Questions Young People Ask Before Marriage, Donald F. Miller, C.SS.R. (Liguori, Mo.: The Liguorian Press, 1956).

*Sex Is Sacred, Lawrence G. Lovasik, S.V.D. (Techny, Ill.: Divine Word Publications, 1958).

Strategy in Courtship, John A. O'Brien (Notre Dame, Ind.: Ave Maria Press, 1954).

Teenagers and Kissing, Ernest F. Miller (Liguori, Mo.: The Liguorian Press, 1957).

What Young People Ask About Life, Love and Marriage, Donald F. Miller, C.SS.R. (Liguori, Mo.: The Liguorian Press, 1959).

When Is Company-Keeping Lawful and Prudent, Donald F. Miller, C.SS.R. (Liguori, Mo.: The Liguorian Press, 1956).

Your Engagement Should Be in Church, Rev. Chester Wrzaszczak (St. Louis: The Queen's Work, 1954).

Youth's Ideal — A Chaste Courtship, John A. O'Brien (Huntington, Ind.: Our Sunday Visitor Press, 1954).

Chapter V ENTERING MARRIAGE

A wedding is a beautiful event in the life of a man and a woman. Since the beginning God intended marriage to be just this. Like any of God's creation, however, marriage just didn't happen. It was planned. "To the lonely Adam, God presented a lovely, new human creature called woman. In wonder and awe they looked at each other and took each other by the hand. Then God gave them their official commission. 'You shall be two in one flesh. Increase and multiply,' He commanded, 'fill the earth and rule over it.' "[1]

To make sure that weddings will always remain beautiful and happy events in the lives of human beings, a number of things have to be planned out beforehand by the intended bride and groom.

Consult With the Pastor

The first thing to remember is that a Catholic marriage is a sacrament and therefore it is absolutely necessary for the engaged couple to consult their pastors. While either pastor can validly officiate at a wedding, it is customarily the pastor of the bride who witnesses the marriage. If only one of the parties is Catholic, the marriage takes place in that person's parish.

When Should This Visit to the Priest Be Made?

Just as soon as both parties have agreed to definite plans of marriage they should consult the respective pastors. This is neces-

Premarital instructions are given to engaged couples to instruct them in the Church's teachings on marriage and assure their well-being and happiness.

John Ahlhauser

sary so that a definite date and hour of one's wedding Mass can be scheduled. This should be done at least two months before the time of the contemplated marriage if both parties are Catholic. When one party is not a Catholic, three months should be allowed so that the necessary premarital instructions can be conveniently given. An appointment with one's parish priest may be arranged by telephone. This visit with one's pastor should be done before printing wedding invitations or making any definite commitments; otherwise, there may be disappointment and embarrassment.

Why Is So Much Advance Notice Required?

A few months of advance notice to one's pastor is necessary because the formalities — paperwork — have greatly increased in recent years. In all dioceses today those who have spent some time in the service or who have changed their residence since the age of twelve (for girls) or fourteen (for boys) must produce two witnesses who have known them since that age who can testify that they are free to marry. This is not always as easy as it appears. Furthermore, the couple must produce fresh baptismal certificates, dated within the past six months, together with First Holy Communion and Confirmation certificates, as well as discharge papers if either or both have been in the service. These documents frequently require some time to trace down and obtain.

Besides the above information, should one of the parties be a non-Catholic it will be necessary for him to take instructions in the

Catholic Faith. In most dioceses today the average number of instructions varies between twelve and twenty-four. They are given on the average of two per week.

Furthermore, shortly before the day of marriage itself, it is necessary for both the future bride and groom to answer under oath in the presence of a priest the following or similar questionnaire.

The bride (or bridegroom) must be interrogated separately by the priest who records the answers given under oath.

1. Do you believe in the sanctity of an oath? Do you realize the gravity of perjury and its serious consequences?
2. (*Touching the Holy Gospels*) Do you solemnly swear to tell the whole truth and nothing but the truth in answering all the following questions?
3. Name? Address? Date and place of birth? Profession or occupation?
4. Father's name? Mother's maiden name? Father's religion? Mother's religion?
5. Were you ever baptized? In what religion? When and where? What religion do you practice?
6. Did you make your First Communion? When and where?
7. Were you reared a Catholic? Did you receive a Catholic education? Where and for how long?
8. Did you receive Confirmation? When and where?
9. In what parish do you reside? How long have you been living there? Have you lived in any other parish for six months or more after the age of 12? If so, give the name and address of two Catholics, known to their pastor, who can testify about you during your stay in these parishes.
10. Have you ever been married, or attempted marriage even civilly? How often? With whom? When? Where and before whom? Is your husband (husbands) dead? If so, an authentic document of death must be presented. Was your former marriage(s) dissolved or declared null by the Church?
11. Have you ever made a vow? Of virginity? Of perpetual chastity? Of temporary chastity and the time is not elapsed? Of never marrying? Of entering religion?
12. Have you ever made a profession in any Religious institute?
13. Are you related to the person you intend to marry? State the degree of relationship: By blood? By marriage? By public honesty?
14. Have you baptized your intended husband, or been his sponsor?
15. Was your intended husband ever married before? If so: During the lifetime of his wife did you attempt marriage with him? Or while she was alive, promise to marry him? Or cause, or cooperate in any way in causing her death?
16. Are you at present a practical Catholic? Is your intended husband? In what religion was he baptized? What religion does he practice? Do you or does he belong to the Masons or any other condemned

99

society? Are you or he conscious of being under any censure of the Church?

17. How long have you known your intended husband? How long have you been engaged?

18. Are you entering this marriage freely and of your own accord? Are you being compelled by any person, circumstance, etc.? Is your intended husband marrying you freely and of his own accord? Is he being compelled by any person, circumstance, etc.?

19. Do you understand the nature and obligations of marriage? Does your intended husband? Have you or he ever suffered from any mental disturbance? Have you any physical defect preventing the proper fulfillment of your duties as a wife?

20. Do you intend to enter a permanent marriage that can be dissolved only by death? Does your intended husband agree to enter such an indissoluble union?

21. Do you intend to be faithful to your husband for life?

22. Do you intend to lead a married life in conformity with the teaching of the Catholic Church regarding birth control? Does your intended husband agree to live such a Christian life?

23. Are you entering this marriage without condition or reservation?

24. When do you intend to be married? Who will be the two essential witnesses? Are they both Catholics?

25. Are the banns to be published? If not, why not?

26. Have you consulted your parents about this marriage? If not, why not?

27. Do you understand that when you sign this document you preclude the possibility of ever contending that this marriage is invalid as far as you are concerned?

28. Do you now affix your signature in testimony of the truth of all the above answers, realizing that you are under oath?

Where Will the Marriage Take Place?

Ordinarily, the marriage will take place in the church of the bride, unless there is a serious reason for making some other arrangements. In some places, the groom and bride are interviewed by their respective pastors as to their freedom to marry. In others, the bride's pastor interrogates both.

What About Witnesses or Attendants?

The witnesses of a Catholic marriage must be a Catholic man and a Catholic woman; if there are to be any non-Catholic members of the bridal party, please speak to your pastor concerning this situation. The number of members in the bridal party should also be discussed with the pastor. A large party gets cumbersome.

A flower girl and ring bearer are impractical unless they are at least six years old. Normally a group of six, including the bride and groom, is the most practical.

What About Special Requests?

Sometimes the couple to be married have a friend whom they wish to serve as organist, singer, or acolyte. They should be reasonable about such requests. Permitting the bridal couple to supply their own organist and singers may be welcomed by one pastor, whereas another pastor may run the risk of trouble with his regular organist and choir members if he grants such permission. Organist and singers at a wedding are, of course, optional unless there is to be a high Mass.

It may also happen that either the bride or groom would like to ask a relative or friend in the priesthood to officiate at the wedding. Again it is up to the pastor who has the canonical right to assist at the marriage, to grant the permission if he wishes and to delegate the priest requested. If the pastor chooses not to grant permission for an outside priest, he is perfectly within his rights; and the couple must bow to his decision.

It may happen, because of sentimental or other reasons, that a couple may wish to be married some place other than in their parish church, for instance, in a college chapel or in another city. Again the permission depends upon the pastor of the bride. Many pastors are very hesitant to grant permission for marriages outside the parish, and rightly so, because the pastor has a strict responsibility for everything that pertains to the spiritual welfare of his people. It is possible for abuses to creep in and for parishioners to want to run hither and yon to get married for the flimsiest reasons. It is always easier for the couple to get permission to bring in an outside priest to officiate at the marriage than it is to obtain permission to be married by that same priest at another church or chapel.[2]

When Can You Get Married?

Strictly speaking, a Catholic marriage can take place at any time of the day or night, including Advent and Lent, and with or without Mass. The special Nuptial Mass and Nuptial Blessing, which is given during Mass, are not permitted during Advent and Lent without a dispensation from the Bishop. During these two times, wedding ceremonies should be kept simple in accordance with the penitential character of the season.

This does not mean that a couple can rush to the priest of a church and be married immediately at any time they wish. In addition to the documents and instructions required, ordinarily they must give the pastor notice quite a bit ahead of time so that he can find a time for the wedding which will be convenient for them and which will not disrupt regular parish functions.[3]

101

What Are Marriage Banns? Where Will They Be Announced?

The publication of marriage banns is a matter of Church Law. This is a formal public proclamation as to the individual's eligibility to marry. Ordinarily these banns will be read in the respective bride's and groom's parishes on the three consecutive Sundays or holydays prior to the wedding. These banns are also announced in every parish in which the bride and groom have lived since the age of twelve or fourteen respectively. The faithful should make known any real reason they may be aware of why the couple should not marry. For a sufficiently serious reason, the Bishop may dispense from the announcing of banns.

What About Wedding Attire and Music?

All attire of those in the wedding party should be in perfect accord with the rules of decency. Modesty and simplicity should be the guide in selecting the gowns of the bride and attendants. A modest bride is a beautiful bride. There is no room at a Catholic wedding for gaudiness or vulgarity of attire.[4]

Only approved Church music is allowable. "The so-called traditional music of *Here Comes the Bride* from Lohengrin and the *Wedding March* by Mendelssohn and other secular songs like *Because* or *O Promise Me,* etc., are not to be used in church according to the decrees of Pope Pius X."[5]

May We Have a Professional Photographer Take Candid Shots?

Pictures by a professional (not amateur) photographer are usually allowed of the wedding party to and from the altar; however, local custom and the pastor's pleasure must be considered. Most priests will not tolerate photographers in the sanctuary. Some find the popping of flash bulbs so distracting that they won't even let them in the church. A professional photographer, of course, realizes that a Catholic marriage is a solemn sacred ceremony, not a style show or a sporting event. It is suggested that the wedding party have a formal portrait taken after the marriage ceremony at some professional studio. The house of God is a house of prayer, not a place for posing for pictures.

What About Wedding Invitations?

A wedding invitation is the first formal notice of the great event. For a Catholic wedding, it is fitting that the design and wording of one's invitation express the sacramental significance of the contract.

As soon as the exact date has been set, the prospective bride and groom should see to it that the invitations are prepared, printed (engraved), and addressed. Both individuals should begin early in drawing up the invitation list so as not to exclude any important relative or friend. The invitations should be mailed approximately three weeks before the ceremony. A reputable stationery store can give appropriate advice on the format. Should the couple decide to send wedding announcements instead of invitations, these too should contain mention of the sacrament received. Such announcements are sent immediately after the wedding takes place. They can be prepared beforehand for mailing.

What Type of Wedding Shall It Be?

In choosing the type of wedding a couple wishes to plan consideration should be given to three items: (1) the amount of one's budget, (2) the couple's personality, and (3) the place (church) where the ceremony is to take place. These three factors will determine whether the wedding is to be a completely formal affair — or what degree of formality the couple desires or can afford. Whether a person's marriage is an elaborate or quiet affair, a Catholic marriage should possess the fullness of liturgical celebration given by the Church. What does this mean?

From a Catholic point of view, a marriage is celebrated with a nuptial Mass. It is a nuptial Mass which gives solemnity to a Catholic marriage. This wedding Mass can be as elaborate or as quiet as the couple desires, but a Catholic marriage should always take place in connection with the nuptial Mass. Some parishes will definitely insist that all weddings take place at a nuptial high Mass.

In deciding whether or not one's wedding will be simple, elaborate, or somewhere in between, due consideration should be given the expense of the affair. Before this can be resolved, the family of the bride will have to be consulted since much of the expense, according to custom, will fall on the bride's family.

Duties of the Bride and the Bride's Family

According to authorities the first responsibility generally assumed by the bride's family is to have a luncheon or dinner for the engaged couple. Sometimes this is done after the engagement is announced and on other occasions the dinner is given announcing the engagement. The next important steps are then generally the following:

1. Engage the proper parish priest and church where the wedding is to be held.
2. Make arrangements for the invitations and announcements with the engraver. Be sure that they are sent out at least three weeks before the wedding to allow ample time for replies.
3. Make preliminary arrangements with the florist, caterer, musicians, and photographer. This is necessary to avoid any conflict of dates that may arise in their working schedule.
4. Start assembling your guest list. Make certain that there are no duplications existing, which could easily occur when the bride and groom have mutual friends.
5. Select the bridal attendants and ushers. It is better to do this jointly so that the couples will match up.
6. Choose the bridal costume and decide on the type of gowns to be worn by the bridal attendants.
7. Start shopping for the bridal trousseau.
8. Hire the necessary transportation (frequently a limousine) for the bridal party in the event there aren't enough automobiles available for this purpose.
9. In the event the parents of the groom live out of town make necessary hotel or club reservations for them.

The Groom . . . and His Responsibilities

As the groom is expected to derive at least half of the pleasure from the marital relationship, he should contribute at least that amount of work in planning the wedding. In most instances he is not required to do this — but tradition requires that he perform a number of duties, as follows:

1. Immediately before or after the engagement he buys the engagement ring (and wedding ring if he chooses at this time).
2. A short time before the wedding he applies for the license. State

104

laws governing marriage must be checked. Be certain that all papers are ready for the necessary compliance.

3. Figure out the wedding list for his family and friends. Make certain that there are no duplications with the bride's list.
4. Choose the best man and the ushers. Notify them of the type of wedding that is to be held. When acceptance is received, notify the attendants of the attire to be worn.
5. Buy a gift for the future bride and gifts for the attendants and ushers. The following are suggested as gifts for the men: money clips, week-end shaving kits, fountain pens, billfolds, cuff links, and brief cases. (In the event the groom cannot afford it, no breach of etiquette exists when gifts are not bought for the ushers and attendants.)
6. Attend to his personal wardrobe. Be certain that there are sufficient clothes for the honeymoon trip and that arrangements have been made with the best man to have his luggage taken from his home either to railroad station or automobile before reception.
7. Make arrangements for living quarters for his new family.
8. Plan the honeymoon trip. All necessary reservations including hotel and travel should be made as early as possible, especially if it is a June wedding.
9. Plan the bachelor dinner, and set the date. The latest that it should be held is three days before the wedding.
10. Give the pastor's stipend to the best man.
11. Attend the wedding rehearsal.
12. Arrange for bouquets, boutonnieres, etc., for the bride and the bridal party.

Paying the Bills

As the wedding is almost entirely planned and conducted by the bride's parents — and since the invitations to both the ceremony and reception are issued in their name — they naturally pay for the major cost of the wedding.

The respective lists are noted below.

What the Bride's Family Pays for

1. The bridal trousseau, both personal and household
2. The bride's wedding outfit
3. The wedding invitations and announcements
4. Organist, soloist, choir for the ceremony; music for the reception
5. The wedding reception or breakfast (this includes the food, flowers, champagne, or other beverages)
6. All floral decorations in the church, home, or elsewhere
7. Gifts for the maid of honor and all the bridesmaids
8. The bridesmaids' bouquets (groom may pay for this, if he wishes)
9. All wedding photographs

105

10. The wedding cake and souvenir napkins
11. Transportation for wedding party to and from the church

What the Groom Pays For

1. The engagement and wedding rings (if double-ring ceremony, the bride pays for bridegroom's ring)
2. The marriage license
3. Bachelor's dinner
4. Wedding gift for the bride
5. Gifts for the best man and ushers
6. If a formal wedding — ties, gloves, and boutonnieres for the best man, ushers, and himself
7. Bride's bouquet
8. Corsage to his mother and new mother-in-law
9. Pastor's stipend
10. Transportation to wedding for best man and himself
11. All honeymoon expenses

State or Civil Requirements

Along with the rules of the Church regarding marriage, an engaged couple must fulfill certain state or civil requirements. These laws differ from state to state, since the Constitution of the United States left complete authority over marriage legislation to the respective states. There are some similarities among the various states, however. All states require a marriage license ($2 to $5), and most states now require a medical certificate (blood or Wassermann test) from both parties showing freedom from communicable diseases (venereal disease) before granting a license. All states have laws requiring parental approval for the marriage of minors. Thirty-one states require this permission when the prospective bride is under 18 and the husband is under 21. All states have a minimum-age requirement for allowing couples to get married even though parental consent is given. In 23 states of the Union this minimum age is 18 for the prospective groom; in 24 states it is 16 for the prospective bride. Lower minimum-age requirements — as low as 14 for males and 12 for females — are found in the remaining states. Most states prescribe a minimum waiting period of from one to five days between the date of application for a marriage license and its issuance or availability for use. Other states have a similar waiting period between the issuance of the marriage license and the date of the wedding. In all states, however, the marriage license must be issued in the same state where the parties are to be married. In some states this applies also to counties. All states agree in prohibiting marriage of relatives within the direct line of blood relationship; they differ, however, in their laws for other kinds of relationships. Twenty-two states prohibit marriages between members of different races (miscegenation). This includes marriages between white persons and Negroes, Orientals, or Indians. Some states, like Wisconsin, now require adult witnesses. For complete information of your state's laws on marriage, it is suggested that you extend an invitation to your district attorney to address your class. An excellent booklet available on the various laws of states regarding marriage is that edited by Irving Mandell, entitled *Law of Marriage and Divorce* (New York: Oceana Publications, 1957).

Preparing for the Sacrament

Amid all these preparations, the young couple will do well to consider their spiritual preparation for the great day. A Catholic marriage is a sacrament. It should be approached reverently and in the state of grace. Catholics should go to confession before the ceremony and if possible receive Holy Communion at their wedding Mass. The same recommendation is offered to the other members of the wedding party. No better investment can be made to secure God's help and blessing. If it is possible for the prospective bride and groom to make a short retreat or day of recollection, so much the better. In all events, the night before the ceremony should be spent quietly without any kind of excess which would get the marriage off to a bad start.

In preparation for the honeymoon and marital life, a good Catholic doctor may be consulted by the couple. Friendly but competent medical advice will be of great value in helping them understand better what to expect and how to conduct themselves in the great intimacy of marital love and its responsibilities.

It is customary for the parish priest to hold one or two rehearsals of the ceremony, the last one usually on the night before the wedding, so that all will know how to conduct themselves. At this time, if he has not already done so, the pastor or the assistant pastor will require certain information which he must enter into the official Marriage Record Book. This includes the full names of the contracting couple, as well as their ages, and also the names of the parents and the two official witnesses. If a dispensation was required, this also is recorded. He must also make a notation of the marriage on the official Parish Baptismal Records of the bride and groom, and send this information

107

to the pastor or pastors if the Baptism of one or both took place else-where. This information must be available, so that it can be transcribed into the official records promptly after the ceremony has taken place.[6]

The Marriage Ceremony

To anyone who has ever witnessed a Catholic marriage at a nuptial Mass, there is no more beautiful wedding ceremony. To en-ter a union of love within the great act of love of Christ Himself, namely, the Holy Sacrifice of the Mass, is the most hallowed and sacred act a couple can perform. This should be an essential part of every Catholic marriage. On one's wedding day, it's the nuptial Mass that matters.

A close look at a Catholic marriage ceremony reveals the beauty of the simplicity of this sacrament. It consists of several distinct ceremonies: There is the allocution of the priest, the mutual con-sent given by the contracting parties — the essence of the sacra-ment — the blessing and conferring of the ring(s), the nuptial blessing, and the final exhortation and prayer of the priest. Let's examine these one at a time.

Allocution of the Priest

No exhortation is so familiar to Catholics as the one given on

The Sacrament of Matrimony is not conferred by the priest; the bride and groom confer the sac-rament on each other. This fact testifies to the dignity of Matri-mony.

the day of marriage. While the words may be familiar, they do not cease to be serious or beautiful for those about to enter into the sacrament of matrimony. These words should be read by the prospective couple far in advance of their wedding day. Throughout their married life they can refer to them from time to time. The *Roman Ritual* reads as follows:

Dear friends in Christ: As you know, you are about to enter into a union which is most sacred and most serious, a union which was established by God Himself. By it, He gave to man a share in the greatest work of creation, the work of the continuation of the human race. And in this way He sanctified human love and enabled man and woman to help each other live as children of God, by sharing a common life under His fatherly care.

Because God Himself is thus its author, marriage is of its very nature a holy institution, requiring of those who enter into it a complete and unreserved giving of self. But Christ our Lord added to the holiness of marriage an even deeper meaning and a higher beauty. He referred to the love of marriage to describe His own love for His Church, that is, for the people of God whom He redeemed by His own blood. And so He gave to Christians a new vision of what married life ought to be, a life of self-sacrificing love like His own. It is for this reason that His Apostle, St. Paul, clearly states that marriage is now and for all time to be considered a great mystery, intimately bound up with the supernatural union of Christ and the Church, which union is also to be its pattern.

This union, then, is most serious, because it will bind you together for life in a relationship so close and so intimate, that it will profoundly influence your whole future. That future, with its hopes and disappointments, its successes and its failures, its pleasures, and its pains, its joys and its sorrows, is hidden from your eyes. You know that these elements are mingled in every life, and are to be expected in your own. And so, not knowing what is before you, you take each other for better or for worse, for richer or for poorer, in sickness and in health, until death.

Truly, then, these words are most serious. It is a beautiful tribute to your undoubted faith in each other, that, recognizing their full import, you are nevertheless so willing and ready to pronounce them. And because these words involve such solemn obligations, it is most fitting that you rest the security of your wedded life upon the great principle of self-sacrifice. And so you begin your married life by the voluntary and complete surrender of your individual lives in the interest of that deeper and wider life which you are to have in common. Henceforth you belong entirely to each other; you will be one in mind, one in heart, and one in affections. And whatever sacrifices you may hereafter be required to make to preserve this common life, always make them generously. Sacrifice is usually difficult and irksome. Only love can make it easy; and perfect love can make it a joy. We are willing to give in proportion as we love. And when love is perfect, the sacrifice is complete. God so loved the world that He gave His Only begotten Son; and the Son so loved us that He gave Himself for our salvation. "Greater love than this no man hath, that a man lay down his life for his friends."

No greater blessing can come to your married life than pure conjugal love, loyal and true to the end. May, then, this love with which you join your hands and hearts today, never fail, but grow deeper and stronger as the years go on. And if true love and the unselfish spirit of perfect sacrifice guide your every action, you can expect the greatest measure of earthly happiness that may be allotted to man in this vale of tears. The rest is in the hands of God. Nor will God be wanting to your needs; He will pledge you the life-long support of His graces in the Holy Sacrament which you are now going to receive.

The Consent

Immediately following the allocution, the officiating priest in the presence of two Catholic witnesses asks the prospective groom and bride separately if they wish to be united in the bonds of matrimony. By their simple answer, "I will," the two administer to each other the sacrament. The formula of the *Ritual* is as follows:

Addressing the bridegroom, the priest asks:

"*N.,* will you take *N.* here present, for your lawful wife according to the rite of our Holy Mother Church?" The groom answers: "I will."

The priest then asks the bride: "*N.,* will you take *N.* here present, for your lawful husband according to the rite of our Holy Mother Church?" The bride answers: "I will."

The priest then asks the bride and groom to join their right hands and repeat separately after him the following words: "I, *N.,* take thee, *N.,* for my lawful wife (husband), to have and to hold, from this day forward, for better, for worse, for richer, for poorer, in sickness and in health, until death do us part."

Immediately after this, the priest says: "I join you together in matrimony, in the name of the Father, and of the Son, and of the Holy Spirit. Amen." Then, in some places, he turns to those present and says: "I call upon all of you here present to be witnesses of this holy union which I have now blessed. 'What God has joined

110

together, let no man put asunder.' " Then he sprinkles the couple with holy water. By these words, the priest, in his capacity of official witness for the Church, bears witness to the fact that by the mutual consent of the two the reception of the sacrament has been enacted.

The Ring Ceremony

Once the consent of the couple has been given the ring ceremony follows. The priest turns to the altar and blesses the ring, which symbolizes the unbroken fidelity and loyalty which should be characteristic of marriage.

> The marriage ring, worn on the left hand, is a visible indication to all others that the wearer of the ring is married and, therefore, not free to bestow intimacy and affection on any one other than the marriage partner. Customs differ somewhat with the ring ceremony. In some marriages only one ring is used. This is blessed first by the priest and then given to the bridegroom, who slips it on the finger next to the little finger of the left hand of the bride. At the same time the bridegroom says: "With this ring I thee wed, and promise unto you my fidelity."
>
> In other marriages two rings are used, one each for both bride and groom. This custom which has much to recommend it, seems to be spreading. In the double-ring ceremony the priest says the following prayer: "Bless, O Lord, these rings which we are blessing in Thy Name, so that they who wear them, keeping faith with each other in unbroken loyalty, may ever remain at peace with Thee, obedient to Thy will, and may live together always in mutual love, through Christ our Lord. Amen." In bestowing the ring on each other, the bridegroom and bride each repeat the following prayer: "In the name of the Father, and of the Son, and of the Holy Spirit. Take and wear this ring as a pledge of my fidelity."
>
> Through the blessing of the priest, the ring becomes a sacramental; and, like other sacramentals of the Church, it should be treated reverently and can be used to dispose one for grace.[7]

A new indulgence granted by Pope John XXIII to promote married love and fidelity has recently been issued. Married persons who devoutly kiss the wife's wedding ring on the day of marriage and recite the following or another similar prayer may receive a 300-day partial indulgence. The prayer to say before kissing the ring is: "Grant us, O Lord, that loving You we may love one another and live according to Your holy law." Married members

The wedding ring is a sign of unbroken fidelity and loyalty. Pope John XXIII granted a new indulgence to married persons who kiss the wife's wedding ring on the day of marriage.

of the wedding party, certainly the parents of the bride and groom, should avail themselves of this new indulgence, immediately after the wedding ceremony.

Once the ring ceremony has been completed the couple receive a series of blessings from the priest officiating. The priest says:

> Almighty and everlasting God, Who by Thy power didst create Adam and Eve, our first parents, and join them in a holy union, sanctify the hearts and bodies of these Thy servants, and bless them; and make them one in the union and love of true affection. Through Christ our Lord. Amen.

In some places, it is customary for the priest then to extend his hands above the couple and pray:

> May Almighty God bless you by the Word of His mouth, and unite your hearts in the enduring bond of pure love. Amen.
> May you be blessed in your children, and may the love that you lavish on them be returned a hundredfold. Amen.

112

May the peace of Christ dwell always in your hearts and in your home; may you have true friends to stand by you, both in joy and in sorrow. May you be ready with help and consolation for all those who come to you in need; and may the blessings promised to the compassionate descend in abundance on your house. Amen.

May you be blessed in your work and enjoy its fruits. May cares never cause you distress, nor the desire for earthly possessions lead you astray; but may your hearts' concern be always for the treasures laid up for you in the life of heaven. Amen.

May the Lord grant you fullness of years, so that you may reap the harvest of a good life, and, after you have served Him with loyalty in His kingdom on earth, may He take you up into His eternal dominions in heaven. Through our Lord Jesus Christ His Son, Who lives and reigns with Him in the unity of the Holy Spirit, God, world without end. Amen.

The Nuptial Mass

Following the marriage ceremony proper, all of which takes place usually in the sanctuary of the church, the nuptial blessing is given. All the prayers of the Mass have a special fitness toward making marriage meaningful. Frequently copies of the nuptial Mass specially printed are distributed to all who assist at the Mass. This enables them to follow the Mass and ceremonies better. It also serves as a fitting souvenir booklet of the wedding itself. Should a couple decide to have their own special missals printed for their day of marriage, The Leaflet Missal, 55 East 10th Street, St. Paul 2, Minnesota, puts out a very attractive pamphlet called *The Mass on the Day of Marriage,* which can be used.

How beautiful is the nuptial Mass! Knowing that it is God Himself who joins man and woman together in the great sacrament of marriage, the priest prays the Introit prayer that God may be with the newly married couple all the days of their life. He says: "May the God of Israel join you together, and may He be with you. . . . And now, O Lord, make them bless Thee more fully."

The Epistle finds the priest reading the beautiful words of St. Paul to the Ephesians, in which the union of husband and wife is said to symbolize the union of Christ and His Spouse, the Church.

The first sentence of the Epistle seems to start an instruction to the wife to obey, but the Epistle turns out to be a very strong sermon for the husband. He is made the head of the home. There must be a

113

central authority in any institution, but he is the head "as Christ is the head of the Church." The husband, then, must be the protector of his wife and home; he must be willing to lay down his life for them. It is true that Saint Paul says, "As the Church is subject to Christ, so also let wives be to their husbands," but he follows that with, "Husbands, love your wives, just as Christ also loved the Church, and delivered himself up for her, that he might sanctify her . . . in order that he might present to himself the Church in all her glory, not having spot or wrinkle or any such thing, but that she might be holy and without blemish" (Ephesians 5:24–27). A husband who loves his wife in this way will never need to remind her that he is the head of the house, for he will be Christlike in all his plans for it.

St. Paul is not satisfied with this much admonition; he continues: "Even thus ought husbands also to love their wives as their own bodies" (Ephesians 5:28). This is strong language, for who would hurt his own body or fail to think of its needs, even of its legitimate pleasures? The wife, then, is to be thought of first and all her proper needs or desires fulfilled first. The husband will nourish and cherish her "as Christ also does the Church."

This doctrine has social meaning too. In case of conflict of loyalties, there is no doubt left as to the husband's first duty according to the words of God Himself which Saint Paul quotes: "For this cause a man shall leave his father and mother, and cleave to his wife; and the two shall become one flesh" (Ephesians 5:31).

The Epistle ends with the words, "Let each one of you also love his wife just as he loves himself; and let the wife respect her husband" (Ephesians 5:33). In some translations the last phrase reads, "Let the wife fear her husband." The word *fear* is to be interpreted in the same way as we interpret it when we speak of the gift of the Holy Spirit called the fear of the Lord. There we mean that our love for God should be such that we fear to offend Him. So, too, the wife ought to love her husband in this manner. This will not be difficult for her if she becomes, in truth, another Christ.[8]

The Gospel is taken from St. Matthew and proclaims the unity and indissolubility of marriage: "They shall be two in one flesh. . . . What therefore God hath joined together, let no man put asunder."

It is assumed in the missal, of course, that the newlyweds will unite themselves with the very person of Christ in the great sacrament of the Eucharist. It is customary that everyone in the bridal party, along with the parents, relatives, and friends of the couple, also receive Holy Communion. In no other way could they bring an abundance of God's blessing upon the young married couple than by receiving Holy Communion for the intentions of the newlyweds at the nuptial Mass.

114

The Nuptial Blessing

Just before Holy Communion, however, the newly married couple receive the bridal blessing better known as the nuptial blessing. Just as the Epistle served to remind the new husband of his duty to be another Christ to his wife and home, so the nuptial blessing serves to remind the wife of her duties. This solemn blessing of marriage consists actually in three prayers. Two of them are said after the *Pater Noster* of the Mass. The third is recited by the priest over the bridegroom and bride just before giving the Last Blessing of Mass. But let's take a closer look.

Immediately after reciting the *Pater Noster* the priest turns toward the husband and wife and prays:

> Let us pray. Listen with favor, O Lord, to our prayers; and in Thy goodness maintain the ways which Thou hast established for the continuation of the human race, so that the union which has been founded by Thy authority may be preserved by Thy aid. Through our Lord Jesus Christ, Thy Son, Who lives and reigns with Thee in the unity of the Holy Spirit, God, world without end. Amen.
>
> Let us pray. O God, Who by Thy mighty power hast made all things where before there was nothing; Who, having put in order the beginnings of the universe, didst form for man, made to Thy image, an inseparable helpmate, woman, so that Thou didst give woman's body its origin from man's flesh and teach that it is never right to separate her from the one being whence it has pleased Thee to take her:
>
> O God, Who has consecrated the union of marriage making it a sign so profound as to prefigure in the marriage covenant the mystery of Christ and the Church:
>
> O God, Who dost join woman to man, and give to that society, the first to be established, the blessing which alone was not taken away in punishment for original sin nor in the doom of the Flood:
>
> Look with kindness on this Thy servant who is now to be joined to her husband in the companionship of marriage and who seeks to be made secure by Thy protection.
>
> May this yoke that she is taking on herself be one of love and peace. May she be faithful and chaste, marrying in Christ, and may she always imitate the holy women. May she be the beloved of her husband, as was Rachel; wise, as was Rebecca; long-lived and loyal, as was Sarah.
>
> May the author of sin have no mastery over her because of her acts. May she hold firm to the Faith and the commandments. Faithful to one embrace, may she flee from unlawful companionship. By firm discipline may she fortify herself against her weakness. May she be grave in her modesty, honorable in her chastity, learned in the teachings of heaven.

115

May she be rich in children, prove worthy and blameless, and may she attain in the end to the peace of the blessed, the Kingdom of heaven.

May she and her husband together see their children's children to the third and fourth generation and enjoy the long life they desire. Through our Lord Jesus Christ Thy Son, Who lives and reigns with Thee in the unity of the Holy Spirit, God, for ever and ever. Amen.

Just before the Last Blessing of the Mass, the priest again turns to the bridegroom and recites the third prayer of the nuptial blessing. Its words are:

May the God of Abraham, the God of Isaac, the God of Jacob be with you, and may He fulfill in you His blessing; so that you may see your children's children to the third and fourth generation and afterward possess everlasting and boundless life. Through the help of our Lord Jesus Christ, Who with the Father and the Holy Spirit lives and reigns, God, for ever and ever. Amen.

In many dioceses, immediately after this third prayer the officiating priest may address a few last words to the bridal party to be faithful to each other, to love each other and God their entire wedded life. He may say this in his own words or recite the following prayer:

O God, who hast ordained and sanctified the holy state of matrimony for replenishing the earth, for mutual consolation, and as a type of the union of Christ and His Church, give to these here present who have this day entered into this sacred relation, grace both thankfully to accept its blessings and faithfully to fulfill its duties. Deliver them from all evil temper, from every heedless action, which may in any way embitter or weaken the tie by which Thou hast bound them together. Make them true and affectionate, studious to please, and ready to deny their own will and inclination in all things. Let not the trials and crosses of this life induce them to murmur, nor let their earthly prosperity cause them to forget Thee, the author and giver of all blessings; but by patience and meekness, by prayer and thankfulness, may all blessings be sanctified unto them, and fit them for an eternal union with Thee. Through the same Christ our Lord. Amen.

It should be kept in mind that the nuptial blessing can only be received once. This blessing is not given to those who contract mixed marriages, or to widows who are contracting marriage for the second time. If it was omitted for some reason when the marriage was contracted, e.g., because of marriage during Lent, it can and should be received as soon as possible. Should the non-

116

In some dioceses it is a custom for the bride and groom to dedicate their marriage to the Blessed Virgin after the nuptial Mass.

Masterhand, Inc.

Catholic become converted to the Faith, a couple who contracted a mixed marriage may then have their marriage blessed.

A Beautiful Custom

A popular custom in some dioceses is for the bride and groom to dedicate their marriage to the Blessed Virgin immediately after the nuptial Mass is completed. While the ceremony will vary from place to place, essentially it is made up of the bride placing a bouquet of flowers on the Blessed Virgin's altar and the bridegroom and bride reciting silently a prayer of dedication. An appropriate prayer for this occasion for both the husband and wife has been edited by Rev. Irenaeus Herscher, O.F.M., St. Bonaventure University, St. Bonaventure, New York.[9] The prayers express the hopes and dreams of the petitioners for a happy, holy married life and are a confirmation of faith in the One who instituted the Sacrament of Marriage. We reprint the prayers here:

A Bride's Prayer

O Father, my heart is filled with a happiness so wonderful, I am

117

almost afraid. This is my Wedding Day. I pray Thee that the beautiful joy of this morning may never grow dim with the tears of regret for the step I am about to take. Rather may its memories become more sweet and tender with each passing anniversary.

Thou hast sent me one who seems all worthy of my deepest regard. Grant unto me the power to keep him ever true and loving as now. May I prove indeed a helpmate, a sweetheart, a friend, a steadfast guiding star among all the temptations that beset this impulsive heart of mine.

Give me skill to make home the best loved place of all. Help me to make its light gleam brighter than any glow that would dim its radiance. Let me, I pray Thee, meet the little misunderstandings and cares of life more bravely.

Be with me as I start my mission of womanhood, and stay Thou my path from failure all the way. Walk with us even unto the end of our journey. O Father, bless my Wedding Day, Hallow my Marriage Night, Sanctify my Motherhood if Thou seest fit to grant me that privilege. And when all my youthful charms are gone, and cares and lessons have left their traces, let physical fascination give way to the greatest charm of companionship.

And so may we walk hand in hand down the highway of the valley of the shadow which we hope to lighten with the sunshine of good and happy lives.

O Father, this is my prayer. Hear me, I beseech Thee. Amen.

A Bridegroom's Prayer

O Heavenly Father, on this, my Wedding Day, I sense as never before Thy sacred Presence. It seems like the first glorious Sabbath in Paradise, when all was good and beautiful, when the universe lay at Thy feet in reverent awe, when the first man and the first woman listened to Thy voice in their pristine joy and innocence.

Behold the woman Thou gavest me as my companion for this life's journey, kneels trustfully at my side. I thank Thee for joining our paths, and for granting us the privilege of sharing Thy power in perpetuating the work of Thy Hand. I know that she is Thy gift to me, and I vow in my deepest soul to love her, treasure her, and keep her with unswerving fidelity until my dying breath. May the love which knits our souls together today, never lose its ardor, its charm, its sweetness, and may spiritual wisdom and maturer understanding ever strengthen our holy bond as the days roll by, and as the bloom and vigor of youth give way to the infirmities of advancing years.

In joy and sorrow, in triumph and failure, I will stand by her side, not as her lord and master, but as a devoted friend and protector, sharing with her lovingly all I have and hold. I will build her a home, enduring, beautiful, peaceful: she shall be my queen, my comfort, the pride of my life.

Over this home we will write the Holy Name of Jesus. Grant, O

118

Heavenly Father, that the charm of this beautiful Cana Day may abide in it forever, and that Jesus and His Blessed Mother may be our constant guests. May the same Divine Saviour fashion our mutual love after the pure love which He bore to His Bride, our Holy Church; and as He presented "to Himself the Church in all her glory, not having spot or wrinkle or any such things," so may I be permitted some day to present to Thee this bride of mine to whom I have pledged constant fidelity before Thy altar.

O Father, this is the prayer of my heart. Bless us and keep us in Thy holy grace. Amen.

The Wedding Reception

Following the ceremony at the church, it is customary for the newly married couple to proceed to the home of the bride's parents or to some other suitable place where they may receive their relatives and friends and partake of a breakfast or luncheon. This is the worldly side of the marriage celebration, and its simplicity or elaborateness will depend upon the financial means of the bride's family. If the affair is prolonged with dancing, usually the bride and groom will leave shortly after the repast to change to traveling clothes and leave for their honeymoon trip. It sometimes takes a great deal of ingenuity and careful planning to escape the pranksters and practical jokers who, from a misguided sense of humor, try to embarrass and plague the newly married pair in every way possible. This is where true and dependable friends in the persons of the best man and bridesmaid can render real assistance.[10]

SUGGESTIONS FOR READING

A Check List for Your Wedding, Msgr. James A. Magner (Notre Dame, Ind.: Ave Maria Press, 1959).

God Bless the Newlyweds, Daniel A. Lord, S.J. (St. Louis, Mo.: The Queen's Work, 1949).

A Guide to Catholic Marriage, Clement S. Mihanovich, Gerald Schnepp, and John L. Thomas (Milwaukee: The Bruce Publishing Co., 1954).

*Happy Marriage, John A. O'Brien (Garden City, N. Y.: Hanover House, 1956).

How to Arrange for Your Wedding, Gerard Breitenbeck, C.SS.R. (Liguori, Mo., The Liguorian Press, 1957).

Marriage Guidance, Edwin F. Healy, S.J. (Chicago: Loyola University Press, 1948).

*Marriage Is Holy, Abbé H. Caffarel (Chicago: Fides Publications, 1957).

Modern Manners, Carolyn Hagner Show (New York: E. P. Dutton & Co., Inc., 1958).

Chapter VI MARRIAGE GAMBLE

One of the major problems to arise in this pluralistic society of ours is the problem of mixed marriages. With interfaith dating becoming more and more common, it is becoming commonplace for Catholics to enter into marriage with a non-Catholic partner. Sociologists report that today one out of every three marriages involving Catholics is now mixed. Too few of those entering such unions realize what a gamble they are taking. Thus the reason for this chapter: to analyze the dangers of mixed marriages.

Forbidden by the Church

The attitude of the Catholic Church toward mixed marriage is expressed with utter frankness in the Code of Canon Law (C. 1060). "Everywhere and with the greatest strictness the Church forbids marriages between baptized persons, one of whom is a Catholic and the other of a schismatical or heretical sect; and if there is added to this the danger of the falling away of the Catholic party and the perversion of the children, such a marriage is forbidden also by the divine law." It is precisely this law as well as the others we have already considered in previous chapters that is commanded of Catholics by the Sixth Commandment of the Church which reads: "To observe the laws of the Church concerning marriage."

Forbidden by Others

The attitude of the Catholic Church toward mixed marriage is similar to the attitude of other religious organizations to such unions. All major religious denominations and/or organizations have gone on record opposing them. As early as 1932 the Federal Council of the Churches of Christ in America, now better known as the National Council of Churches, declared that "persons contemplating a mixed marriage should be advised not to enter it." Dr. Leland Foster Wood, formerly secretary of the Council's Commission on Marriage and the Home, stated at that time: "In warning young people against the pitfalls of mixed marriage we are taking a position rather similar to the Roman Catholic Faith."

In 1948 the general conventions of the Protestant Episcopal Church adopted a resolution as follows:

> Resolved, that this convention earnestly warns members of our Church against contracting marriages with Roman Catholics under conditions imposed by modern Roman Catholic common law, especially as these conditions involve a promise to have their children brought up under a religious system which they cannot themselves accept; and further, because the religious education and spiritual training of their children by word and example is a paramount duty of parents and should never be neglected nor left entirely to others, we assert that in no circumstances should a member of this Church give any understanding as a condition of marriage, that the children should be brought up in the practice of another communion.

In May, 1950, the General Assembly of the Presbyterian Church of the United States announced that it had joined the Protestant Episcopal Church in going on public record as opposed to mixed marriage with its inevitable dangers. Individual denominations have also gone on record opposing interfaith marriages. Typical of many such warnings is that sounded by the Southern Baptist Convention in San Francisco in June, 1951: "We, with our Roman Catholic friends, give public warning of the dangers to harmonious home life in mixed marriage."

Not too long ago Jame A. Pike, Bishop of the Protestant Episcopal Diocese of California, presented his argument against marriages of mixed religion in his book *If You Marry Outside Your Faith*. No Catholic with any experience will argue with the five reasons he presents and explains for all the failures of such unions. Noting that 66 per cent of such marriages meet with ill success he stated that:

1. Such marriages lack a commonly held basis of ideas, purposes and motivation.
2. Such marriages lack the resources of marital health provided by common worship of God.
3. Such marriages rob the parents of a common spiritual relationship to their children.
4. In such a marriage, one parent has to renounce his (or her) right to give to the children his own spiritual outlook.
5. In such marriages, if one of the parties is a Roman Catholic, the question of birth-prevention is bound to be an acute and continuing source of conflict and difficulty.

In 1956 the *Ave Maria* magazine's special report on mixed marriage found that all religious groups oppose religious intermarriage as a general principle and in many specific ways also. Opposition varies from the strictest prohibition to a kind of nominal displeasure with the situation, but in all cases there is at least the feeling that it is generally better for a person to marry within his own faith.

Now without in any way implying that all interfaith marriages are doomed to failure because of problems that will and can arise in such situations, those contemplating such marriages should take a good look at the many problems they will be facing before entering such unions.

Problems Relating to Marriage Ideals

Those contemplating a mixed marriage should consider well the problems relating to the ideals of marriage. There is a big difference, for instance, between a Catholic and a non-Catholic's viewpoint of marriage. A Catholic recognizes marriage as a sacrament as well as a contract. This is not always the case with the non-Catholic, who more often than not permits divorce and remarriage.

In mixed Catholic-Protestant marriages the rate of divorce and separation is about three times higher than in marriages where both parties are of the same faith. Three separate studies in Michigan, Maryland, and Washington, covering a total of 24,184 families have verified this condition. Mixed marriages are unstable and should be avoided at all costs.

Dr. Clifford Adams, directing the Marriage Counseling Service at Pennsylvania State College, School of Education, stated several

John Ahlhauser

Marriages between Catholics provide the children with a common spiritual relationship to their parents.

years ago in an article in the *Woman's Home Companion* that "My records show that 70 per cent of mixed marriages now end in divorce or separation." And Dr. Adams ought to know about this, for he counsels over 4000 students a year.

Another problem soon to raise its head in marriage is the problem of birth control and the means used in spacing children. For the Catholic, contraception of any kind is forbidden under pain of mortal sin. The only method of birth control a Catholic may practice is self-control or rhythm (which shall be discussed in detail later). In contrast to this position, a non-Catholic frequently condones contraceptive measures of family limitation.

Problems Concerning the Marriage Ceremony

The marriage of a Catholic to a non-Catholic is a rather drab affair, liturgically speaking. The priest officiating at the ceremony

123

wears no liturgical vestments. There is no nuptial Mass, no nuptial blessing, and no mutual reception of Holy Communion. Not even the wedding rings are blessed before they are exchanged. Only the brief ceremony of pronouncing the mutual vows of marriage takes place before the communion rail (if in church) or in the rectory. All of this is the Church's way of expressing her disapproval of such a union.

Problems Affecting Home Life

A mixed marriage creates many problems of living in marriage. The reason is that Catholicism permeates the entire life of the Catholic party. It is not just a Sunday affair. The use of sacramentals such as holy water, statues, crucifix, and religious pictures are commonly found in Catholic homes. In a mixed marriage, these religious articles and outward symbols of Catholicism could prove distasteful and embarrassing to the non-Catholic spouse. Even if they are accepted, they are tolerated, never fully understood by the non-Catholic party. This could have repercussions on the children's attitude toward sacramentals.

No matter how kind and considerate the couple may be, religious differences will eventually lead to quarrels. Intellectual disputes are bound to occur when two individuals differ in such an important life factor as religion. A popular non-Catholic columnist of some years ago pointed up the seriousness of this problem: "It is merely a fact that just as no wars have been so bloody as holy wars and no persecutions so cruel as those done in the name of religion, so there is nothing about which husbands and wives can quarrel so bitterly, nothing which can so completely estrange them as a difference in creed."[1]

Even where the non-Catholic partner belongs to no particular denomination, or affiliation, religious quarrels will arise between husband and wife because of the apathy of the one and the worry of the other. For example, the non-Catholic may see no reason for attendance at Sunday Mass, the Catholic party knows better, etc.

Another cause of religious disputes between the members of a mixed marriage is the sacrament of penance. For a non-Catholic the confessional is nonessential in telling God that you are sorry

124

for your sins. For the Catholic party, confession is at least an annual obligation. Going to confession presents great problems where moral issues such as artificial birth control affect married life. At times the Catholic may have to choose between his partner and his Faith. A Protestant Episcopal rector in advising a young man of his parish against a mixed marriage, pointed up this situation some time ago.

> In matters of faith again, you, as a Protestant, may find yourself resenting the confessional — always a bogey to men like yourself. Your wife must continue going to confession. No evading that, and the confessor occupies a more or less judicial position where the married, as well as the unmarried, are concerned, and here is where mixed marriage troubles generally begin. For sooner or later the question of children will crop up, and self-control versus birth control will be a serious issue to be faced. Your wife, as a Catholic, will not listen to any birth control argument through the media of contraceptive measures. Her faith teaches her that such things are shameful and vicious. . . . And the man who marries her will have to recognize her view of faith and morals, especially in the close intimacies that exist between husband and wife. Make up your mind to this, otherwise you may look for disillusion and disgust, followed on your part by a desire for divorce.[2]

Church support becomes the occasion of still further problems for a mixed marriage couple. The non-Catholic as an active church member will wish to contribute to his respective church, the Catholic partner will wish to contribute to her respective parish church. With battle lines neatly drawn, the arguments are frequent. This double Sunday giving is but a part of a problem. Children born of a mixed marriage must be educated in a Catholic school if one exists in the area. This requires the burden of double taxation for the support of parochial as well as public schools. Too often this financial burden causes the non-Catholic to go back on his premarital promises of educating all children in Catholic schools.

Difficulty arises too over reading matter that is brought into the home. A good Catholic family is expected to subscribe to some good Catholic reading. Frequently the non-Catholic spouse will not like to lay out money for publications which do not support his own beliefs. When it comes to entertainment, here again Catholics are urged to observe the listings of the Legion of Decency. While these listings take into account the natural law of avoiding an occasion of sin, the average non-Catholic does not consider them binding in conscience. In fact he considers them a limitation of freedom.

Catholics may wish to participate in certain Catholic societies that may be a source of disagreement for the non-Catholic partner. Such organizations as the Holy Name Society, the St. Vincent de Paul Society, the Altar and Rosary Society, and the Legion of Mary are open only to Catholic membership. This excludes the mixed marriage partner from participation. So often this exclusion is reversed as well. The non-Catholic may belong to some fraternal organizations (e.g., Masons) that are forbidden to Catholics. This frequently results in religious quarrels.

A brief study of the above circumstances readily shows that a mixed marriage by its nature is adverse to peaceful domestic life. A Catholic contemplating marriage with a person not of his faith should give this matter marked consideration. Marriage is for a lifetime. A mixed marriage may mean a lifetime of "cold war" over religion.

Mixed Marriage Breeds Religious Indifference

Mixed marriages very often lead to a gradual lessening of religious practices, and then to laxity, religious indifference, and the loss of the Faith. At least this is the conclusion born from so many sociological studies of the problem. Take the survey made by Murray H. Leiffer, professor of sociology at Garrett Biblical Institute, in cooperation with 22 churches and the partners of 743 mixed marriages some years ago.

Of 444 husbands of Catholic-Protestant marriages interviewed, 124 acknowledged that they had not attended church for a year, while 110 admitted that they had severed all religious connections. Out of 449 wives interviewed, 60 had already broken away completely, 91 had not attended church services for a year, and only 107 claimed to attend as often as every other Sunday.

John A. O'Brien's noted study, *The Truth About Mixed Marriages,* conclusively shows that out of every ten Catholics entering into mixed marriages, six are ultimately lost to the Church.

Studies of mixed marriages also show that children of such

126

marriages become definitely lost to the Catholic Faith.

In 1951 the YMCA made a study of this problem. Its survey revealed that in cases where both parents were Catholic, 92 per cent of their sons were also practicing Catholics, and where both were Protestants, 68 per cent of their sons were practicing Protestants. But where one parent was Protestant and the other Catholic, only 34 per cent of their sons were practicing members of either faith. This means that 66 per cent were lapsed Catholics and/or failed to be raised in the Faith.

You may ask, "What faith benefits from mixed marriage?" The answer to that question is no religion, or the religion of indifference which has its chief dogma that one religion is just as good as another. Mixed-faith marriages have done much to foster the growth of this modern heresy.

It is worth noting here that Catholic women are more likely to enter an interfaith union than Catholic men. In a study by the Catholic Bishops' Committee on Mixed Marriages covering 7 archdioceses and 43 dioceses from 1932 to 1941, the ratio was 60–40, 60 women to 40 men. Father Joseph Fichter, S.J., in his celebrated study of a Southern parish, found the ratio to be 73–27 in the case of valid mixed marriages.

A Real-Life Decision

A close study of interfaith marriages readily shows that they seldom contain true happiness or success without definite sacrifice of spiritual values. Alice Case gives a personal experience of this fact.

I was 19, Bob was 22. We had a bright, shining future. Why spoil everything by arguing about religion? Rather, we carefully avoided the subject because neither dared admit to the other how completely we expected to win. As I look back over the years, I marvel at the atrocious conceit I displayed when I went so far as to tell my mother that I was certain Bob would turn Catholic if I so much as mentioned it. Ah, 19! A wonderful age.

The night I met Bob's parents was the beginning of the end of my dream. They joked about "signing up a minister" if their son continued to spend so much time at the home of his future in-laws. I must have given some sign at the mention of minister because Bob's father said, "You would naturally adopt the religion of your husband, wouldn't you?"

127

I don't remember my exact answer but later Bob told me of the terrible disappointment his parents felt at his being interested in a "headstrong girl who refused to follow her man." That was the opening wedge. Bob's parents used every argument at their disposal to influence him in insisting that I be the one to change religion. At first he was too much in love to see me in the poor light they used. But gradually, by appealing to his male ego, they made him feel that it was a point of honor for a man to force his bride to accept his religion. Meanwhile, I was struggling against open combat with two people whom I scarcely knew except as future (?) in-laws.

Much as I had dreamed of orange blossoms, I could not bring myself to toss my long years of Catholic upbringing to one side and be married by a Methodist minister. I was adamant. I refused to study the Methodist beliefs; I wanted no part in their ceremonies. In fact, I tried to defend Catholicism until each date became a long session of argument which left me confused and bitter. I cried and beat my fists into my pillow on a good many nights after Bob left me with his stubborn refusal to be "led around by a woman."

Finally I sought advice. Perhaps I was wrong in my choice of confidants but I went to visit a relative who had given up her religion to marry a man who proclaimed himself to be an atheist. I had not talked with Aunt Patty for years inasmuch as she was considered the "black sheep" of our family. But I felt close to her now since we had our common ground.

"Tell him to go fly," Aunt Patty said without hesitation. "No man is worth giving up anything as personal as religion. I know." She and her husband appeared compatible on the surface but Aunt Patty said they existed in a state of truce. She was constantly being nagged by her conscience and he was forever cramming his erratic beliefs down her throat. There were no children and Aunt Patty thanked God for not complicating a bad situation. I could see that after eight years this marriage was something less than I desired. I left Aunt Patty with a genuine concern for her sanity. She was nervous, excitable, loud and not at all serene as I remembered her. With a shudder I faced my own dilemma.

Fall had arrived and I entered nurses' training as I had planned. Bob and I continued to see each other occasionally but it was as if we were strangers meeting for the first time. There was a stiff formality about our relationship which annoyed me. We had been so gay and carefree. Such fun we had had . . . until we began this mad wrangle over religion. I told him my feelings on this subject one night just before Christmas. I was home for a few days and we were trying to recapture the old zest and spontaneity while all our school friends were gathered for the holiday season.

"It's no use, Bob," I said. "I can't punish myself by dating you any longer. This is leading us against an impossible wall. Neither will give in and we may as well face it."

"Can't we just go on enjoying each other's company?" he asked.

"Must we settle the future today?" He was irritated and I knew it.

One thing led to another and we had a violent argument ending in bitter accusations, a slammed door and a break up. I cried myself to sleep and went back to the hospital the next day to work during my vacation . . . anything to forget Bob.

My superintendent of nurses sensed trouble and I poured out my story to her. A kindly soul, she offered to introduce me to several people whom she felt could advise me. I was willing to meet anybody and listen to their views if it would ease the pain I felt over losing Bob.

During that week I had tea with a wonderful priest who gave me a lovely sterling cross to wear on a chain to remind me that I was truly dedicated to Christ. He said for me to live my life as usual but to avoid any talk of religion with Bob.

"If you see him, and I think you will," he said with a twinkle in his eye, "don't talk. Show him. Show him a picture of a Catholic girl and let him decide. Remember, my child, a picture is worth a thousand words."

The full meaning didn't penetrate until much later but I felt strangely rested and relaxed as I fingered the beautiful cross.

I met a girl my own age who had given up her church two years before to marry her loved one. At the time of her marriage, she said nothing mattered except Bill. But two years had dimmed the splendor of the relationship and the Sunday morning church bells gave her severe headaches. She was still very much in love but she was paying a terrible price. Her parents rejected her; her conscience made her miserable and her baby was not baptized, a cross which she bore daily in fear. Her faith meant more to her now that she was denied the practice of it. I listened, pitied and left the girl to her sadness.

Bob called me early the next week and asked for "just one date . . . to straighten things out."

I granted him that much and as I dressed for the evening, I prayed hard to the Blessed Virgin. I prayed for guidance. I didn't trust myself without her help.

As it turned out, I needed all the help I could get. Bob was contrite, apologetic and very humble. He acted so meek and considerate of my wishes that I was taken completely by surprise when he drove to a spot overlooking the city and began making love to me with a violence which frightened me.

"I've missed you so much I can't live without you," he said. "We'll both have to grow up and forget this childish squabbling. Let's announce our engagement right away and be married in June."

Stunned, I dared not venture a question. Did he mean *he* would give in? Just in time, I recalled Father Boler's advice. I was not showing a very clear picture of a Catholic girl as I accepted his caresses almost eagerly. It took terrific strength and will power to draw away from Bob whom I realized I loved even more than I dared think about. But I did. I sat primly on my side of the car and said, "Bob, we couldn't live forever on passion. I would grow to hate you if I chose you over my religion. And it wouldn't be fair to you, either. You deserve a girl who can marry you on your terms willingly. Since there is really nothing to straighten out, will you please take me back?"

To say he was startled would be the understatement of all time. He was furious. But he drove me back and said good-night with a great show of polish. I was certain that it was the last time I would ever see him and I went to my room and sat in a big chair dry-eyed and peaceful like a tired soldier after a long battle.

Thus I entered my second year of training . . . free and unattached. I dated a few fellows but always I compared them with Bob and they never measured up. I worked hard and tried to forget him.

I kept in touch with Father Boler during these difficult months and his good humor often pulled me out of a slump when I allowed my self-pity to show. He visited the hospital often to call on the sick and I looked forward to his red cheeks and shock of white hair popping above the row of charts on the ward where I worked.

It was on one of these visits that he leaned over to my ear and said, "I'd like to have you come to the rectory tomorrow afternoon . . . sort of a little celebration going on that I think you'd enjoy."

I said I'd come and promptly put it from my mind. But I walked the short distance the next day with feelings of curiosity as well as pleasure at being invited out.

Father met me at the door himself. His eagerness was as plain as day. He quickly took my coat and almost pushed me into his little study where I looked directly into the eyes of Bob who sat before the low tea table as though he owned the place.

"I'm glad you could come. We're celebrating my baptism," he said.

The rest is easy. Bob had stubbornly decided to find out what magnetism the Catholic Church held . . . if it could come between him and the girl he was sure loved him. And he found out. He took instructions eagerly and has not been sorry yet . . . or so he told me on our 17th wedding anniversary this year![3]

Marriage, Mixed or Unmixed

Marriage, mixed or unmixed, that is the question for many these days. Those who are unconvinced that the above arguments are sound or who feel that they are too emotional, ought to ask themselves a few questions before the ring on their finger ends up in their nose. By the time some individuals consider these questions, however, it is already too late. Being in love with a non-Catholic, the questions which follow, however obvious and convincing to others, will usually have little effect upon them. Being a little blind or dazzled, however, should not prevent one from noting very basic reactions in the prospective non-Catholic husband or wife. If you are going with a non-Catholic and getting serious ask yourself the following questions:

1. How does this person react to Catholic doctrine as he becomes aware of it? Is he hostile? Is he amused? Is he disdainful? If he is any of these things, the marriage is a bad risk.

2. Is he interested, if uncommitted in the Catholic faith? Does he ask reasonable questions and listen politely to replies? Does he respect your religious practices, even while disagreeing with their form or purpose? Does he perhaps voice a vague "wish that he could believe all that," because it must be wonderful to have such faith? Does he believe in the support of religion in general? Does he show in his manner of life respect for or belief in a good basic moral code? If he does all of these, a course of instructions from one's parish priest will result in the non-Catholic eventually joining the Catholic faith. If not, this partner will seldom cause trouble or difficulty in the practice of religion of the Catholic party.

3. When the prospective spouse takes instructions, does he become angry at the necessity of doing so? Does he feel your Church is ordering him about unjustly? Does he react badly to priests in general? (This also applies to women — and perhaps even more, since children will be in their care.) If any of these reactions is among the usual ones for the bride and groom-to-be, one should look long before leaping. This is not to misjudge the motives of these individuals, who are acting true to their own beliefs, after all. It is natural for them to be upset if the priest's instructions seem to them an invasion of their rights and conscience. It takes a sensitive individual, who loves another deeply, to enter into his mind through the mind of his religion. He could not do it at all, were it not for love. If he does it for love, and is repelled or resentful love will not be enough to carry the pair through a lifetime without damage to religious beliefs. Because if we resent the religious background of our beloved, we do our best to "see" him outside of it. Trying to see him without his religion, we strip him of something which is part of him. Those who hate our religion, while saying they love us, mean they would cut out the hateful part if they could. If they cannot, they may spend a lot of time trying to get us to cut it out ourselves, and sometimes they may succeed.

4. How does this non-Catholic feel about children? Is he willing to have a large family, if it should turn out that way? Could he, if a man, support a large family without constantly blaming his wife for having a religion which makes the possibility of such a family almost a foregone conclusion? Could she, if a woman, enter with good will into the rearing of a large family, without feeling that she has sacrificed herself unwillingly on the altar of her husband's religion? If their attitudes are positive and hopeful, realistically ready to bear the probable burden of marriage along with its blessings, the prospects are good.

131

However, if there is much discussion and preoccupation before marriage as to keeping the family small, it is safe to assume there will be even more discussion and difficulty afterward. A large family may or may not result from a particular union, but if a couple wills against it at the outset, there is cause for concern during marriage.[4]

A serious appraisal of the above questions should help you make the Church's attitude toward mixed marriage your attitude. Look before you leap. There are two ways to avoid a mixed marriage: (1) make sure to associate with eligible Catholics of the opposite sex, and (2) guard against the beginning of serious love in friendly association with non-Catholics of the opposite sex.

Why Grant Dispensations?

The prohibition of interfaith marriages is an ecclesiastical law, although at times it may be also forbidden because of divine law. When a mixed marriage involves serious and irremovable spiritual risks to the Catholic party or to children who might be born of the union, the marriage is forbidden. The Church gives permission for an interfaith marriage only if:

1. Natural and divine laws do not forbid the marriage.
2. There is a genuinely grave reason for the dispensation, e.g., where marriage is necessary because, due to sinful intimacy, a child is to be born, or where it is necessary to avert or remove a great scandal or a grave spiritual danger.
3. Both the Catholic and non-Catholic make certain promises, and there is moral certainty that these promises or solemn agreements will be carried out faithfully.

The Pre-nuptial Promises

The promises made by the partners in a mixed marriage are called the pre-nuptial agreement. They are usually drawn up as a contract, signed, and witnessed. Recent studies show, however, that these promises are not kept in about 30 per cent of all mixed marriages. Moreover, there is no practical way to make the non-Catholic keep his promise. In a recent decision (1957) the Ohio Supreme Court ruled in effect that agreements made by parties to a mixed marriage for the Catholic rearing of their children are "void and unenforceable." This means that pre-nuptial promises

By marrying a partner of one's own faith, the Catholic has the benefit of assistance in the responsibility of raising children in his Faith.

John Ahlhauser

are valid only so long as the non-Catholic partner wishes to keep them.

The following are the promises both parties agree to keep prior to their marriage: The first are directed to the non-Catholic party; the second are to be signed by the Catholic party.

PRE-NUPTIAL PROMISES

(To be signed by the Non-Catholic Party)

I, the undersigned, not a member of the Catholic Church, wishing to contract marriage with ...., a member of the Catholic Church, propose to do so with the understanding that the marriage is indissoluble, except by death; and on my word of honor I solemnly promise, without any reservation, tacit or expressed:

1. That I will not interfere in any way with the free exercise of my spouse's Catholic religion, and in particular I will remove from my Catholic spouse any danger of perversion regarding Catholic faith and morals.

2. That all children, both boys and girls, who may be born of this union, shall be baptized only in the Roman Catholic Church, and that they shall be educated according to the teachings of the same Church, that is, solely in the Catholic Faith, both at home and through faithful attendance and participation in the formal program of religious instruction provided by the Catholic Church. They shall attend Catholic schools if such are available.

133

3. That I will keep the promise I have just made concerning the baptism and education of the children in the Catholic Faith, even if my spouse and I are separated by (his) (her) death or by any other means.

These promises and covenants herein contained shall be binding on my respective heirs, next of kin, executors, administrators, and/or subsequent guardians and their successors.

Signed at .... this .... day of .... 19.....

(Parish Seal)   ....
                                       (Signature of Non-Catholic Party)

In the presence of the following two witnesses:

1. ....   2. ....

(To be signed by the Catholic Party)

I, the undersigned, a Catholic of (Parish) ...., wishing to contract marriage with .... a non-Catholic, hereby solemnly promise, if the Church finds sufficient reason for granting me a dispensation:

1. That I will have all our children, both boys and girls, baptized only in the Roman Catholic Church, and I will educate them, according to the teachings of the same Church, that is, solely in the Catholic Faith, both at home and through faithful attendance and participation in the formal program of religious instruction provided by the Church. I will send them to Catholic schools if such are available.

2. That I will practice my religion faithfully and, by the edifying influence of a good Catholic life, I will endeavor to bring my partner to the true Faith.

These promises and covenants, herein contained shall be binding on my respective heirs, next of kin, executors, administrators, and/or subsequent guardians and their successors.

Signed at .... this .... day of .... 19.....

(Parish Seal)   ....
                                       (Signature of Catholic Party)

In the presence of the following two witnesses:

1. ....   2. ....

134

Instruction Necessary

One of the conditions required of the non-Catholic party before being allowed to enter into marriage with a Catholic is a course of instructions on the fundamental points of Catholic belief and practice. Six instructions usually comprise the course, although some dioceses today are requiring twelve, others as high as twenty-four before allowing the mixed marriage to take place. The Catholic party is required to sit in on them also. The Church has good reason for this instructional requirement.

> If a non-Catholic is to marry a Catholic and agrees not to hinder the Catholic partner from practicing his or her religion and agrees also to the Catholic upbringing of all children who may be born to the marriage, certainly the non-Catholic ought to know something about the fundamental beliefs and practices of the Catholic Church.[5]

Serious Problem

With 85,000 to 100,000 Catholics marrying non-Catholics every year, the problem of mixed marriages is not to be taken lightly. Along with the Catholic Church, more and more Protestant Churches are recognizing the grave harm they cause. Officials of all Churches as well as marriage counselors of all faiths advise today's youth to marry their own kind. A mixed marriage is a marriage gamble. Very few end up winners for a lifetime.

Another Mixed-Marriage Problem

Another mixed-marriage problem that has blossomed with the increase of integration is racial intermarriage or miscegenation — the marriage of a white to a Negro. While the Church imposes no diriment or prohibitive impediment to such marriages, it does command her ministers to respect the law regarding such unions. In several states such marriages are illegal. It may take several decades before society will give its complete approval. Prejudice has a way of living on. But an enlightened, educated society will some day establish interracial justice and overlook the color of skin as love does in marriage. For the fear of intermarriage is much like a ghost. It lacks substance and form. Two Christians no matter what their color receive the sacrament of Christian marriage when they marry, not a sacrament of interracial marriage.

SUGGESTIONS FOR READING

Can Mixed Marriages Be Happy?, Donald F. Miller, C.SS.R. (Liguori, Mo.: Liguorian Pamphlets, 1956), 29 pp.

If I Marry Outside My Religion, Algernon D. Black (New York: Public Affairs Pamphlet, 1954).

If You Marry Outside Your Faith, James A. Pike (New York: Harper & Brothers, 1954).

"I Love You But . . . ," by a Catholic husband and a Protestant wife, *The Sign,* 1952, 15 pp.

*Life Together, Wingfield Hope (New York: Sheed and Ward, 1943).

*One Marriage Two Faiths, James H. S. Bossard and Eleanor S. Boll (New York: The Ronald Press Co., 1957), 180 pp.

Program for Catholics in a Mixed Marriage, Donald F. Miller, C.SS.R. (Liguori, Mo.: The Liguorian Press, 1965), 22 pp.

The Race Question and the Negro, John LaFarge, S.J. (New York: Longmans, Green & Co., 1944).

Shall I Marry a Catholic?, James A. Magner (Huntington, Ind.: Our Sunday Visitor Press, 1946), 28 pp.

"What You Should Know About Mixed Marriage," Stan Frank Hamel, *Ave Maria,* Notre Dame, Ind., Vol. 84, November 24, 1956, pp. 8–13. (Can be purchased as a reprint.)

Why Marriages Go Wrong, James H. S. Bossard and Eleanor S. Boll (New York: The Ronald Press Co.).

Chapter **VII** *PARTNERS IN LIVING*

There is no human act in which a person reveals himself or involves himself so totally as in love. In love the best that is in man is brought out to the best advantage. How true this is of marital love! In the sacrament of marriage a man and a woman become one with Love Himself. Whatever brings a husband and wife closer to one another (mutual consent, devotion, and sacrifice) can bring them closer to God; and whatever brings them closer to God brings them closer to one another.[1]

Marriage Requires Mature Personality

One of marriage's chief contributions to those who enter into it is the enrichment of the personality of partners. This is so because love urges one's personality to go beyond itself. If the marriage has constant sharing and there is mutual giving, husband and wife together become finer personalities than either could have been alone. The strengths of one offset the weaknesses of the other. When in one person there is deep need for comfort, affection, and reassurance, the other gives with generosity. Each contributes love, respect, and happiness to the other. Partners with mature personalities in the making always give of themselves in marriage. This is not a 50–50 sort of arrangement, but a total 100–100 living of giving. In marriage, husband and wife belong entirely to each other — one in mind, one in heart, and one in affections. This unity of love is essential to marital fulfillment and success.

The Honeymoon

To help the newly married couple make the new and more intimate adjustments to each other that marriage requires, a honeymoon of some fashion is planned. "Very commonly the honeymoon takes the form of a trip. This affords a change in environment and removal from old associations. It has importance also in that it affords restful quiet. All this should be helpful in making memorable and pleasant the important transition from courtship to marriage, from the exciting or hectic anteroom to the deeper and more real joys of married life."[2]

The honeymoon trip, so much a part of today's marriage, is of fairly recent origin. In planning such a trip, newlyweds should keep in mind that they are beginning a long journey through life together. A honeymoon, therefore, is no time for strenuous traveling and sight-seeing, especially if the time at their disposal is short. It should be long enough to escape the horseplay of their friends and short enough so that they will not become bored with each other. Because of the strain and tension during the days preceding their wedding, newlyweds should seek a place of rest and quiet. Getting off on the right foot in marriage is important.

In making honeymoon plans, the couple should not only eliminate fatiguing sight-seeing, they should face up squarely to the problem of finances. To avoid financial difficulties, it is well for them to form a budget at the outset. Overspending on a honeymoon is no way to start a marriage.

Making use of the matter of the sacrament and the contract of marriage also has its problems. Newlyweds will have no difficulty here if they remember that sex adjustment takes time, patience, respect, and consideration for the other person's feelings and attitudes. Haste, lack of the most tender consideration, ignorance of each other's sex nature, and an absence of complete trust in each other can shatter the happiness of the honeymoon, if not the happiness of marriage itself. That is why it is all important for those about to marry to consult an intelligent Catholic doctor and priest to learn the positive side of chastity in marriage.

Some newlyweds spend their honeymoon in the privacy and comfort of their own apartment or home. They do this to eliminate

138

In planning a honeymoon trip, newlyweds should keep in mind that they are beginning a long journey through life together.

H. Armstrong Roberts

the problems of fatigue and finances that so frequently take their toll of those beginning married life. There is something to say for this type of honeymoon. Providing adequate privacy is assured, money the couple save which otherwise would have been spent on traveling and hotel accommodations can now be spent on home or apartment furnishings. It has frequently happened that honeymooners have returned home only to wish that they had not made such an expensive wedding trip. Before embarking on the road of life together, a smart couple should weigh well both types of honeymoon.

Adjustment in Marriage

The big problem in the early days, months, and even years of married life is adjustment. The word "adjustment" comes from two Latin words *ad* and *juste* which mean "justice toward." Adjustment, therefore, means full willingness to recognize, accept, and promote the entire personality of one's spouse so that both will be able to bear the burdens and responsibilities of married life. Adjustment also has reference to the couple's acceptance of God's plan for marriage. There is no room for selfishness in His plan. That is why the best marital adjustments are those that are made

139

by unselfish, generous people. Where the "unselfish spirit of perfect sacrifice guides their every action," a married couple is assured of success.

Complementary Differences

God made man and woman partners not competitors in marriage. How important it is to realize this fact. Before describing the various marital adjustments that will have to be made by both partners, therefore, it is essential that the partners themselves realize that they differ not only biologically but also psychologically. What God has made distinct, let no man confuse.

Philosophers down through the centuries have pointed out the complementary differences of men and women.

> Man . . . has initiative, power and origin. Woman has intuition, response, acceptance, submission and cooperation. Man lives more in the external world . . . it is his mission to rule over it and subject it. Woman lives more in the internal world. . . . Man is more interested in the outer world; woman in the inner world. Man talks about things; woman more about persons. Man fashions the products of the earth; woman fashions life. . . . Man makes sacrifices for things which are in the future and which are abstract; woman . . . is more inclined to make sacrifices for persons and for that which is immediate. Because more objective, man is inclined to give reasons for what he loves and what he does; woman, being more subjective . . . is more inclined to love just for love's sake. Man's reasons for loving are because of the qualities and attributes of the beloved. Man builds, invents, conquers; woman tends, devotes, interiorizes. The man gives; the woman is a gift.[3]

According to Dr. Alphonse Clemens, director of the Marriage Counseling Center of the Catholic University of America, there are some very differing traits of men and women in our culture that should be considered. Without such knowledge marital adjustment is extremely difficult, if not impossible. The various traits of men and women are as follows:

Men	Women
Men prefer generalities.	Women prefer details.
Men are more objective.	Women are more subjective.
Men tend to be stern.	Women tend to be tender.
Men tend to be forceful.	Women tend to be tactful.
Men prefer essentials.	Women prefer accidentals.
Men are more passionate.	Women are more romantic.
Men are more materialistic.	Women are more spiritual.

140

Men are more self-contained.	Women are more social.
Men are more egoistic.	Women are more altruistic.
Men tend to dominate.	Women are more submissive.
Men are more steady.	Women tend to moodiness.
Men are content with the prosaic.	Women prefer the poetic.
Men are more conceited.	Women are more jealous.
Men are more pugnacious.	Women are more tenacious.[4]

From comparing these differences it can be said that ideally every woman possesses the psychological qualities for motherhood: a great capacity for generous and unselfish love, a loving attention to details, a strong intuitive sense, tenderness, patience, long-suffering; while every man manifests the qualities required of fatherhood, namely: strength, clear and logical thought, wisdom to command, resolute and determined will, courage. In practical living, however, it is important to remember that few "pure" types of the masculine and feminine traits can be found. It is perhaps more accurate to say that the perfect human being is a composite of both. There are times when a man should know how to be tender, meek, sympathetic, patient, and understanding. And he does not become less a man for so doing. No man is "just like a man."

The same holds true for a woman. No woman is just another member of her mysterious sex. She has personal feminine characteristics similar to those of her sisters, but nevertheless quite different. At times she may and must display some very definite masculine traits.

Marriage, a Discord or Symphony in Relationships

Getting married is one thing, establishing a happy home quite another. A Christian home is not an outright gift of God; it must be built up by the contracting parties themselves, upon the fixed principles of the law of God. No matter how well matched the newlyweds may seem to be, no matter how well they think they know and understand each other, there will be great need for mutual adjustments in every phase of married life. This requires a great amount of sacrifice. The priest reminds the couple of this at the marriage ceremony. "Sacrifice is usually difficult and irksome. Only love can make it easy; and perfect love can make

141

it a joy. We are willing to give in proportion as we love. And when love is perfect, the sacrifice is complete."

Making marriage a symphony of good living takes time. It is not achieved overnight. It sometimes takes 25 hours a day, as newlyweds are soon to discover, because some days are very long. This adjustment to living harmoniously with one another is best made alone, and by the newlyweds themselves. To paraphrase Sacred Scripture, it is good for them to be alone during this period. If they are forced to live with in-laws, there is usually a serious hazard to peace and happiness. Doting parents do the young couple no great favor in offering them an upstairs apartment. It is almost axiomatic that newlyweds do better when away from the prying eyes and free advice of parents or other in-laws. This is no reflection against in-laws. They may be well intentioned, but studies show that God's command to man to leave father and mother and cleave to his wife is still the best.

Little Things Mean a Lot

The first important duty of newlyweds is to get acquainted. Living under the same roof gives them their first real opportunity to do this. If they are unwilling to make the concessions that are necessary to bring harmony between two dissimilar natures, there is very little chance of success. The emotionally immature person is fundamentally selfish, but unselfishness is a key habit in seeking happiness. Differences will occur, and both partners must make a high resolve to sink their differences. In every case it takes intelligence, character, and time to become an excellent husband or wife. Fortunately nature defers the advent of a child, and in ordinary cases nine to twelve months pass before newlyweds are permitted to become fathers and mothers. This gives time for the mutual adjustments which must be made. Not that adjustments and the need for virtue are exclusively marital characteristics. In every human relationship there must be a harmonious give-and-take between individuals; each must adapt to the other. The same characteristics which make a good child, a good parent, a good employee, a good employer, or a good neighbor will make him or her a good husband or wife.

142

Thoughtfulness is a good indicator of the vitality of a marriage. Do not let the passing of the years allow this trait to pass out of your married life.

H. Armstrong Roberts

Two important virtues sorely needed by both husband and wife are patience and charity — patience, to bear each other's shortcomings willingly; and charity, to help each other unselfishly in family tasks for the mutual good of the family.

"The Gift of the Magi," a short story by O. Henry, vividly points up how natural it is for two people in love to think first of each other. Briefly, a poor couple, newly married and in love, faces a penniless Christmas. The husband pawns his one good possession, a gold watch, to buy his wife a beautiful comb. She in turn sells her luxuriant hair to buy him a handsome watch fob. Without the magic of love, this story would be a masterpiece of irony. With it, however, each succeeds in giving the other a priceless, precious gift — the devotion of a selfless marriage.

How to Handle a Tense Situation

Tensions will and do arise in marriage. It is important, therefore, that both husband and wife learn right from the outset of married life how to handle such situations. The first thing to keep in mind is that each partner has a right to his likes and dislikes, which may be different from the other's. Understand your part-

143

ner's way of looking at a situation. Never make a decision when emotionally upset. Leave the place of a tense situation. Develop a saving sense of humor. This is invaluable in tight situations. Never attribute an ulterior motive to another's actions. Few people are truly malicious. Before declaring war on your spouse, talk out your problems. St. Paul warns about never letting the sun go down on an argument, and his advice is as modern as today. Psychologists and marriage counselors all agree that lack of communication between husband and wife is the beginning of the end. "Who is to blame?" is not so important as "How can we set this situation right?"

Money Matters

Riches are by no means essential for the happiness of marriage, but there should be enough money on hand to provide a home, if only in a small way, and a reasonable certainty of being able to meet the expenses of the new household. Many young men and women today are partners in earning until their children come. Sometimes it becomes necessary for the mother to continue as a wage earner even after the children are born, but this should be

H. Armstrong Roberts

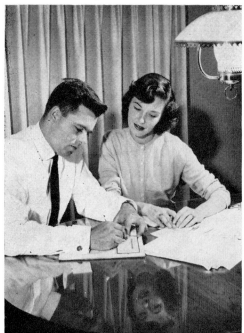

Too many marriages are shipwrecked by financial crises or at least imperiled by them. A realistic attitude toward family finance must be considered a requirement for successful marriage.

the rare exception. Ordinarily the family income is earned solely by the husband. It should be remembered, however, that both husband and wife should decide how the family income is to be portioned out — how much for housekeeping and clothes, how much for luxuries, entertainments, and holidays, and how much for the work of God's Church and the needs of others. This is only just, because marriage is a partnership. It is essential, therefore, that newlyweds know how to budget their income. Listed below are typical expenditures of young couples whose take-home pay from the husband's job ranges from $425 to $575 a month in the first year of marriage.[5] These figures can help determine where adjustments in a family's expenditures should be made. If the wife works, net proceeds (after job expenses) from her job should be used to build up a reserve for starting a family or buying a home, rather than for raising the standard of living.

	Per Month
1. Food, including meals away from home	$80–100
2. Rent, or mortgage payments	75–100
3. Transportation and automobile	40–55
4. Clothing, plus cleaning and repairs	30–40
5. Personal insurance and taxes	30–35
6. House furnishings and payments	25–30
7. Education, hobbies, recreation	20–25
8. House operation, supplies, utilities	20–25
9. Personal care (barber, beauty shop, etc.)	20–25
10. Contributions (church, charity, etc.)	15–35
11. Medical and dental care, drugs	15–20
12. "Special" (tobacco, alcohol, etc.)	15–20
13. Savings for vacation and Christmas	15–20
14. Savings (or debt payment)	25–45

Keeping and Making Friends

Marital adjustment also requires that the couple make every effort to be courteous and agreeable to each other's friends. Sarcastic comments or criticisms of a partner's friends or any minor objections to their visiting the home because of personal dislike should be avoided. "Marriage does not mean that one gives up the right to keep friends he or she had before marriage. It is taken for granted, of course, that neither partner to a marriage would encourage a visit to the home by any friend who might sow seeds of

145

discord in the home or be an occasion of scandal to the children."[6] Marriage partners should realize from the outset that at times relatives will arrive unannounced, even at mealtime. Common courtesy should be practiced at all such times.

Two in One Flesh

Unity in marriage implies many adjustments — social, psychological, practical, spiritual, and physical. This occurs because marriage is the partnership of two whole lives, not of parts of two lives. Marriage has a spiritual side because true love is spiritual and comes from God; it has a social side because husbands and wives and children have to live in a wide world of human beings like themselves; it has a psychological and practical side because not only does it require many mental adjustments, but takes plenty of common sense to face problems like work and money and to keep the home together. It also has a bodily side. In this world, soul and body are united, and the soul cannot do without the body, any more than the body without the soul. Because of this, it is important that the newly married couple possess a healthy attitude toward sex. It is essential that both husband and wife recognize that the use of sex in marriage is virtuous. It was for this reason that God designed its use. Though we are naturally reticent about the basic fact of marriage, it is nevertheless true. Sex was designed by God for marriage. That is why any use of sex outside of marriage is a betrayal of the trust God has given to man. For the unmarried, this means that the deliberate arousing of sensual desire or feeling or the consenting thereto is a degradation of sex that goes contrary to the will of God.

God's Purpose

It is not from anthropology, not from biology, not from any merely human source that we learn the true meaning of sex. It was not human society, but God Who instituted marriage, and He Himself tells us its purpose. In the inspired account of the creation of man we read that God created man in His image — male and female He created them. Then God blessed them and said to them, "Be fruitful and multiply; fill the earth and subdue it."[7]

God might have willed that new human bodies come into existence other than the way they do. He could have willed that human bodies periodically divide, as do one-celled animals, and two new beings exist where formerly there had been one. But God willed otherwise. In creating sex, God gave to man a share in His own creative power. He willed that husband and wife become His cocreators in marriage. This was the chief purpose of sex, namely, creation of new life. His second purpose was to unite the souls of man and woman through the union of their bodies in a pleasurable act. Sexual intercourse in marriage, therefore, is of itself the closest possible union of two human beings — a union which is meant to give fulfillment to both body and soul. This unique union is God's reward to men and women who enter into marriage and cooperate with Him in the creation of new life.

It is because of this that Pius XII could write:

> The Creator Who in His goodness and wisdom has willed to conserve and propagate the human race through the instrumentality of man and woman by uniting them in marriage, has ordained also that in performing this function (marital intercourse), husband and wife should experience pleasure and happiness both in body and soul. In seeking and enjoying this pleasure, therefore, couples do nothing wrong. They accept that which the Creator has given them.[8]

Marriage Is Sex Sacramentalized

For a Christian, sex in marriage has a far greater meaning than pleasure and production. It is part of the very matter of the sacrament. By its proper use in marriage the couple receive an increase of sanctifying grace in their souls. In the sacrament of marriage Christ unites husband and wife to each other and to Himself, gives them an increase of divine life and a pledge of all the graces they will need throughout life to deepen their union with one another and with Him.

> In His sacraments Christ uses the good things of nature in order to bring us His divine life and His graces. He makes use of water to signify and to effect the rebirth which He gives us in Baptism. In marriage, it is the love of husband and wife which He so uses. Their very union, the expression of their love, is the means He uses to give them an increase of His life. As they grow in love for one another, as they give love to one another, they grow in love for God and increase in holiness. Each endearing act, therefore, each demonstration

147

of affection, each sacrifice made for one another is the vehicle of God's grace, because their very love is part of a sacrament.[9]

It is sometimes difficult for young people who have not had gradually unfolded to them the beauty of God's plan for sex to realize this at first. But it is true nevertheless. Christ raised the contract of marriage to a sacrament. In so doing He deepened and enhanced the natural union of marriage, already uniquely intimate, into a virtuous act. To use sex properly in marriage, therefore, is a positive act of the virtue of purity. On the other hand, whenever sex is indulged in solely for its own sake apart from marriage, its use is sinful.

> The vague feeling sometimes met with that even within the marital bond sexual relations are indecent or little short of sinful, or only reluctantly tolerated, is in no sense Catholic teaching and can find no shadow of support therein. God placed in men and women mutual sex attraction. God purposely attached to the exercise of sex strong sensual pleasure so that men and women would be led to accept the responsibilities of marriage. Within marriage the sex relation is perfectly legitimate in itself and so too is all pleasure taken in it by married couples. The married couple assume the responsibilities and sacrifices of marriage and have the right to its satisfactions. A healthy attitude toward sex implies that one has made a successful adjustment from the misconceptions of childhood to the reality of sex as God created it.[10]

The true Christian approach, therefore, to the marital act should be one of awe at a reality sacred in itself. "How it is possible for two people, a man and a woman, to communicate with each other so deeply and intimately and, in the communication, to cooperate with God in the procreation of a child is a mysterious and never-to-be-understood fact. No amount of scientific frankness will help the human being to enter any more deeply into the mystery."[11]

Parenthood

No marriage is fully perfect that has not a baby in it. This is so because procreation and education of children is the primary end and the greatest blessing of marriage. Everyone contemplating marriage should realize this. For this reason it is presumed that those preparing for marriage know how new life is created.

Briefly, the life story of every child begins with conception,

148

A baby is a living parable. It tells as no poet can the story of God's infinite wisdom and love and life's real values.

which takes place within the mother's body. Conception is the meeting of an egg cell of the mother with one of the fertilizing cells of the male substance or semen which comes from the body of the father in sexual intercourse.

The egg cells come from the ovaries, paired organs which lie within the pelvis of the mother, one on each side of the womb or uterus. Once a month approximately, in connection with the menstrual flow or monthly period an egg cell is released from one of the ovaries, and is drawn toward the uterus through the fallopian tube. The womb is connected with the outside of the body by a passage called the vagina.

Corresponding to the female ovaries are the male testes, which lie outside the body of man in a purselike sac called the scrotum. In these the male cells are formed and in the act of sexual intercourse pass through the penis, which has been introduced into the vagina, and so reach the uterus. If a male cell then meets an egg cell, the two cells combine to form a fertilized ovum. This is called fertilization or conception. It is precisely at this moment that God gives life or a soul to the matter.

Fertilization normally takes place in the fallopian tube as the ovum passes through it into the uterus. The uterus is where the baby lives while he is growing inside the mother's body. Shortly after reaching the uterus the fertilized egg becomes attached to the lining of the uterine wall and there begins its development into a human being. A saclike membrane filled with fluid, called the "bag of waters," forms around the developing baby to protect him from any jolts or bumps he might get from mother's actions during pregnancy.

The meeting place for the blood vessels of the mother and the baby is the placenta, an organ which develops in the lining of the uterus. The baby is connected with the placenta by the umbilical cord. Through the umbilical cord blood vessels run from the baby out to the placenta and back to the baby. The mother's blood does not actually circulate through the baby. Food, water, and oxygen from the mother's blood stream, and waste products from the baby's blood stream, pass to and fro through the blood vessel walls in the placenta, which is often called the afterbirth because it passes out of the uterus normally after the birth of the baby.

The development of the baby normally takes about nine months. During these months doctors have recorded various phases of the child's development as it grows in the uterus of the mother. At two months, for example, the baby, medically termed "fetus," is about one inch long and weighs $\frac{1}{30}$ of an ounce. He has a big head and a human face, with eyes, nose, and mouth; he has fingers and toes, elbows and knees. His sex organs have started to develop, and his bones have begun to form.

At three months the baby is a little over three inches long and weighs about one ounce. Teeth are beginning to develop in the jawbone.

Hair begins to grow on the skin and head at four months. The baby is now six and one-half inches long and weighs about four ounces. The eyes, ears, and nose are well formed.

At five months the baby can usually be felt by the mother and

150

heard through the stethoscope of the doctor. At this time the average baby is about ten inches long and about eight ounces in weight.

At six months the baby is about twelve inches long and weighs one and one-half pounds. Eyebrows and eyelashes appear on the baby's head. If born at this time, the baby never survives.

At seven months the baby is about fifteen inches long and weighs about two and one-half pounds. At this stage of life the baby is viable, that is to say, capable of living apart from his mother should premature delivery occur. An incubator will, of course, be required. Despite aids, many babies born at this time die.

At eight months the baby weighs approximately four pounds and is about sixteen and one-half inches in length. At nine months or about termination (childbirth) the baby is about twenty inches long and weighs from seven to seven and one-half pounds on the average.[12]

Some Medical Problems

Modern medicine has achieved great things in our times. One of its achievements is reducing the number of deaths of both mothers and babies at childbirth. In 1933, 6.2 mothers died for every 1000 live births in the United States. This means that 1 mother died for every 162 live births. By 1960 the maternal death rate dropped to 1 mother for every 3100 births. The infant mortality rates have been reduced from 99.9 per 1000 live births in 1915 (1 out of 10) to 27.1 per 1000 live births in 1957 (1 out of 37).[13]

While doctors are able to determine by various tests whether a woman is pregnant or not, science has not yet found a foolproof method of determining the sex of the baby. Expectant parents who speculate about this, however, should keep this biological fact in mind. It is the father's cells which determine the sex of a child. Male sperm cells are of two types — X and Y, one which will produce a girl baby, and one which will produce a boy baby. The mother's egg cells are always constantly the same — X.

The Rh Factor

A modern medical problem connected with childbirth which

has been exaggerated in our time is the Rh factor. The Rh factor is present in the blood cells of most people. If you have it, you are Rh positive; if you don't, you are considered negative. An expectant mother who is Rh negative and whose husband is Rh positive may develop certain conditions which can affect a baby who has inherited Rh positive blood. This usually happens only if the mother has had previous transfusions with Rh positive blood, or if she has had more than one pregnancy with Rh positive babies. (Babies which possess Rh negative blood are not affected.) A few Rh women may, under these circumstances, develop substances in their blood called antibodies, which while they are not a danger to the mother, can cause a rare type of severe anemia in the Rh positive babies. This is a rare complication (less than one mother out of two hundred), since only a few Rh negative women form antibodies, and most have normal babies. Statistics show less than 5 per cent of Rh negative mothers will have babies who have any difficulty at childbirth.[14]

The So-Called Dilemma Case

Should the child have any difficulty at childbirth, or should the mother have any medical complications with childbirth, every effort is made by medical science to save both persons. Both have equal rights to life. Under no circumstance does a doctor take the life of a mother under pretense of saving her baby or vice versa. Somehow this old wives' tale has been perpetuated down to our present day, but it is unfounded in fact. For a doctor to choose between the life of the mother or the baby is a hypothetical situation and in practice it does not exist.[15]

Adoption

"Adoption is the privilege of raising someone else's child as your own. Annually some 100,000 couples receive a child from a social service agency and take on the role of adoptive parents. Another 200,000, encouraged by the word 'approved' stamped in bold letters on their applications, hopefully wait in line. Spread across the country are 700,000 disappointed would-be adoptive parents who

152

fail to qualify under the rigid restrictions imposed by the 500 licensed private agencies and state welfare departments."[16] This means that there are approximately ten to fifteen applicants for every child put up for adoption. Selections of suitable parents for the child are carefully made by social workers. An adoption agency's principal assignment is to find homes for children, not children for homes. This frequently takes time. A year, perhaps longer, usually passes before an approved couple receives a child.

Frequently a couple tires of waiting for a child and turns to the black market. Each year at least 20,000 babies are sold or placed in homes under questionable procedures. In 1955 Senator Estes Kefauver and a Senate judiciary committee startled the country by dragging this black-market operation out into the open. According to their findings, the black market is a $35,000,000-a-year business with couples paying from $1,000 to $10,000 and higher for a baby. Placement by such procedures are usually performed by unscrupulous lawyers and doctors who prey on the misfortune of young girls in trouble.

Ten times more widespread is gray-market adoption. "Gray-market adoptions are 'under-the-counter' placements of babies and young children, private deals worked out by go-betweens, who may include friends, relatives, doctors, lawyers, clergymen. There is no question of willful wrongdoing, and certainly nobody profits from this financially as in black-market transactions. But these placements hover between legality and illegality, hence the term 'gray.' This is because adoption statutes are complex and differ widely from state to state."[17]

While adoption practices of agencies may leave much to be desired, black-market and gray-market adoption procedures have nothing to recommend them. When adoptions are the product of independent placements, the blind frequently lead the blind. Good intentions are no substitute for trained and experienced personnel. That is why while it may require some time, sound medical and counseling services by authorized adoption agencies, public or private, are the only way to make sure the right home is found for the right child.

153

Sterility in Marriage

Marriage does not always guarantee having children. One of today's problems among many a devoted husband and wife is the problem of sterility. "Statistics seem to show that fifteen per cent of all married couples will never have children because of some involuntary sterility for which apparently there is no remedy. An additional nine or ten per cent of married couples will have at most one child because sterility will set in after the first birth."[18]

Sterility does not void a marriage and should never be confused with impotency. Sterility means that either husband or wife or both lack the necessary qualities for the conception of a child. Impotency, on the other hand, means the inability to have marital relations because of some physical or psychological defect or abnormality.

Involuntary sterility (not to be confused with direct sterilization which shall be considered in the next chapter) in married couples may be due to many causes, some known, some unknown. Sterility may be due to nervousness, tension, fatigue, the result of heredity, the operation of natural laws, a known disease, or a surgical operation. Individuals suffering from sterility should seek out expert medical advice. Frequently doctors will recommend the use of the rhythm method. It was precisely for this reason — to alleviate sterility — that this method was originally designed. Today, however, rhythm is usually practiced for another reason — not to help husband and wife have children but to keep them from having them. (This natural method of birth control will be discussed in more detail in the next chapter.)

Artificial Insemination

During the past fifteen years, 10,000 to 50,000 pregnancies have allegedly occurred in the United States by artificial insemination. The general term of "artificial insemination" is used to include any process outside the purely natural marital act which might be employed to bring about the conception of a child. There are two ways of bringing about a "test-tube" baby, as artificial insemination is popularly called. One is by using the seed of an unknown "donor" in cases where the husband is sterile (AID), the other, when the husband supplies the seed but in an unnatural way (AIH). Both forms are sinful because they violate the natural law of the contract of marriage. "No substitute for human intercourse is morally right as a means of effecting insemination. And this verdict stands no matter how successful artificial procedures have proved in breeding livestock. Animals have sexual functions like human beings, but human beings are not brutes nor can their reproductive activities be dealt with exclusively on the animal level."[19] It is for this reason that artificial insemination has been called "artificial adultery."

Pope Pius XII in 1949 informed doctors that "artificial insemination outside of marriage must be purely and simply condemned as immoral. Only the marriage partners have mutual rights over their bodies for the procreation of a new life, and these are exclusive, nontransferable, and inalienable rights. So it must be out of consideration for the child."[20] He went on to say, however, that certain forms of medical help within marriage designed to assist the proper act of husband and wife toward attaining fulfillment may be morally used.

Later he cautioned:

> The church rejects the attitude which would pretend to separate in generation, the biological activity in the personal relation of the married couple. The child is the fruit of the conjugal union when that union finds full expression by bringing into play the organic functions, the associated sensible emotions, and the spiritual and disinterested love which animates the union. It is in the unity of this human act that we should consider the biological conditions of generation: Never is it permitted to separate these various aspects to the positive exclusion either of the procreative intention or of the conjugal relationship. The relationship which unites the father and the mother to their child finds its root in the organic fact and still more in the deliberate conduct of the spouses who give themselves to each other and whose will to give themselves finds its true attainment in the being which they bring into the world.[21]

Natural Childbirth

When a mother gives birth to her baby in full awareness of what is going on and cooperates in the process from beginning to end, that action is popularly known as "natural childbirth." Natural childbirth or, as it is sometimes termed, "painless childbirth" or "childbirth without fear" has come into its own in recent years. This has been due mainly to the efforts of Dr. Grantly Dick-Read, a British obstetrician, who discovered that the pains of childbirth were frequently caused by the unnecessary and frequently unfounded fears of mothers regarding childbirth. Since his discovery that fear is caused by lack of understanding of the entire birth process, there has been increased effort by medical authorities to educate women for childbirth. While knowledge leads to understanding and this in turn to confidence, it must not be concluded that childbirth becomes automatically painless with some schooling on the subject. It merely points up the fact that pregnancy should be a most healthful time in a woman's life, not a time of unwarranted fears and anxieties.

SUGGESTIONS FOR READING

Adoption Is It for You?, Children's Service Society of Wisconsin, 734 North Jefferson Street, Milwaukee, Wisconsin.

"Artificial Insemination and the Law," Rev. Anthony F. LaGatto, *The Catholic Mind,* June, 1956, p. 323 ff.

"Artificial Insemination and Society," Rev. Anthony F. LaGatto, *The Catholic Mind,* Vol. 54, July, 1956, p. 396 ff.

*Childbirth Is Natural, Barbara Francis (Notre Dame, Ind.: Ave Maria Press, 1952).

*Childbirth Without Fear, Grantly Dick-Read, M.D. (New York: Harper & Brothers, 1944).

*Fundamental Marriage Counseling, John R. Cavanagh (Milwaukee: The Bruce Publishing Company, 1957).

How to Face the Problems of Married Life, Donald F. Miller, C.SS.R. (Liguori, Mo.: Liguorian Pamphlets, 1956).

If You Adopt a Child, Helen and Carl Doss (New York: Henry Holt and Co., 1957).

New Problems in Medical Ethics, Dom Peter Flood, O.S.B. (Westminster, Md.: The Newman Press, 1954).

Ten Signs of Love in Marriage, Donald F. Miller, C.SS.R. (Liguori, Mo.: Liguorian Pamphlets, 1956).

When the Honeymoon's Over, Godfrey Poage, C.P. (St. Louis, Mo.: The Queen's Work, 3115 South Grand Blvd., 1948).

Why Not Adopt a Child?, Thomas Tobin, C.SS.R. (Liguori, Mo.: Liguorian Pamphlets, 1956).

Chapter VIII *FAMILY PLANNING*

Marriage as a natural process exists for the procreation and education of children as well as for the good of the spouses and the welfare of society. While this statement is true, it is also true to say that in recent years limiting the natural process or family planning has become a burning issue all over the world. Much attention has been given this problem in our day because of various "population explosions" in various parts of the world. One of the results has been great confusion over such terms as "planned parenthood," "artificial birth control," "natural birth control," "birth prevention," "contraception," "family limitation," and "rhythm," all of which have been used interchangeably in the press and ordinary conversation. The purpose of this chapter, therefore, is to give the teaching of the Catholic Church regarding family planning based upon natural and divine laws, and to offset the confusion now existing through ignorance or misinformation.

What's in a Name?

What is family planning? By family planning we mean restricting in some way the number of children to be born in a given family. Contrary to what those outside the Church seem to think, the Catholic Church does not hold that married couples are under the obligation to bring into the world the maximum number of children or to bring an ever increasing bumper crop of babies into the world. The Church merely insists that married couples use the

The family is the basic unit of society. Where family life flourishes, that nation is strong.

proper, legitimate method in limiting or planning their family. The proper, legitimate method of family planning is natural birth control (self-control), better known as periodic continence or the rhythm method. This method involves limiting marital sex relations to such times when through the operation of the laws of nature a woman cannot ordinarily conceive.

Planned parenthood, on the other hand, is the voluntary limitation of possible offspring by artificial or mechanical means. While both methods are aimed at controlling or regulating the birth of children, the first is achieved by cooperating with nature, while the latter is intrinsically evil because it frustrates nature. Planned parenthood, or artificial contraception, frustrates the primary purpose of the marital act, namely the begetting of children. It places emphasis on the secondary ends of marriage, while deliberately preventing the primary from being fulfilled. Instead of viewing sex for life as it was designed by God, it advocates life for sex — a reversal of the natural law. It takes a faculty designed by God for the continuation of the human race and makes of it solely an instrument of pleasure.

158

Nothing New

The practice of family planning in the sense of voluntarily limiting the increase of population is not new or peculiar to our age. A glance at history reveals that various methods of family limitation have been tried from the earliest of times. The most common methods employed have been infanticide, sterilization, onanism, abstinence, and abortion. And while it may surprise the modern reader, history shows that the Greeks were familiar with contraceptive drugs as early as 100 B.C., while mechanical contraceptive devices so prominent in our day date from the second century after Christ.

Infanticide

The earliest and most common method was infanticide, that is, destroying the newly born infant by abandonment or exposure. This was common practice among the Greeks and Romans and in other parts of the ancient world. It was practiced in the Middle Ages and is still common among primitive and savage people. In Sparta a special tribunal examined every newly born infant and determined whether or not it was to be permitted to live. Even the noble Plato advised the exposure of unwanted children. And Aristotle, the most versatile of ancient scholars, suggested that the size of the family be determined by the state and that all children born beyond the limits set by the authorities be exposed. Seneca, the Roman philosopher and moralist, advised that all children born of tainted or diseased parents be mercifully put to death.[1]

Sterilization

Sterilization is a process of rendering men and women barren by means of a surgical operation, X ray, or intravenous injection. This sterility is not to be confused with involuntary sterility which happens either naturally or accidentally. This sterility concerns itself with the direct prevention of procreation by unlawful means. There are three types of direct or voluntary sterilization. They are eugenic, punitive, and therapeutic.

Eugenic Sterilization

Eugenic sterilization is a distinctly modern development. In the first decades of the twentieth century the eugenic movement, spurred on by Darwin's evolutionary theory and the scandalous record of several generations of the Jukes and Kallikak families, whose members compiled a terrifying score of crime and insanity all of which was naïvely assumed to be inherited, proposed that a thoroughgoing program of sterilization of the unfit would usher society into a golden age in which antisocial behavior would approach the vanishing point. Twenty-eight states were quick to pick up the program. By 1949 more than 50,000 sterilizations of the feebleminded and the insane had been effected.

At first glance the eugenist's idea to promote a healthy citizenry by ridding the human race of the mentally deficient (i.e., morons, imbeciles, and idiots) may appear good and necessary. To achieve a good end by an immoral means, however, is sinful. Eugenic sterilization is against the moral law, or the right of an individual to contract and enjoy marriage. And while such marriages are not advised, they cannot be forbidden because of the natural law. Eugenic sterilization, therefore, violates the right of an innocent human being to bodily integrity.

Besides being sinful, sterilizing the unfit does not and will not guarantee a perfectly healthy citizenry. At least this has been the conclusion of reputable authorities who have found that at least 50 per cent of the cases of feeblemindedness arise from nonhereditary causes. The remaining 50 per cent of the unfit may be attributed to hereditary causes. Feebleminded offspring come from feebleminded parents as well as from normal parents who are carriers of feeblemindedness (recessive genes). To sterilize the entire feebleminded group without sterilizing all others for the next 2000 years, therefore, would merely reduce feeblemindedness from the proportion of 1 per 1000 to 1 per 10,000. The only sure way of stamping out all feeblemindedness is to sterilize everyone. But this is absurd.[2]

Punitive Sterilization

Punitive sterilization is performed on criminals (sex offenders, unwed mothers, etc.) as a punishment for their crimes. Since the State has the power to punish, even with capital punishment, some argue that the State can also sterilize as a punishment.

160

This argument seems logical until one investigates why the State has the right to punish criminals. Punishment acts as a strong deterrent to crime. When capital punishment is enforced with true justice, major crimes diminish considerably. Since the State has the duty to take care of the rights of its citizens, and since protecting their lives and property is part of this duty, the State may, if it so decides, take the lives of those who have forfeited their right to life by some major crime.

Punitive sterilization or sterilization as a punishment does not act as a deterrent to future crime. When it is imposed upon sex criminals, it does not keep them from ever repeating their crime. It merely prevents the conception and birth of offspring after the crime has been committed. This appears to be more of an incentive to further crime than a preventative. For this reason, as well as the fact that the State has no right to destroy a natural faculty of man without sufficient reason, punitive sterilization is wrong.

Therapeutic Sterilization

Therapeutic sterilization is used to protect or restore the health and well-being of an individual. This may be done by the removal of certain organs or by some treatment which destroys temporarily or permanently the functioning of organs necessary for procreation. There are two types: indirect and direct.

Sterilization is indirect when the operation, or whatever treatment takes place, is needed and intended to remove diseased organs or to restore a person's general health. Such sterilization, like any other operation required for the sake of health, is perfectly lawful. In such cases the Law of Double Effect must be applied.

Four conditions are necessary for the lawful performance of an action from which both good and bad results are foreseen:

1. The original action must be morally good or indifferent in itself.
2. The good effect must not be the result of the bad effect, but both the good and the evil effects must be the immediate result of the original action, or the evil effect must follow from the good effect rather than vice versa. Evil cannot be used to obtain a good result.
3. There must be a proportionately serious reason for doing the original action and permitting the evil effect. The good effect must be of equal or greater value than the evil.

161

4. The evil result which is foreseen must not be intended nor approved, but only permitted.

Therapeutic sterilization which is direct is never lawful. It is contrary to the fundamental nature of marriage to perform preventative sterilization for either the private or the social good. Therefore, regardless of how lofty one's motives may be, for example, to prevent pregnancy or to avoid undesirable offspring, this type of therapeutic sterilization may never be performed.

Birth Control Pills

A radically new way of limiting the size of a family is birth control pills. These chemical compounds have quite legitimate uses. When used to test ovarian function, correct menstrual disorders, and prevent abortions (miscarriages), these pills are completely unobjectionable. When these oral steroids are used to bring about sterility for contraceptive purposes they are just as immoral as surgical procedures. Pope Pius XII declared in a talk to a group of blood specialists (September 12, 1958) that the use of medicine for contraceptive purposes is morally wrong. No amount of rationalization will ever justify the use of these pills for contraceptive purposes.

Onanism

Onanism is a form of birth control which receives its name from the man who practiced this unnatural act as recorded in Chapter 38 of Genesis. "Onan knowing that the children should not be his . . . spilled his seed upon the ground . . . and therefore the Lord slew him because he did a detestable thing." While some authorities refer to onanism as the most common form of contraception still practiced by man today, it is nevertheless sinful. It is a masturbatory act against the virtues of chastity and justice required in marriage. It is because of this that St. Augustine could write in the fourth century: "Intercourse even with one's legitimate wife is unlawful and wicked where the conception of the offspring is prevented. Onan, the son of Juda, did this and the Lord killed him for it."

162

Abstinence

The most perfect form of controlling birth is abstinence or continence (self-control) voluntarily practiced totally or partially by married couples. According to the natural law, it is not sinful for husband and wife voluntarily and mutually to abstain completely or to limit the use of their marriage privileges to certain times for a variety of reasons, some of which may have nothing to do with the possibility or expectation of conception. The natural law demands only that there is no interference with the proper method and end of the marriage privilege whenever it is used. Periodic continence and total abstinence, while not impossible, oftentimes require heroic virtue on the part of both husband and wife.

The Rhythm Method

The practice of periodic continence in our times has popularly become known as the rhythm method. First discovered by two scientists — Ogino of Japan and Knaus of Austria, rhythm refers to a systematic method of performing marital relations on certain days of the month. The method is built around the rhythm of fertility and sterility which occurs in the monthly cycle of a woman's menstrual period. According to a woman's menstrual cycle, there are days of the month when she is quite likely to conceive a child and other days when she will not conceive. The days on which conception is quite likely to occur are called "fertile." Those on which conception will not take place are called "sterile." The rhythm method consists in following a systematic method of performing marital relations only on "sterile" days and abstaining on "fertile" days. By this method, therefore, pregnancy may be postponed or avoided altogether. This is the only method of family planning or birth control approved by the Church. For as Pope Pius XI has stated: They are not

> considered acting against nature who in the married state use their right in the proper manner although on account of natural reasons either of time or of certain defects, new life cannot be brought forth. For in matrimony as well as in the use of matrimonial rights there are also secondary ends, such as mutual aid, the cultivating of mu-

163

The **affection** of a parent for its offspring is a reflection of God's love for His creatures.

tual love, and the quieting of concupiscence which husband and wife are not forbidden to consider so long as they are subordinated to the primary end and so long as the intrinsic nature of the act is preserved.[3]

How Rhythm Is Justified

The rhythm method or the practice of periodic continence may be used *only* by married people who have a serious and legitimate reason for avoiding pregnancy. The mere fact of having had a certain number of children does not justify a husband and wife in deciding to use rhythm continuously thereafter. Those who desire to practice rhythm must fulfill three conditions. They are easily remembered by the mnemonic phrase WAR:

W — Willingness of both parties. Both husband and wife must agree to its use.

A — Ability to practice continence must be had by both. In other words, there is little danger of incontinence (self-abuse, etc.) on the part of either husband or wife during the fertile periods.

R — Reason. Only a serious motive or reason, deriving from external circumstances, can make it lawful for husbands and wives to adopt the practice of rhythm for either a short or long time.

164

When it comes to reasons, everyone SEEMS to have a reason. Because of this, it is helpful for a married couple to seek spiritual counsel from a priest, in order that selfishness be ruled out and a prudent decision made. The reasons for practicing rhythm have to be based on social, economic, eugenic, or medical conditions. These reasons can be easily remembered by the mnemonic word SEEMS:

S — A Social Reason, such as necessary travel and location at a new job or home, or professional responsibilities that involve husband and wife, may make it advisable to avoid pregnancy.

E — An Economic Reason. Poverty, or the problems of space in the home, of food or clothing, medical and dental care, education, etc., may be serious enough for a couple to practice rhythm.

E — A Eugenic Reason would exist if there were a great probability of bringing forth defective children into the world.

M — A Medical Reason could necessitate the use of rhythm. Too many children too closely spaced together, or organic damage suffered by the mother during childbirth, or a severe miscarriage are medical reasons for avoiding conception for a time. In all cases, however, the family doctor is the one to advise.

S — Selfishness is never a reason to practice rhythm.

Objections to the Use of Rhythm

The main objection that can be brought against the use of the rhythm method is the fact that all married people have an obligation to procreate, that is, to provide for the conservation of the human race, unless they are excused for serious reasons. In 1951, Pope Pius XII, in a talk to a group of Italian midwives, stated:

> The individual and society, the people and the state, the Church itself depend for their existence in the order established by God on fruitful marriage. Therefore, to embrace the married state, continuously to make use of the faculty proper to it and lawful in it alone, and on the other hand, to withdraw always and deliberately with no serious reason from its primary obligation, would be a sin against the very meaning of conjugal life.[4]

Married couples should at best seek only the spacing of children, not permanent avoidance of conception, because they do have an obligation to procreate. How many children are married people obliged to have? On this point, theologians disagree. Four or five children seem to be sufficient to fulfill one's obligation to the human race.[5]

Whether married people feel obliged to have children, or whether they feel excused from having them, there are certain moral limits set by the Church. The Church insists that both the social and personal goals of marriage be fulfilled. As Pius XII has said:

> The truth is that matrimony as a natural institution, by virtue of the will of the Creator, does not have as its primary, intimate purpose the personal improvement of the couples concerned, but the procreation and education of new life. The other aims, though also connected with nature, are not in the same rank as the first, still less are they superior to it. They are subordinated to it. This holds true for every marriage, even if it bear no fruit.[6]

Any method of birth prevention (rhythm included) therefore, frustrates a natural need. John R. Cavanagh, M.D., noted psychiatrist and marriage counselor, recently expressed it this way.

> All methods of conception control (and this would include the use of periodic continence) make of the sex act a purely physical reaction, since the act is thereby deprived of its primary creative element. True mating calls upon the total personality, the mind, will, and feelings. It is the occasion for experiencing a true harmony of instincts and aspirations. Anything which separates the procreative element from the pleasure element in the sex act and makes sex pleasure an end in itself destroys the "oneness" and the "we" of marriage.
>
> If the mates no longer find in the sex act, thus deprived of its purpose, a reason to go along with the natural order, the act will tend to lose its appeal. It is likely, under these circumstances, to become a source of discord, of deceit, and of emotional conflict. It is no longer a true mating act. Such false mating impedes the couple's progress toward their true destination as helpers in creative activity, and leads to psychic disorders.[7]

Abortion

By the word "abortion" is meant the interruption and termination of pregnancy by the expulsion of a nonviable fetus from the mother's uterus. A nonviable fetus is one that is so immature that it is unable to survive outside the uterus of the mother. The loss of a child is more apt to happen before the end of the seventh month of gestation. Sometimes this occurs spontaneously, because of some illness or accident or by a pathological condition within the woman. In popular language this is known as a miscarriage or premature birth. More often abortion is voluntarily performed induced by the application of some kind of force or the use of medicine. There are two types: therapeutic abortion and criminal abortion.

166

Therapeutic Abortion

This type of abortion is usually produced by a physician to preserve the health, welfare, or perhaps the life of the mother. Such direct taking of life of an unborn child is never justified even to save the life of the mother, because no matter what it is called, direct abortion is always murder. Besides being a violation of the natural law, it is a serious sin and forbidden under pain of excommunication (Canon 2350). The Church has always proclaimed that once life has begun in the womb, it is as sacred as any self-sustaining life. The claims of mother and unborn child to life are equal. One cannot be taken to save the other.

Indirect abortion is another matter. There are times when it may be necessary for a physician to perform an operation on a mother or to administer medicine to safeguard her life and the expulsion of the fetus takes place as an unwanted secondary effect. If the reasons are serious, indirect therapeutic abortion is permitted. In all cases the principle of Double Effect must be applied. In no case does the Church teach that the life of a child must be preferred to that of the mother's or vice versa. Doctors must make every effort to save both.

Criminal Abortion

A criminal abortion is one which is produced voluntarily and intentionally merely to terminate an undesirable and/or undesired pregnancy. It is called a criminal abortion because it willfully destroys human life and must therefore be classified as murder and is considered a criminal offense in most countries today. Any person becoming guilty of this offense or assisting in producing this type of abortion is subject to criminal prosecution. Because of this, criminal abortion is usually carried on in secret, like the illicit narcotics trade. Estimates of the number of criminal abortions performed in the United States alone range from 200,000 to over 1,200,000, costing from 50 to 100 million dollars annually. It is also estimated that about 10,000 to 20,000 women's deaths occur each year in the United States as a result of this practice.[8]

Many times criminal abortion is performed under the title of therapeutic, for example, in order to save the parents' embarrass-

167

The improvement of land after one year of irrigation is shown in these pictures. Alfalfa and grain grow on land formerly covered with sagebrush. The solution to the problem of the world's expanding population is cooperation with God's laws.

ment; but no matter how well sounding the name, direct abortion is just plain murder. It is against the precept of God and the law of nature which reads: "Thou shalt not kill."

Contraception

While methods of contraception were used centuries before the time of Christ, the modern movement of birth control is generally regarded as beginning with the publication of the famous essay on population by the English clergyman Thomas Malthus, *An Essay on the Principle of Population,* which appeared in the year 1798. Malthus was deeply concerned with the economic distress of the great masses of working people in England at that time, and he feared that the human race would increase more rapidly than the available or potential food supply. To maintain a proper balance between the two, he suggested a curtailment of population by controlling conception. The remedy which he suggested was moral restraint which would be achieved by late marriage and abstinence.

The Malthusian theory, spurred on by economic depression and overpopulation scares, found a spokesman in the United States in Margaret Higgens Sanger, in the year 1913. Convinced that her mother died because of too many pregnancies (she was the mother of eleven children) and that the only way abortion could be elimi-

168

nated was by artificial methods of birth control, Mrs. Sanger founded what has become the Planned Parenthood Federation of America. Unlike Thomas Malthus, who stressed "moral restraint," Mrs. Sanger "screamed from the housetops" the limitation of family size through contraception. Local birth-control clinics were established with the motto "Every Child a Wanted Child." Today PPFA clinics in the United States number about 570 in 36 states and the District of Columbia, and boast that over $1,000,000 is spent annually on contraceptive research.

The Attitude of Protestant Churches

The attitude of Protestant churches to planned parenthood has undergone a noticeable change in the past 30 years. Before 1930 practically all denominations were one with the Catholic Church in opposing every form of birth control, because such practices were opposed to the natural law. But public opinion has a way of swaying principles at times. With birth-control philosophy saturating society, Protestant churches changed their outlook on contraceptives. In 1930 the Lambeth Conference of Anglican bishops throughout the world adopted a resolution which marked a beginning of an about-face position on birth control and preventatives for non-Catholics. The resolution read in part as follows:

> Where there is a clearly felt moral obligation to limit or avoid parenthood the method must be decided on Christian principles. The primary and obvious method is complete abstinence from intercourse as far as may be necessary in a life of discipline and self-control lived in the power of the Holy Spirit. Nevertheless in those cases where there is such a clearly felt moral obligation to limit or avoid parenthood and where there is morally sound reason for avoiding complete abstinence, the conference agrees that other methods may be used, provided that this is done in the light of the same Christian principles. The conference records its strong condemnation of the use of any method of contraception control from motives of selfishness, luxury, or mere convenience.[9]

The Federal Council of Churches in the United States succumbed to the teachings of Margaret Sanger in 1931 when its committee on marriage and home issued a comprehensive statement on the whole problem of parenthood, the Christian view of sex, overpopulation, and the use of contraceptives. While there was some opposition to the new position, the majority of members agreed and issued the following statement:

> A majority of the committee holds that the careful and restrained use of contraceptives by married people is valid and moral. They take this position because they believe that it is important to provide for the proper spacing of children, the control of the size of the family, and the protection of mothers and children; and because intercourse between the mates, when an expression of their spiritual union and affection is right in itself. They are of the opinion that abstinence within marriage, except for a few, cannot be relied upon to meet the problem, and under ordinary conditions is not desirable in itself.[10]

In 1952 the Lutheran churches in America openly backed the PPFA religion of free motherhood by issuing this statement which reads in part as follows:

1. A Christian husband and wife know that children are the natural and desirable fruit of their marriage in fulfillment of God's command, "Be fruitful and multiply."
2. Every child born into the world should be a wanted child. To be unwanted by its parents is a fate more cruel to the child than is poverty, low social standing, or nearly any other handicap.
3. Married couples have the freedom so to plan and order their sexual relations that each child born to their union will be wanted both for itself and in relation to the time of its birth. How the couple uses this freedom can properly be judged not by man but only by God.
4. The means which a married pair uses to determine the number and spacing of the births of their children are matters for them to decide with their own consciences, on the basis of competent medical advice and in a sense of accountability to God.
5. No moral merit or demerit can be attached to any of the medically approved methods for controlling the number and spacing of children. Whether the means used be those labeled "natural" or "artificial" is of far less importance than the spirit in which these means are used.[11]

The Position of the Church

The position of the Catholic Church toward planned parenthood, artificial birth control, birth prevention, contraception, or whatever other name it goes by, is contained in the words of Pope Pius XI given in 1931: "Any use whatsoever of matrimony exercised in such a way that the act is deliberately frustrated in its natural power to generate life is an offense against the law of God and of nature, and those who indulge in such are branded with the guilt of grave sin."[12]

The essential evil of contraception, therefore, consists in the fact that it is intrinsically evil; that is to say by its very nature it is opposed to the natural law, since it is contrary to the nature and dignity of man in the exercise of his sex faculties and subverts the sacredness of marriage. Sex is for life, not life for sex.

The natural law is a rule of moral conduct prescribed by our very nature. Contraception is contrary to this law because our reason tells us that the special privileges of married life have the procreation and education of children as their primary purpose. Contraception involves the unnatural use or perversion of man's sex faculties. It perverts marital intercourse from co-operation (potential if not actual) with God into a mere means of sensual gratification. It reduces husbands and wives to the level of mutual instruments of indulgence.

A Comparison

In the decadent days of Rome there were palaces that promoted orgies of eating and drinking. When the guests had gorged themselves to the full on various delicacies, they made use of a room called a vomitorium where a slave tickled their palates with a feather until they regurgitated all their food. Then they began all over again. This action was sinful because the nourishment of the body, which is the primary purpose of eating, was deliberately frustrated. There was a morally unjustifiable interruption of the due process of nature. The natural process of eating is mastication, deglutition, digestion, assimilation, and nutrition. The last three of these were excluded in a deliberate and disordered fashion. Such orgies were wrong because they were unnatural. Man eats to live, not lives to eat.

The parallel between Roman gluttony and contraception in any form should be quite easy to see. In marriage sexual intercourse tends naturally to conception, gestation, and parturition. By contraception, these are deliberately excluded. The secondary purposes of marriage are made an end in themselves. Contraception takes a faculty designed by God for the continuation of the human race

171

and makes of it solely an instrument of pleasure. But sex is for life, not life for sex. That is why, in summary, from the Church's viewpoint, artificial prevention of conception (this includes mechanical, chemical, and oral means of contraception) is an act intrinsically evil, opposed to the natural law, and will never be justified under any circumstances whatsoever. Natural birth control (continence or rhythm), on the other hand, is not an intrinsically evil act. The morality of this form of family planning depends upon the circumstances under which it is practiced. As already mentioned, for serious reasons the spacing of children by limiting marital sex relations to such times when through the operation of the laws of nature a woman cannot ordinarily conceive is definitely lawful.

Will the Church Ever Change Her Mind on Contraception?

Non-Catholics frequently ask this question. The answer, of course, is definitely negative! The Church cannot change her position on contraception any more than she can change her basic position on the nature of man. Both positions are unchangeable; they are here to stay. Just because some of her members commit sin, the Church does not change God's laws. Artificial prevention of conception is always and under all circumstances immoral and grievously sinful.

The Problem of Overpopulation

By the end of this century the United Nations estimates that between six and seven billion people will inhabit the earth. "Will we be able to provide for our ever expanding world population with adequate sustenance and a decent way of life?"

The informed Catholic answers "Yes!" The population challenge is a problem of the ratio, or balance, between population size and the productivity of the world. The approach to this problem must always be moral and rational. That is why immoral solutions such as mass sterilization, abortion, and contraception so openly advocated by many today are wrong. The true solution lies in increasing production by technical assistance, discovery of new foods and materials, immigration of populations to undeveloped lands, aid

172

from "have" to "have not" nations, promoting a later age of marriage, the elimination of polygamy and concubinage, the development of a greater love for the vocations to celibacy, the encouragement of absolute or relative continence within marriage, and stricter divorce laws.

SUGGESTIONS FOR READING

A for Abortion, Rt. Rev. Msgr. Thomas J. Cawley (Scranton, Pa.: The Catholic Light, 1954), 24 pp.

"Catholics and Birth Control," *Ave Maria,* John Reedy, Vol. 85, May 18, 1957, pp. 4–5.

**The Catholic Viewpoint on Overpopulation,* Anthony Zimmerman, S.V.D. (New York: Doubleday & Co., 1959).

Genetics Is Easy, Philip Goldstein (New York: Lantern Press, 1956).

Happy Marriage, John A. O'Brien (Garden City, N. Y.: Hanover House, 1956).

"Important Facts About Abortion," *Reader's Digest,* Vol. 68, February, 1956, pp. 53–56.

Love and Marriage, Ralph L. Woods (New York: J. B. Lippincott Co., 1958).

**Marriage and the Family,* Clement S. Mihanovich, Gerald J. Schnepp, John L. Thomas (Milwaukee: The Bruce Publishing Co., 1952).

Marriage and Rhythm, John L. Thomas, S.J. (Westminster, Md.: The Newman Press, 1957).

Mutual Agreement on Rhythm, Donald F. Miller, C.SS.R. (Liguori, Mo.: Liguorian Pamphlets).

Overpopulation — A Catholic View, Msgr. George A. Kelly (New York: Paulist Press, 1960).

Parenthood, Daniel A. Lord, S.J. (St. Louis: The Queen's Work, 1946).

**Planned Parenthood — God's Plan,* G. Gibbons, C.SS.R., and H. O'Connel, C.SS.R. (Liguori, Mo.: Liguorian Pamphlets, 1960).

"Rhythm . . . Morality and The Method," *Information,* Daniel J. Bradley, M.D., September, 1959, pp. 14–20.

Rights and Wrongs in Marriage, Donald F. Miller, C.SS.R. (Liguori, Mo.: Liguorian Pamphlets, 1958).

**Sins of Parents,* Charles Hugo Doyle (Tarrytown, N. Y.: The Nugent Press, 1951).

The Rhythm of Sterility and Fertility, Leo J. Latz, M.D. (Chicago, Ill.: Latz Foundation, P.O. Box 152, 1956).

Those Dangerous Babies, Rt. Rev. Msgr. Thomas J. Cawley (Techny, Ill.: Divine Word Publications, 1959).

What They Ask About the Church, J. D. Conway (Chicago: Stratford Press, 1958).

When Is Rhythm Allowed?, T. E. Tobin, C.SS.R. (Liguori, Mo.: Liguorian Pamphlets, 1960).

Why Is Birth Control Wrong?, Donald F. Miller, C.SS.R. (Liguori, Mo.: Liguorian Pamphlets, 1956).

Chapter IX MARITAL UNREST

The United States enjoys the dubious distinction of having the highest divorce rate in the world. Each year, it is estimated that about a half-million marriages are broken by divorce, separation, desertion, or annulment. Nor does this figure tell the complete story. "No one knows how many unhappily married husbands and wives do not attempt to escape from their union via legal or extralegal means. While it is true that most Americans are happily married, some more so than others, it is quite apparent that a large number are not satisfied in their marriage relationship."[1]

Since marriage is a permanent contract dissolved only by the death of one's spouse, the extent and degree of marital breakup and marital maladjustment demands an explanation. What are the reasons for a couple once apparently in love to seek a divorce? What impels the husband or wife to walk out on a marriage and to disappear from his spouse, children, relatives, and friends? What prompts a couple to seek a separation or an annulment? These and other questions will be considered in this chapter.

Divorce

Divorce may be defined as the unhappy opposite of a wedding.[2] It is the severing of the bond existing between husband and wife, so that they live apart, no longer enjoy marital rights or privileges, and cease to be a pair. It legally gives the couple the right to contract a new marriage with different partners.

The purpose of careful preparation for marriage is to insure happiness in marriage and to prevent the anxiety, heartaches, and wounds left by divorce.

Arguments for divorce are plentiful. They range from the ridiculous to the pathetic and the insane:

"She took an hour and a half to make up her face."
"He was a vegetarian and this upset her diet."
"He came to breakfast in his long underwear."
"She got the chicken-pox while they were on their honeymoon."
"He was more fond of his pet rooster than of her."

From the headlines in the newspapers it is easy to see that the arguments for divorce all boil down to this: whatever makes married life hard or unpleasant is sufficient justification for breaking the marriage bond.

Seeking the causes of this American scandal is a complex task. The reasons given in divorce courts are rarely the real reasons for marriage failures. People simply pick the easiest legal ground — usually some catchall like "mental cruelty." And since 90 per cent of divorces are uncontested, the real reasons for ending the contract seldom come out into the open.[3]

Writers on the subject of divorce and marriage failures have listed many reasons for breaking up housekeeping. Some are serious, some are trivial. Frequently more than one exist in any given divorce case.[4] The reasons given for divorce are:

175

1. Excessive drinking
2. Adultery — infidelity — lust
3. Irresponsibility or immaturity
4. Incompatibility of temperament
5. In-law troubles
6. Sexual incompatibility — problems arising from limiting the size of the family
7. Mental illness — ill-health
8. Religious differences — mixed marriage
9. Financial difficulties — insufficient income
10. Hasty marriages — improper preparation especially during war years
11. Easy availability of divorce
12. Working wives
13. Cultural incompatibility
14. Exploitation, misrepresentation, and debasement of marriage in print, on the stage, in the movies, radio, and TV
15. Selfishness and exaggerated individualism

In the last analysis, however, it can be said that most marriage failures result from haste and lack of preparation for the vocation of marriage, or from weakness of personality and character and the consequent failure to adjust in marriage.

It Takes Two to Tangle

While women are granted three-fourths of all divorces in the United States, this does not mean to imply that the woman in the majority of divorce cases is sinless and without fault. To make a success of marriage a great deal depends on each partner's personality. A partner may have difficulties in his personality which make it hard for him to get along with others. More frequently than not both partners are at fault in a divorce action. Emotional immaturity, combined with the lack of self-sacrifice, causes many a couple to fail to work together as a team. To point up this fact, recently a survey was taken in which husbands and wives were asked to list the most annoying marital grievances of their partners.

ONE OUT OF FOUR MARRIAGES ENDS IN DIVORCE

A brief study of this list shows convincingly how important mature preparation for marriage is for marital success.

MARITAL GRIEVANCES LEADING TO DIVORCE[5]

Order Listed by Husbands	Order Listed by Wives
1. Nags me	1. Selfish and inconsiderate
2. Not affectionate	2. Unsuccessful in business
3. Selfish and inconsiderate	3. Untruthful
4. Complains too much	4. Complains too much
5. Interferes with hobbies	5. Does not show his affection
6. Slovenly in appearance	6. Does not talk things over
7. Quick-tempered	7. Harsh with the children
8. Interferes with my discipline	8. Touchy
9. Conceited	9. Has no interest in children
10. Insincere	10. Not interested in home
11. Feelings hurt too easily	11. Not affectionate
12. Criticizes me	12. Rude
13. Narrow-minded	13. Lacks ambition
14. Neglects children	14. Nervous or impatient
15. A poor housekeeper	15. Criticizes me
16. Argumentative	16. Poor management of income
17. Has annoying habits	17. Narrow-minded
18. Untruthful	18. Not faithful to me
19. Interferes in my business	19. Lazy
20. Spoils the children	20. Bored with my small talk
21. Poor management of income	21. In-laws
22. In-laws	22. Easily influenced by others
23. Insufficient income	23. Tight with money
24. Nervous and emotional	24. Argumentative
25. Easily influenced by others	25. Insufficient income
26. Jealous	26. No backbone
27. Lazy	27. Dislikes to go out with me
28. Gossips indiscreetly	28. Pays attention to other women

The Deserted Child

While it is true to say that more divorces occur among childless couples than those with children,[6] it is also true to say that the one who suffers most in a divorce action is the child. A divorce cuts the ground from under the child. It sets him grimly apart from his friends and classmates, from everyone else who still has a whole family to belong to, a whole family to back him up.

Some 300,000 children are involved in divorce each year. This means that each year in the United States thousands of children

177

Divorce is hard enough on the man and wife; the child is treated to the spectacle of seeing his home blow up before his eyes. The character you are building now is your greatest heritage to your children.

are being crippled emotionally by divorce. A deserted child suffers frustration. His need for satisfying human relationships is thwarted. In a divorce which is bitterly contested, the child is treated to the spectacle of seeing his home blow up before his eyes.

The father and mother that he is supposed to love, respect, and imitate as examples of good living are exposed as jealous, selfish, spiteful, greedy, bitter people so wrapped up in their private hates that they have no feeling left for him but the desire of each to alienate him from the other.

Occasionally parents give the knife in the child's feelings an exquisite twist by allowing him to see that they regard him (and his brothers and sisters) as an intolerable burden, one which either parent is glad to shift to the other.

When his own parents make it clear that they don't want him, it is not too hard for a child to take out his resentment on the adult community of which those parents are a part. He finds outlets for his resentment and frustration. This explains in part why investigation of the family background of our problem school-children and our youthful delinquents shows that in alarming numbers they are the products of broken homes.

Even where the divorce is a friendly one (if this is possible) and both parents assure the child that they are still the best of

178

friends but not happy together any more, the child is left feeling that he matters very little to either of his parents. If they did care they would put up with each other's disagreeable company for the sake of giving him his normal heritage of a home where he belongs, with his own mother and father to take care of him.

Divorce Breeds Divorce

The damage divorce brings to home life is far from ended with the payment of alimony. Divorce has a way of continuing itself not only among the divorced, but also among their children.

> Parents who rush into divorce in the illusion that they are "making things better for the children" seldom realize the pattern they are establishing. Court and marriage-clinic records show that children of divorced parents are far more likely to turn to divorce when their own marriages hit rough spots later on than are children whose parents stuck together through thick and thin. They have a pattern for failure in marriage but none for success.[7]

A successful marriage is a lifelong career, not a state achieved once and for all times when a couple steps away from the altar. Consideration, patience, tolerance, common understanding, the ability to overlook small faults, and a sense of humor are all essential to the success of marriage. If married persons commonly realized this, our nation would not be plagued with divorce and broken homes as it is today.

The Church Speaks

The Catholic Church has ever been the guardian of marriage. Since her foundation, she has taught the unity, indissolubility, and sanctity of the marriage bond. Despite the free-love ethics of the world, the Church still proclaims that marriage is now and for all time unbreakable. She does this because Christ commanded her to do so.

The mind of Christ toward the indissolubility of marriage is quite clearly pointed out in the Gospels and tradition.

"Have you not read that He who made man from the beginning made them male and female?" Christ asked the Pharisees, "For this cause shall a man leave father and mother, and shall cleave to his wife, and they two shall be in one flesh. Therefore, now they are not two, but one flesh, WHAT THEREFORE GOD HATH JOINED TOGETHER, LET *NO MAN* PUT ASUNDER" (Mt. 19:4–8).

In St. Mark's Gospel, we have Jesus saying that "Whosoever shall put away his wife committeth adultery against her. And if the wife shall put away her husband, and be married to another, she committeth adultery" (10:11–12).

St. Luke quotes Him to the same effect: "And he that marrieth her that is put away committeth adultery" (16:18).

St. Paul the Apostle underscores all this for the benefit of the early Christians. Writing to the Romans, he says: "For the woman that has a husband, while her husband lives is bound to the law; but if her husband dies, she is loosed from the law of her husband. Therefore, while her husband lives, she shall be called an adulteress if she be with another man; but if her husband is dead, she is delivered from the law of her husband, so that she is not an adulteress, if she is with another man" (7:2–3).

"To them that are married, not I, *but the Lord commands,"* he writes to the Corinthians, "that the wife depart not from her husband. And if she depart, that she remain unmarried, or be reconciled to her husband" (1 Cor. 7:10–11).

This, of course, has been Christian teaching from the beginning. Hermas, one of the earliest Christian writers, said, around the year 160 — only 60 years after the death of St. John the Evangelist: "If a man have an adulterous wife, let him put her away and let the husband remain by himself; but if he puts his wife away and marry then, he also commits adultery."

At about the same time (165) St. Justin Martyr wrote: "Whoever marries a woman that has been put away by another, commits adultery."

St. Clement of Alexandria (150–216): "The Bible declares it to be adultery if a person marries another while his or her partner is still alive."

St. Jerome (340–420) wrote: "As long as the husband is alive, even though he be an adulterer . . . and is deserted by his wife for his crimes, he is still her husband and she may not take another."

180

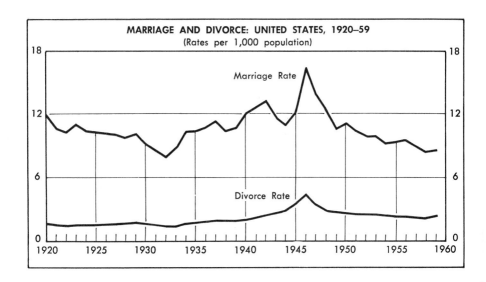

MARRIAGE AND DIVORCE: UNITED STATES, 1920–59
(Rates per 1,000 population)

Adultery

The Catholic Church condemns adultery. Adultery is the exchange of sexual relations between two people, one or both of whom are married to someone else. It is first of all an offense against the virtue of purity, which dictates that sex be used only within the limits of a legitimate marriage, i.e., between husband and wife. It also involves a sin against justice, whereby husband and wife have given their bodies, each to the other until death. And finally there is a sin against charity. Each is leading the other astray, contributing to the other's delinquency through bad example. ADULTERY IS A TRIPLE SIN. It is not necessary, incidentally, that the marriage act be completed before there is a serious sin of infidelity. Any yielding on this point, physically or mentally, is a grave matter as far as God is concerned. "Thou shalt not commit adultery." "Whosoever shall look on a woman to lust after her hath already committed adultery with her in his heart." A divorced person, therefore, may not begin company keeping.

Legal But Immoral

Unfortunately there are some Catholics, who, despite the clear teaching of the Church and the many safeguards and helps which

181

they have in the Catholic Faith, get a divorce and remarry while their first partner lives. They rationalize their consciences by thinking that if the State approves, God approves. What a mistake! God made marriage a perpetual contract, and GOD ALONE, or one to whom He has given the authority, can dissolve a marriage (see "Dissolution of Marriage Contract," pp. 50–51). God has not given this authority to the State. Hence when the State passes a law permitting divorce and remarriage, that law is null and void in the eyes of God. It is as St. John Chrysostom wrote over a thousand years ago: "Do not cite the civil law made by outsiders, which command that a bill be issued and a divorce granted. For it is not according to these laws that the Lord will judge thee on the Last Day, but according to those which He Himself has given."

Seven Danger Signals in Marriage

Just as a doctor can diagnose symptoms of a possible serious illness, marriage counselors can detect when a marriage is heading for trouble. According to Msgr. George A. Kelly, author of *The Catholic Marriage Manual,* it is also possible for husbands and wives to detect these signs. There are seven danger signals in marriage for which a couple should be alert:[8]

1. **Inability to Communicate.** One of the most conspicuous signals is an inability to communicate with each other. Not being able to talk things over is the beginning of the end of marriage.
2. **Drinking to Excess.** This is a contributing factor in two out of every five disturbed marriages that counselors are asked to help. A marked sign of immaturity, progressive steps on the road to alcoholism weaken self-control so important in a happy marriage.
3. **Difficulties in Expressing Affection.** When there is a marked decrease in displays of affection, kindness and gentleness, indifference to each other's physical needs may also follow. This could lead to adultery. Courtship throughout marriage is all important for successful living.
4. **Lack of Responsibility.** The man should be the breadwinner; the woman the homemaker. Whenever either begins to show weakness or indifference in his or her respective role in marriage, it marks the beginning of not caring at all about making marriage a success. A successful marriage finds husband and wife working together as a team.
5. **Increased Faultfinding.** When a man or woman finds more and more things to criticize — perhaps the mate's way of speaking, eating habits, conduct in the company of friends, or way of dress — it is a sign

of basic dissatisfaction, a decrease in the harmony needed for the success of marriage.

6. **Inability to Enjoy Each Other's Company.** When either partner begins to spend more and more recreational hours away from home and each other, this is a red light — a sign to stop and consider what lies behind the inability to tolerate each other.

7. **Indifference to Religious Duties.** When one or both become indifferent to religious duties such as repeated missing of Mass on Sunday or failure to receive the sacraments in accordance with the laws of the Church, there is a lessening of the sense of solidarity which every marriage needs in order to survive.

To prevent minor difficulties in marriage from growing in intensity until they threaten the breaking of the marriage bond altogether, couples would do well to heed the advice of marriage counselors about making an annual marital checkup. A few hours on each anniversary given to a conscientious consideration of minor difficulties in marriage will help to prevent a breakup and will promote renewed "togetherness." Annual Cana Conferences and Christian Family Movement activities which are being conducted in more and more parishes around the country, afford an excellent opportunity for a couple to take stock of their marriage. Retreats for married couples are also becoming increasingly popular for those who want to enrich their married life.

As stated before, marriage is not a reform school. This is something to be remembered by all married couples and those about to enter into marriage. Nine-tenths of all the trouble in marriage is caused by all the little irritating, annoying, insulting, incessant demands of the partners on each other. Both the husband and the wife have to adjust to each other in many ways. This adjustment has to be made between what was expected or hoped for and what actually is. Divorce is no solution to marriage problems. The solution lies in the couple's willingness to accept responsibilities "for better or for worse, for richer or for poorer, in sickness and in health until death."

Some Misunderstandings

Knowing that the Church never permits divorce, some Catholics are thoroughly confused and puzzled when it appears as if the Church seems to go back on her word. Roger and Susan were married before their pastor in their parish church. Less than a year later Roger obtains an uncontested divorce and marries Elizabeth before her parish priest in another Catholic church. How is this possible?

To clarify this case as well as others, it would be helpful here to review the diriment impediments already mentioned in this book. Wherever these obstacles to a valid marriage exist, there actually is no marriage, no matter how solemnly the ceremony was performed, and regardless of whether or not these invalidating reasons were known at the time.

Because so much confusion arises in these cases it would be well for us to clarify such terms as "annulment" and "separation."

Annulment

The word "annulment" means that a given marriage is really no marriage at all. "Since marriage is a natural contract, the requirements of natural law must be present for the validity of a particular marriage. Also, marriage is a sacrament, and the Church lays down certain requirements for the valid reception of the sacrament. If these requirements are not fulfilled in a particular marriage, the marriage is invalidated. The validity of a marriage calls for a declaration of nullity."

> The Church presumes that every marriage that takes place before her properly authorized minister is valid until the contrary is proven. No matter how certain an individual may feel about the invalidity of his marriage, he must present the matter to the proper ecclesiastical authorities for judgment. Each regularly constituted diocese has its own matrimonial court with competent judges, lawyers, and officials and an established procedure for handling all marriage problems presented to it. After the matrimonial court has carefully studied the case, held hearings, and summoned witnesses where necessary, a declaration of nullity either will be granted or refused. If the annulment is granted it means that the marriage was null and void from the beginning.
>
> Thus there is a wide difference between divorce and annulment. Divorce is the dissolution of the marriage bond. Annulment is the declaration that there never was a bond, and, therefore, the two parties are free to contract marriage anew. Divorce puts asunder those whom God joined together, whereas annulment declares that the two never were joined together in marriage by God.[9]

184

Separation

The Canon Law of the Church regarding separation from bed and board states this general principle: "The married couple is obliged to live together in conjugal relations unless a just cause frees them from the obligations" (Canon 1128). A just cause would exist if living together would be a grave danger to faith or to life, or if the partner has been guilty of adultery or is living a criminal or scandalous life.

> Such a separation, even if intended to be only temporary, should be made only after careful consideration and advice and with the permission of the local bishop through the chancery office. If a permanent separation is intended, the chancery's explicit permission must be sought.
> In such cases of separation, sometimes called partial divorce, it is understood that both partners remain husband and wife, and it is always the hope of the Church that a reconciliation may be possible after a lapse of time. In no case is either of the partners free to contract a new marriage or even to keep steady company with anyone of the opposite sex while the other partner lives.
> Sometimes it is necessary to obtain a civil separation or divorce to enforce the separation legally, to obtain separate maintenance, or to decide custody of children. In such cases the permission of the bishop is required, and every effort must be made to avoid scandal.[10]

Separation is not the same as desertion. Desertion is the abandonment of one's home, spouse, or family. The husband or wife simply walks out on a marriage. Despite this abandonment, the innocent party may never validly marry again unless a death certificate of the missing party is presented to Church authorities.

Where There's a Will

The words of the marriage ritual, "for better, for worse; for richer, for poorer; in sickness and in health," warn us that all human living is not without tribulations. Happiness in marriage is an achievement and depends upon the will of both husband and wife. That is why Christ raised marriage to the dignity of a sacrament. Aware of the weakness of human nature, He enabled husband and wife to draw upon an infinite amount of grace to make marriage a success. Thus, no matter how poor one's preparation for marriage, no matter how unwise one's choice of mate,

185

no matter how crushing one's disappointment and disillusionment with marriage, every Christian with the grace of God can make a success of marriage.

SUGGESTIONS FOR READING

About Divorce, Daniel A. Lord, S.J. (St. Louis 18, Mo.: The Queen's Work, 3115 South Grand Blvd., 1946).

*The Catholic Marriage Manual, Rev. George A. Kelly (New York: Random House, Inc., 1958).

Divorced Catholics Tell Their Story, Donald F. Miller, C.SS.R. (Liguori, Mo.: Liguorian Pamphlets, 1957).

Happy Married Life, Lester M. Dooley (Island Creek, Mass.: Mirimac Book Department, 1955).

Marriage and the Family, Edgar Schmiedler, O.S.B. (New York: McGraw-Hill Book Co., Inc., 1946).

Marriage Is Holy, Henry Cafferel (Chicago: Fides Publishers Association, 1957).

Program for Divorced Catholics, Donald F. Miller, C.SS.R. (Liguori, Mo.: Liguorian Pamphlets, 1956).

*Sins of Parents, Charles Hugo Doyle (Tarrytown, N. Y.: The Nugent Press, 1951).

The Truth About Divorce, Morris Ploscowe (New York: Hawthorne Books, Inc., 1955).

Why Marriages Fail, John A. O'Brien (Notre Dame, Ind.: Ave Maria Press, 1958).

*Why Marriages Go Wrong, Bossard & Boll (New York: Ronald Press Co., 1958).

Chapter X LASTING MARRIAGE

Perhaps no one has had the opportunity to observe the characteristics of happy lasting marriages as has the Catholic Church. Down through the centuries she has recognized that in a marriage in which husband and wife truly love each other with self-sacrificing love, where both love children, and where children obey, respect, and love their parents in return, lasting marital happiness is maintained.

Successful Home Life

Lasting marital happiness depends upon the success and happiness of home life, upon the spirit of unity and love that pervades the family. As previously mentioned, without children, home life is incomplete. When the greatest blessing of marriage is missing, the life of a husband and a wife is also incomplete.

The child is the fruit of the union of its parents. It is the blessing of their marriage: the true end of their striving toward unity, which is the very essence of love. Husband and wife reach their completeness in the child. For instance, it brings father and mother closer together, giving them a joint source of love, and they achieve a closer sense of unity in planning for their child's welfare. As husband and wife co-create with Almighty God, their love for each child extends their love for each other, and in each child they can see qualities which they love in each other.

Children help parents to develop the virtues of self-sacrifice and consideration for others. The childless husband and wife must consciously

187

Family morale is the love of the father and mother over-flowing to the children among them and back to the parents. It is the basis of lasting and happy marriages.

cultivate these qualities, for the very nature of their life tends to make them think first of their own interests. In contrast, a father and mother who might have innate tendencies toward selfishness learn that they must subjugate their own interests for the good of their children, and they develop a spirit of self-denial and a higher degree of sanctity than might be normally possible.[1]

Large Families

Since family life is the principal source of human happiness, children contribute greatly to the success of marriage. Over 50 per cent of divorces occur in marriages where there are no children, while an additional 23 per cent occur in marriages with only one child. This in itself speaks well for large families.

A large family provides many distinct advantages over an only-child family. An only child does not occasion as much sacrifice on the part of parents as does a large family which teaches parents

188

to rise above themselves. An only child is ever in danger of being both spoiled and smothered.

> The child may be spoiled because the parents, having no other child, cater to all his fancies and whims. The only child is always the center of attention, with no other children to share it. Thus, the innate selfishness of the child tends to be nurtured and fostered instead of being directed into unselfish channels. At the same time, an only child tends to be smothered because he lives too exclusively with his parents. They are apt to be very choosy about his playmates, and they may prefer to have the child always in their company. It is unhealthy for a child to live in a circle where only grown-ups predominate. Such a child never fully experiences the carefree abandon of childhood and loses something that he may need later in life.[2]

The child in even a moderately large family has more advantages. Large families teach children to live harmoniously with others.

> They must adjust to the wishes of those older and younger than themselves, and of their own and the other sex. In learning to work, play, and, above all, share with others, the child in a large family discovers that he must often sacrifice his own interests and desires for the common good. For this reason, the "spoiled child" who always insists on having his own way is rare in the large family, if he can be found there at all. For the child who will not co-operate with others has a lesson forcibly taught to him when others refuse to co-operate with him.[3]

Family Frictions

This is not to say that large families are frictionless. Family life gives the greatest happiness, comfort, and security to its members only if the bonds of family unity are strongly forged. All members of the family must participate in actual homemaking. There can be no real family life without everyone sharing and co-operating — working together, playing together, praying together.

With differences of personalities, there are bound to be some frictions in family life. In an effort to get at the causes of these difficulties the Youth Research Institute conducted a nationwide poll among teen-agers and parents, pinpointing situations that create family tensions. Like the many causes of divorce, the majority of family-friction situations stem from the lack of maturity and acceptance of responsibility on the part of both children and parents. According to the survey, there were many items both

189

sides wished the other wouldn't do. For every charge children launched at their parents, parents returned complaints of their own.

Things I Wish My Parents Wouldn't Do

1. Ridicule and belittle problems that are important to me.
2. Order me, like a dictator, to do things instead of diplomatically suggesting.
3. Give me a wonderful buildup to other grownups.
4. Keep tabs on me, like private detectives when I've left the house.
5. Override my own decisions.
6. Make promises and break them.
7. Compare me adversely to my brighter friends.
8. Bring up "the good old days."
9. Take sides when I fight with my brothers and sisters.
10. Stay away from home so much.
11. Criticize my friends and what they do.
12. Refuse to understand my enthusiasms like rock 'n' roll, entertainment personalities, my reading and my social habits.
13. Get my phone messages all mixed up.
14. Tell my friends intimate family secrets they shouldn't know.
15. Fight with each other in front of me.

Things I Wish My Children Wouldn't Do

1. Expect us to become their personal servants.
2. Treat us disrespectfully when ordered to do something.
3. Consider it their right to do something because "everyone else does it."
4. Insist on dating and going out whenever they choose.
5. Tell us how to act when their friends come over.
6. Keep their problems to themselves because we "wouldn't understand."
7. Dress and look sloppy . . . and like it!
8. Be late for meals and appointments.

John Ahlhauser

If children are to develop harmoniously, they must live in an atmosphere of affection and love.

9. Feel the whole world is against them.
10. Disregard our rights.
11. Fight with their brothers and sisters.
12. Eat in the living room while watching television.
13. Keep telling us how swell their friends' parents are.
14. Monopolize the phone.
15. Criticize our appearance.[4]

What Parents Owe Their Children

If children are to develop harmoniously, they must live in an atmosphere of affection and love. Therefore, the very first duty of parents toward their children is to provide love in the home. This is easier to say than to do at times, but do it parents must or true family life dies. A child denied love is more underprivileged than one denied food or clothing. This is because all human beings need love. Kind and encouraging words, affectionate smiles, recognition and acceptance by others are important not only to adults but to the growing child who is feeling his way through life. A child needs assurance when he is doing the right thing, or if and when he makes a mistake, he needs understanding parents who will kindly direct him to do what is correct. Psychiatrists constantly point up the fact that many personality disorders which appear in adulthood originate in infancy and childhood because of a lack of love and understanding by one's parents.

According to Msgr. George A. Kelly, director of the Family Life Bureau of the Archdiocese of New York City, children who are not truly loved usually have parents who are overrestrictive, overprotective, or perfectionists.

Overrestrictive parents handle their child like an army recruit. They set down orders which he must follow blindly. They permit no deviation. The child who does not respond to their orders instantly is severely punished. Such parents lack human compassion and often produce children who are either cowed and fearful all their lives, or who rebel against and reject all authority.

Overprotective parents deny their child his normal right to develop his own powers. Although the child is normally healthy, he cannot run on the street because his mother fears that he may fall. He cannot walk to school by himself; his mother must either drive him or walk with him to make sure that no harm befalls him. He sets his eyes on an expensive toy beyond his parents' means; rather than see the little one disappointed, the father digs into his pocket. Parents who

191

save their children from normal knocks and disappointments prevent them from acquiring the self-confidence they need to become independent men and women.

Perfectionist parents are never satisfied with their child. They often maintain a spotless home where the child would not dare leave a toy in the living room. They sharply criticize him when he returns from play with dirty hands. If he stands third in his class, they want to know why he is not first, and they will not rest until he achieves the top position. True, children need, and respond to, inspiration. But perfectionist parents make no allowances for human frailty and short-comings. They demand more than the child can humanly be expected to give.[5]

Actions Speak Louder Than Words

Besides love, understanding, and affection, children need direction — plenty of direction. While this childhood need may many times be verbally taught by parents, the best direction a child receives comes indirectly from the example parents knowingly or unknowingly set for him. This means that

if parents are sincerely religious, if they are patriotic, if they esteem honesty and despise dishonesty and loose living, the child will adopt these attitudes even though parents make no conscious effort to inculcate them. If the parents have social or racial prejudices and look upon others with envy or contempt, the child will pick up their point of view in the same spontaneous and unconscious way. As the child grows older, it is true that outside influences may compete with those of parents and, at times, may even offset their influence; but, for the most part, it is the parents who maintain the chief influence, especially in homes where love and happiness abound. When the child begins to grow independent of the family circle, he is already impregnated with a spirit imbibed from parents which will remain with him until old age.[6]

Training and Discipline

One very important job of parents is the training and discipline of a child. This requires the constant vigilance of both father and mother, if the child is to develop into a responsible person. There is so much to be taught. A child must be trained in habits of cleanliness, orderliness, and promptness. He must be taught to be obedient and to be considerate of others. He must be taught good manners and scores of other traits and habits so essential in helping him become a mature adult.

192

This sort of training for responsibility requires both understanding and firm parents. Understanding parents do not expect a child to perform according to rules and regulations at all times. A child will sometimes fail in his responsibility just because he is a child; but continuous disregard for responsibility is quite different. In this case, parents must make use of firm discipline. Discipline goes hand in hand with training. Good parents always associate these two together in the minds of the young.

In dispensing discipline parents would do well to heed the advice of experts in child guidance. In brief, discipline of children must be firm, consistent, with clear directives, and not changeable. It must be reasonable, that is to say, capable of being carried out by the child. Parents should insist that their orders be carried out promptly and completely. They should not use too many don't's." They should motivate the child by both natural and supernatural reasoning. As the child matures, parents should explain the "why" of discipline.

Should some form of punishment be necessary to enforce correct behavior, it should be given promptly, not delayed. While the most effective type of punishment is to deprive the child of something that he likes very much, in early stages of child development, spanking may be necessary. A young child feels before he learns to reason. In all training, parents should be fair in instilling the virtue of justice. They should never play favorites.

Children and Responsibility

Responsibility should start as soon as the child can understand what is expected of him. At least this is the advice of a noted psychiatrist, Robert P. Odenwald, M.D., who gives the following advice on children accepting responsibility.

1. At an early age children should be given responsibility for doing things for themselves. For example, running an electric train, fixing broken toys, helping in the kitchen in a small way or helping in the house.
2. When parents give the child some duty or responsibility the child must understand what is expected of him; it is perhaps too much for a six- or eight-year-old child to take care of a baby.
3. Parents must give an example of responsibility and must be careful

in their action. A drunken father or a consistently bridge-playing mother are not good examples of responsibility.

4. Never expect too much of your child. In learning responsibility he may fail and repeat his failure until he learns. Too much responsibility at too early an age ruins the mental and emotional balance.

5. Have the child and the adolescent be responsible in participating in the affairs of the family unit and discuss, according to his understanding, family problems.[7]

Education of Children

The proper education of the child begins at home, not at school. The school merely supplements the home, never supplants it. "Formal education in the classroom, no matter how extensive it may be, can never actualize the full potential inherent in the child. Education can never be considered sufficient or complete unless it includes emotional, physical, moral, and religious elements as well as intellectual. These elements of a thorough education are not all to be had in the classroom — unless, of course, one is naïve enough to consider the world a classroom environment."[8] True education is a self-activated process and it begins in the home. Parents must bear in mind that the home is the school of life, the mother's lap the first kindergarten.

> Good education requires that a child should come under both the masculine influence of the father and the feminine influence of the mother. It should, of course, be evident that there must be no conflict of means or aims in these separate influences. The harmonious development of the child requires the love and influence of both father and mother, working together as a team. That is one reason why it is considered a misfortune for children to be left as orphans or to have bad or incompetent parents. Persons other than the parents may do excellent work for the education of young children, but they never can replace the loving care of a devoted father and mother.[9]

The Home Is the Child's First Church

Teaching the child his religious beliefs and prayers is the parent's job. So often this is relegated to the priests and Sisters in Catholic schools. It is not unusual to find children from supposedly good homes entering Catholic schools knowing much about the world, but so little about God. This is a sin of omission on the part of parents. Good parents realize that example speaks louder than

Maytag Corporation

Happy children like the Lennon children, are a testimony to the spirit of unity and love that pervades the family.

words. No matter how excellent the school may be it can never replace the parents. Religion which is learned at home from prudent, intelligent parents sinks in deepest, wears best, and lasts longest.

Sex Education

One of the parent's greatest obligations so sadly neglected is educating children to the true meaning of sex. Ignorance of the facts of life is not innocence. It is frequently the remote cause of many problems later in adult life. Realizing this, good parents begin at infancy to instill in their children the virtue of chastity. They realize that if a child is old enough to ask a question about sex, he is old enough to get a suitable answer. Should the child fail to ask questions, good parents anticipate his needs and impart all the essentials of the subject before puberty. This is usually done by repeated private conversations naturally and spontaneously given as the child grows and develops. As soon as the first baby-talk references can be outgrown, good parents use refined, tech-

195

nical language. Where they find themselves tongue-tied, books, pamphlets, or phonograph records from Catholic sources are used as starters, then discussed.

This gradual unfolding of sex, with all its natural and spiritual implications, helps the child amid occasions of sin in later years. Legitimate curiosity, satisfied in the home, diminishes the influence of undercover distorted sources of information.

Today's Challenge for Parents

The challenge which faces today's parents is the same challenge that has faced all parents. They must guide, teach, and support their growing children in the difficult process which goes on within them as they strive to reach maturity. "This process always represents internal stress and struggle," writes Father John L. Thomas, S.J., associate professor of sociology and author of *The Family Clinic*. "The child must learn the norms, moral rules, and modes of conduct expected by his parents and society. As his powers and faculties develop, he must acquire the habit of controlling and directing their impulses and drives according to approved standards. In this process, his parents are present not only to teach and encourage, more important, they are his models."[10]

What Children Owe Their Parents

So much has been written on this subject of late that we will only briefly summarize the obligations expected of children toward their parents. The basic rule children must follow is this: while they are living under the roof of their parents or are still subject to them, children owe their parents love, respect, obedience, and co-operation in respect to bettering family life. This obligation stems from the natural law as well as the divine law which reads: "Honor thy father and thy mother."

In matters that concern a choice of lifework or the selection of a life mate, the advice and counsel of parents should be sought and carefully pondered. However, the decision in these crucial matters is a personal one which must rest, in the final analysis, with the son or daughter.

Even when children have left the parental home and have "come

196

Assistance with household chores given cheerfully and on one's own initiative is a sign of gratitude and maturity.

of age" they always must have affection and gratitude for their parents and be willing to render to them whatever assistance they may need in their declining years. Sometimes parents can be over-demanding in their expectation of attention from grown-up sons or daughters who have obligations of their own. This may occasionally pose a delicate problem when a son or daughter has to try to strike a just balance between affection and feeling of duty towards an aging parent and the clear obligation to spouse and children and the happiness of their home life.

It is a rule of life that children are not bound to live for their parents and to consecrate their lives to them in the same way that parents are bound to live for their children and consecrate their lives to them as long as the children have need of them. This is one of the renunciations, perhaps the final renunciation, of parental love.[11]

Who's Boss?

While marriage is oftentimes spoken of as a partnership of democratic equality, this does not mean to say that there are not certain definite roles husband and wife must play to make marriage a success. The man is the head, the woman the heart of marriage. St. Paul was only passing on traditional teaching when he said,

197

"Man is the head of the woman as Christ is the head of the Church" (Eph. 23:5).

> All of man's natural aggressiveness, his masculine brawn, his logical mind, make being head easy for him. What is more, nothing gives a man greater satisfaction and sense of fulfillment than a realized sense of importance. Men want recognition. They thrive on it. And their natural instinct in marriage is to be head. If they abdicate the masculine role in the family, they feel guilty; if they are denied it, they are resentful.[12]

Recognizing the husband as the natural head of the family does not imply or mean that he be a despot. Husband and wife are inseparable helpmates. Their relation is not one of superiority and inferiority but one of equality. But just as some division of labor within the home is necessary, so some order is called for. The role of the husband as head of the home is to promote greater harmony and greater love. A divided house cannot stand.

Regarding the wife's position in the home it cannot be too often repeated that the work of the mother in the home is a full-time occupation.

> It is her chief honor and dignity, and only extraordinary circumstances permit her to delegate this responsibility. The formation of the personalities of her children and the making of the home into a vital cell of society is a precious vocation. To delegate this task to hired help in order to make extra cash for luxury items is an unworthy motive. Even more tragic is the current attitude that homemaking is boring work; this tempts the mother to seek outside employment to escape from her home duties.[13]

Unfortunately in some instances the wife must work. Such a situation is rather a criticism of our present society which requires both spouses employed in order to make ends meet. In his encyclical, *On Christian Marriage,* Pope Pius XI spoke strongly against this abuse and offered some recommendations.

> . . . such economic and social methods should be adopted as will enable every head of a family to earn as much as, according to his station in life, is necessary for himself, his wife, and for the rearing of his children, for "the laborer is worthy of his hire." To deny this, or to make light of what is equitable, is a grave injustice and is placed among the greatest sins by Holy Writ; nor is it lawful to fix such a scanty wage as will be insufficient for the upkeep of the family in the circumstances in which it is placed.[14]

The Family Allowance Plan

Because the major portion of the children of the United States are raised by a small number of families and because these families are below the wage level needed to support children in an adequate manner, the Family Allowance Plan is being considered by legislators. In essence the Family Allowance Plan is a system whereby those families which have children (usually two or more) are helped in support of their children by means of financial aid from some outside agency, be it private industry, state or federal government. At present, 39 countries have such plans. Each differs somewhat from the other.

> There are, for instance, differences in the age levels of children under the various plans. Canada considers only those families which have children under 16 eligible to family allowance benefits, while Germany sets 21 as the age limit. There are also diverse sums or monthly allowances allotted to families according to the needs of the families and the amount of revenue available. To cite an example, a plan proposed for the United States by Father Francis J. Corley, S.J., calls for monthly payments of $12 for the third child, $10 for the fourth child and $8 for each succeeding child. In contrast to this, British Guiana pays $5 for each child while the Canadian plan pays from $5 to $8 for each child depending on circumstances. There is no one source for the payments to the families. The plan proposed by Father Corley would be financed by the federal government, while the plan used in British Guiana is financed by Catholic industrialists.[15]

Whether the United States will adopt the Family Allowance Plan remains to be seen. But this much is certain, if it is adopted it will help parents carry the financial responsibilities of training and educating their children according to the American standard of living. It might also serve to avoid the common stigma of relief which is becoming common to many families today.

The Later Years

Only a generation ago, parents could truly feel that their lifework was over by the time their children were married and on their own. But with earlier marriages, smaller families, and greater longevity, men and women today are usually still in the prime of life when their active parenthood roles are over. By the time their last child is married, the average husband and wife now have about twenty additional years to look forward to. This is wholly a new development in family life and represents a great challenge as well as a unique opportunity. It means that numerous middle-aged couples must strive to forge a new life for themselves. With more years together, husband and wife face new dimensions for companionship and for rich enjoyment providing there is some intelligent planning for it.[16]

A husband must never take his wife for granted or vice versa. All through the years both need to reassure one another of their continual love for each other by marks of affection and by the many little tokens of constant thoughtfulness they shared through courtship. These include remembrance of anniversaries, recalling happy memories as well as hopes and disappointments. It necessitates a continued consciousness of working together in a noble enterprise with Almighty God. That is why praying together is important in all stages of married life. It takes not only three to get married, it takes three to stay married!

SUGGESTIONS FOR READING

*Accent on Purity, Joseph E. Haley, C.C.S. (Notre Dame, Ind.: Fides Publishers, 1948).

The Art of Happy Marriage, James A. Magner (Milwaukee: The Bruce Publishing Co., 1947).

*Beginning Your Marriage, Cana Conference of Chicago (Oak Park, Ill.: Delaney Publications, 1957).

*The Catholic Family Handbook, Rev. George A. Kelly (New York: Random House, Inc., 1959).

Christian Marriage, encyclical letter of Pope Pius XI (Washington 5, D. C.: National Catholic Welfare Council, 1312 Massachusetts Avenue, N.W.), 48 pp.

*Examination of Conscience for Married Couples, Edwin C. Haungs, S.J. (St. Louis: The Queen's Work, 1945).

*Marriage, A Medical and Sacramental Study, Alan Keenan, O.F.M., and John Ryan, M.D. (New York: Sheed and Ward, 1955).

Marriage and the Family, John J. Kane (New York: The Dryden Press, Inc., 1952).

Parents, Children, and the Facts of Life, Henry V. Sattler, C.SS.R. (New York: Garden City Press, Image Books edition, 1956).

*Purity, Modesty, Marriage, Joseph Buckley, S.M. (Notre Dame, Ind.: Fides Publishers Association, 1960).

*_Sanctity and Success in Marriage_ (Washington, D. C.: National Catholic Welfare Council, Family Life Bureau, 1956).

Sex-Character Education, John A. O'Brien (New York: The Macmillan Co., 1953).

Stretching the Family Income, Robert and Helen Cissel (New York: Joseph F. Wagner, Inc., 1953).

REVIEW QUESTIONS AND STUDY HELPS

Chapter I

SUGGESTIONS FOR CLASS PROJECTS

1. Have each student interview a religious either personally or by mail; propose suitable questions which would give answers to students' question on the religious life. This will afford a firsthand contact with the religious life. Students may use tape recorders. Wherever possible invite religious to speak to your classes on vocations.
2. Write to famous religious persons asking them why they entered the religious life. Post letters on the bulletin board for all to see and read.
3. Make a scrapbook of the various occupational opportunities your area offers to graduates. Which jobs require more than a high school diploma?
4. Have students interview various employers of their particular locality. Take a poll of what they commonly feel are the most necessary assets one should have who is looking for employment.

Chapter II

REVIEW QUESTIONS AND STUDY HELPS

1. Who determined the essential purposes of matrimony? What is the derivation of the word "matrimony"?
2. What is the essential primary purpose of marriage? Prove it from Genesis.
3. Is more than the mere bearing of children included in this purpose?
4. What are the essential secondary purposes of marriage?
5. What is marriage? When and by whom was it instituted?
6. Was marriage always a sacred contract? Was it always a sacrament? Explain.
7. Why is marriage the concern of the Church? Why does she make laws regulating marriage?
8. What are invalidating or diriment impediments to marriage? Name three. Explain.
9. What are prohibiting impediments? What effect do they have upon marriage? Which one is the most common?
10. What obstacles lie in the way of giving free consent to the contract of marriage?
11. Are the sacramental effects of marriage received only by Christians?
12. If Christians in mortal sin were to make a matrimonial contract, would they really be married? Would it be a sacrament? Would they receive the graces of the sacrament?

13. What obligations do those who enter marriage agree to undertake?
14. What does indissolubility mean in marriage? unity?
15. Show that marriage is as much a vocation as the priesthood and religious life.
16. In the following cases, indicate which show "free consent," which show "defective consent," and which show "forced consent." Give reasons for your answer in each case. Which cases would be valid marriages?

    a) Marrying while intoxicated;
    b) Marriage of two actors in a stage play;
    c) Marriage under threat of death if you refuse;
    d) Marriage with the intention of refusing sexual intercourse;
    e) Marrying in ignorance of the biology of pregnancy;
    f) Marrying while hypnotized;
    g) Marrying because of fear of reprisal from your parents;
    h) Marrying one twin when you wanted to marry the other;
    i) Marriage with the intention of not having children;
    j) Marrying when you are too old to have children.

17. What impediment, if any, exists in the following cases? Name the impediment, indicate whether it is prohibitive or invalidating; tell whether or not a dispensation can be obtained in each case.

    a) A husband, validly married for five years, is in an accident which makes him impotent;
    b) A Catholic wishes to marry a Moslem;
    c) A man and a woman freely elope; later the woman asks for an annulment on the grounds of being kidnapped;
    d) A girl wishes to marry a divorced Jew;
    e) A Sister wishes to leave her congregation and get married;
    f) A woman who knows she is sterile wishes to get married to her sister's widower;
    g) A young man wishes to marry his sister by adoption;
    h) A boy of 14 wishes to marry a girl of 16;
    i) In an accident Shirley baptizes Al, the man she wishes to marry;
    j) A man who is a subdeacon wishes to withdraw from the seminary and get married;
    k) A Negro boy, aged 19, desires to marry a white girl, aged 18;
    l) A Catholic desires to marry a non-Catholic before a Protestant minister.

18. A Catholic has just gone through a marriage ceremony before a justice of the peace. She says, "Oh sure, we are really married. Only we don't have the blessing of the Church. John and I will get our marriage fixed up in Church one of these days." What do you say?

19. A single girl, age 24, who desires marriage very much falls in love with a divorced man and intends to marry him. She comes to you for advice. What would you tell her?

20. A fallen-away Catholic in a bad marriage tells you that if you have enough money, the Church will always grant permission to marry again regardless. What do you say?

Chapter III

1. At what age should marriage preparation begin? Why?
2. "Happy homes breed happy marriages." What do you think of this statement?
3. What is social dating? Compare it with serious dating.
4. At what age should a person get involved in serious dating?
5. What do you understand by the term "going steady"?
6. When is going steady allowable for anyone?
7. What are the moral objections to going steady during high school?
8. What percentage of high school students eventually marry the person with whom they go steady?
9. What are the Polywogs? What do you think of this teen-age organization?
10. Are the schools principally responsible for a teen's dating behavior?
11. Your best friend tells you that she's going steady. Her reason: "Everyone else is doing it." What do you say?
12. Jim tells you that he intends to become a doctor at the same time that he tells you that he's going steady with Jan. They plan on marriage six or seven years after high school graduation. What do you say?
13. Shirley, a new girl in school, is rumored to have had a baby out of wedlock. She approaches you for some friendly advice. How do you act?
14. Draw up a list of dating rules. Ask your parents to do the same. Compare the lists.
15. Interview a social worker, a judge, a lawyer, or some other appropriate official about the dangers of teen-age dating; the benefits of teen-age dating. What important facts do they mention?
16. Who is more responsible for moral conduct on a date, the boy or the girl? Why?
17. Survey your schoolmates (underclassmen) as to their attitude toward going steady. What significant facts do you discover?
18. "Teen-agers are largely responsible for the unwed-mother problem in the United States today." What do you think of this statement?
19. Jane confides in you that her mother and dad are never at home, that she frequently has secret parties where she invites the boys. She asks you to attend her next event. What do you say?
20. What moral obligations does the father of an unwed mother have if any? Should two teen-agers in trouble get married?
21. What is your attitude toward parents who allow their children to go steady in grade school? in high school? What do you think of grade school dances? grade school dating?

Chapter IV

REVIEW QUESTIONS AND STUDY HELPS

1. List in their order of importance to you the nine qualifications for a prospective life mate which have been described in this chapter. Explain your selection.
2. Draw up a list of qualities you would want to find in the person you marry. How do they compare with those mentioned?
3. What do you understand by courtship? Why is it important?
4. What type of suitors should girls avoid most? Why?
5. What type of girls should young men avoid most? Why?
6. How important is prayer during courtship?
7. What is the meaning of true love? How does it differ from infatuation?
8. Is there such a thing as love at first sight?
9. "Love is blind; marriage an eye-opener." What do you think of this statement?
10. What is the greatest hazard of courtship?
11. How does one determine whether kissing is sinful or not?
12. Is petting ever lawful for the unmarried? What about French kissing?
13. Is there any rule regarding kissing that will be helpful to those in love?
14. What do marriage experts say regarding sexual experience before marriage?
15. What do marriage counselors have to say regarding college marriages? What do you think of them?
16. Which is preferable and why: a long courtship and short engagement, or a short courtship and long engagement?
17. What is the purpose of the engagement?
18. How does the formal engagement differ from the informal?
19. How long should an engagement last? What do the experts say?
20. Does an engagement confer any marital privileges? What is a good rule to keep in mind during this time?
21. What are Pre-Cana Conferences? Are any held in your area? If so, in what do they consist?
22. How important are week-end retreats for engaged couples? Do any exist in your area?
23. Find out your parents' attitude to engagements. How long do they say they should be? Why?
24. Survey some of your schoolmates (underclassmen) as to what they mean by the words "love"; "infatuation."
25. What suggestions would you give to a couple to perform during their months of engagement? Why?
26. Jim and Jan were among 10,000 who filled out a questionnaire including such key topics as sex, religion, and politics. Later these two were considered perfectly paired according to Univac. What do you think of this modern way of selecting a life mate?
27. "We know for a fact that we are going to be physically compatible,"

Betty says to you speaking about her premarital sex relations with her boy friend. What do you say to her?

28. "Broken engagements, which drew strong disapproval in the past, perform a useful function in the present." What do you think of this statement?

29. Marriage experts agree that the greatest enemy of success and happiness in marriage is not poverty, bodily weakness, sexual compatibility, parental interference, but emotional immaturity. What marks of maturity do you look for in a life mate?

30. How much should a young man spend on an engagement ring? Must a ring be given?

Chapter V

REVIEW QUESTIONS AND STUDY HELPS

1. Check with a recently married couple to discover whether the information in the text is correct for your area. Let the class know if there are any notable changes.

2. Draw up a list of the actual costs of the items the bride will be responsible for; the groom.

3. Study the prayers of the nuptial Mass. What teachings on marriage and family life do they suggest?

4. Bring into class announcements of marriage. See how they compare. What essentials of information should a good marriage announcement contain?

5. When should an engaged couple go to see their pastor to make preparations for marriage?

6. Which pastor should they consult?

7. What are the banns of marriage? Why must they be announced?

8. When may a marriage take place?

9. To whom can the nuptial blessing be given? How many times can a bride receive this blessing?

10. Describe the wedding ceremony proper.

11. Why should the entire wedding party, including relatives and friends, receive Holy Communion on the wedding day?

12. To whom is the Epistle of the Mass directed? What does it say?

13. Why should a Catholic always get married in connection with a nuptial Mass?

14. Is a nuptial Mass essential to the sacrament of marriage?

15. What are some of the current prices for engagement rings? wedding rings? Check with a local jeweler for your information.

16. Who is the proper minister of the sacrament of marriage?

17. Are there any special requirements as to number, sex, relationship, or religion for the official witnesses of a Catholic marriage?

18. What is the usual stipend or offering made to the officiating priest in your area? For what is the stipend used?

19. What are the civil requirements for marriage in your state?
20. Why is marriage called a sacrament of the living?
21. What does the wedding ring symbolize in the marriage ceremony?
22. What do you think about placing signs or writing on the car of the newlyweds?
23. Why must a couple see their pastor so much in advance of the actual date of marriage?
24. Must bridal apparel contain "something old, something new; something borrowed, something blue"? What about throwing the bridal bouquet? Is there any symbolism to these actions?
25. Should the pastor and assistants be sent a wedding invitation?

Chapter VI

REVIEW QUESTIONS AND STUDY HELPS

1. Interview a non-Catholic as to his Church's attitude toward mixed marriage. How does it compare with the teaching of the Catholic Church?
2. What is your present personal attitude toward mixed marriage? Did the reading of this chapter influence your attitude in any way?
3. If the Church condemns mixed marriages, why does the Church grant dispensations?
4. Why do so many mixed-marriage partners lose the faith?
5. What is your personal attitude toward interracial marriages? Would you marry a person not of your race if you were really in love?
6. Comment on the following statements:
   a) While an interfaith marriage is two or three times as likely to end in divorce or separation as a marriage between people of the same faith, the chances for success are high for any specific couple who approach the problems with intelligence and awareness.
   b) Interracial marriages are more likely to succeed than interfaith marriages.
   c) A mixed marriage robs parents of a common relationship with their children on the deepest level, namely the spiritual life.
   d) In our democratic society, it is entirely unequal to exact promises from the non-Catholic before allowing a mixed marriage to take place between a Catholic and a non-Catholic.
   e) Mixed marriages ought to be avoided at all costs because of their high rate of failure. Therefore dating members of other faiths should be forbidden.
   f) Why struggle over conflicts in religion. An interfaith married couple can resolve their religious difficulties by joining a third neutral religion agreeable to both.
   g) Laws have failed their purpose to prevent intermarriage of races; they have only created a perpetual interracial problem.

h) Religious differences don't matter. Man and woman differ in many ways. It makes marriage interesting. While it isn't always easy to adjust, love always finds a way.

i) Mixed marriages are a source of converts to the Catholic Faith.

j) In a mixed marriage a Catholic runs the risk of not receiving the sacrament of matrimony.

Chapter VII

REVIEW QUESTIONS AND STUDY HELPS

1. What is meant by "Marriage is not a 50–50 sort of arrangement, but a total 100–100 living of giving"?
2. What qualities or virtues in husband and wife will contribute most to harmonious adjustment in marriage?
3. What mistakes could make the "honeymoon" an occasion for unhappiness and disillusionment rather than the joyful occasion it should be?
4. What is meant by "A married couple is assured of success where the unselfish spirit of perfect sacrifice guides their every action"? List ten sacrifices husbands and wives are required to make in marriage.
5. List ten complementary differences of husband and wife. Why is it important that these differences be known by both?
6. Why did God give man the power of sex?
7. What is meant by "Some days in marriage are 25 hours along"?
8. List five ways in which you would handle a tension situation in marriage?
9. What is meant by "Never let the sun go down on an argument"?
10. What is meant by involuntary sterility, and what effect could it have on marriage?
11. What is artificial insemination, and why is it condemned by the Church?
12. What is meant by "It is essential that both husband and wife recognize that the use of sex in marriage is virtuous"?
13. What is the matter and the form of the sacrament of matrimony?
14. What is the Rh factor? How could this affect childbirth?
15. Does a doctor ever have the right of taking the life of a mother to save the baby or vice versa?
16. What steps are necessary in your area before a couple may adopt a child?
17. Explain what is meant by "black-market" and "gray-market" babies?
18. What is the Dr. Grantly Dick-Read method? How is this important in the birth of a child?
19. What place do children have in marriage? Why is adoption important and necessary in a marriage which has not been blessed with children?

Chapter VIII

REVIEW QUESTIONS AND STUDY HELPS

1. What is the teaching of the Catholic Church in regard to the number of children in a family? What is meant by the social and personal goals of marriage?
2. What is the moral argument against contraceptive birth control?
3. What do you understand by the term "intrinsically evil"? Name three other acts which are intrinsically evil.
4. What do you understand by the "natural law"? Why are contraceptive practices opposed to the natural law?
5. What is meant by the term "population explosion"? How does this affect the rise of birth-control propaganda and practices?
6. What common methods have been employed by man to limit the size of a family?
7. What is meant by sterilization? therapeutic? punitive? eugenic? Is sterilization ever lawful?
8. What is meant by the Law of Double Effect? Give an example of how this law is applied.
9. What do you understand by the rhythm method? What conditions are necessary to practice this method lawfully?
10. What is the main objection to the rhythm method?
11. Do contraception and rhythm have any possible evils in common? Explain.
12. What do you understand by abortion? therapeutic abortion? criminal abortion?
13. What methods of birth control were recommended by Thomas Malthus? How do these differ from the methods of the Planned Parenthood Federation of America?
14. Is it ever lawful to permit the death of an unborn child in order to save the life of the mother?
15. What is the attitude of Protestant churches toward contraception? How does their attitude compare with the Catholic Church's teaching?
16. Why is it important for a woman to know about the moral principles of her doctor?
17. What does this phrase mean: "Sex is for life, not life for sex"?
18. What means and methods may be lawfully used to prevent overpopulation in certain parts of the world?
19. Why may artificial contraception have a detrimental effect upon the mental health of its users? Will the Catholic Church ever change its present position on contraception?

Chapter IX

QUESTIONS AND STUDY HELPS

1. What do you understand by the term "divorce" as it is condemned by the Catholic Church?
2. How does divorce differ with separation? annulment? desertion?
3. Under what circumstances may an annulment be granted? Cite three cases.
4. What are the basic reasons for divorce?
5. Clip from the newspaper some recent divorce cases. What were the reasons cited for the divorce action? Are the given reasons the real reasons?
6. What is meant by marital fidelity? How is this assured in married life?
7. In what ways is divorce especially harmful to children?
8. What is adultery? Why is it a triple sin?
9. Where in Sacred Scripture is adultery condemned? in tradition?
10. Why is this true: "Divorce breeds divorce"?
11. What are the seven danger signals in marriage? Why are these important to recognize?
12. What is your state's laws regarding divorce and separation?
13. What procedure has the Church for handling marriage problems of Catholics?
14. Why is divorce on the increase in the United States?
15. What do you think of this statement? "There are no problemless marriages; marriages are a success only because both husband and wife have learned to solve their problems together."
16. How much importance should one give to the selection of a life mate in order to avoid a future divorce?
17. What does this expression mean: "Marriage is not a reform school"?
18. What do you think is the real cause for adultery?
19. What annoying grievances should a husband try to avoid in marriage? a wife?
20. How do lax divorce laws contribute to the increase of juvenile delinquency?

Chapter X

QUESTIONS AND STUDY HELPS

1. What is the most important contributing factor to successful home life? Why?
2. What are the duties and obligations of parents toward their children?
3. What are the duties and obligations of children toward their parents? How long does this obligation last?

211

4. What advantages does a large family have over an only-child family?
5. Survey five underclassmen as to what causes family frictions? How do these findings compare with those listed by the Youth Research Institute?
6. Why is it true to say that the child's first school is his home?
7. Clip from the newspaper examples of good family life; of poor family life. What are the leading contributing factors in each case?
8. How does a parent go about disciplining his child? Can parents ever be too severe? Give examples. Can parents ever be too weak and lax in this duty? Give examples.
9. Should children be spanked?
10. What does this mean: "The husband is the head, the wife, the heart of the home"?
11. What does this mean: "True education is a self-activated process"?
12. Explain: "The home is the child's first church."
13. Do you think today's parents are living up to all that is required of them in educating their children as to the facts of life? Explain your answer.
14. What does old age have to offer husband and wife?
15. Explain: "Life begins at forty."
16. What are your ideas about sex education for the young? When and how should it be given?
17. How is marital love increased as the years go on?
18. How is character formation of children mainly the duty of parents? Why must both father and mother co-operate in this task?
19. How important is it to have the family rosary said daily in the home? How important is it for married couples to join Cana groups or become members of the Christian Family Movement?
20. What is a married couples' retreat? Are there any held in your area?
21. Explain: "The school supplements the home but never supplants it."

212

FOOTNOTES

NOTES — CHAPTER I

[1] Ernest F. Miller, "Teenagers and Vocation," *The Liguorian*, XLIV, April, 1956, pp. 209–210.

[2] John A. O'Brien, *Marriage a Vocation* (Notre Dame, Ind.: Ave Maria Press, 1953), p. 18.

[3] *Quest for Happiness*, Book 4 (Chicago: Mentzer, Bush & Co., 1958), p. 199.

[4] "The Most Important Question," *Vocational Digest*, Holy Cross Fathers, Notre Dame, Ind., reprint.

[5] *Quest for Happiness, op. cit.,* p. 200.

[6] Raymond A. Tartre, S.S.S., "Signs of Priestly Vocation," *Emmanual*, March, 1959, pp. 116–117.

[7] *Ibid.,* p. 117.

[8] *Quest for Happiness, op. cit.,* pp. 202–203.

[9] *Ibid.,* p. 203.

[10] William D. Ryan, *Seven Steps to Tabor* (Chicago: J. S. Paluch Co., Inc.), pp. 8–9.

[11] *Quest for Happiness, op. cit.,* p. 207.

[12] *Ibid.,* p. 209.

[13] "I Am a Catholic Priest," K. C. pamphlet, St. Louis 8, Missouri, p. 7.

[14] Rev. Thomas E. Langer, "What Is a Priest?" *Our Sunday Visitor*, March 13, 1960.

[15] *Quest for Happiness, op. cit.,* p. 217.

[16] *Ibid.,* p. 220.

[17] Ida Mae Kempel, "God Can't Have Her!", *The Family Digest*, March, 1958.

[18] "God's Career Women," Msgr. Walter L. Fasnacht.

[19] Edward V. Stanford, O.S.A., *Preparing for Marriage* (Chicago: Mentzer, Bush & Co., 1958), pp. 22–23.

[20] Pius XII, *Woman's Duties in Social and Political Life* (New York: Paulist Press, 1945), pp. 7–8.

[21] Pius XII, *On Holy Virginity* (Washington, D. C.: National Catholic Welfare Conference, 1954), pp. 3–4.

[22] *Quest for Happiness, op. cit.,* p. 233.

[23] Ernest F. Miller, C.SS.R., "Teenagers and Single Life," *The Liguorian*, July, 1956, pp. 396–397.

[24] This essay was penned by Rose Mary Harry, a social worker of the Washington, D. C., area, upon request.

[25] Miller, *op. cit.,* p. 397.

[26] 1 Cor. 7:32–35.

[27] Raymond Bernard, S.J., "Secular Institutes," *America*, June 23, 1956, p. 301.

[28] Mary A. Grice, "God's Secret Service," *Our Sunday Visitor*, February 19, 1961, pp. 1–4.

[29] The author is indebted to the Catholic Youth Organization of the Archdiocese of Milwaukee (207 East Michigan Street, Milwaukee 2, Wisconsin) for the use of this material on careers.

NOTES — CHAPTER II

[1] Brother Gerald J. Schnepp, S.M., and Rev. Alfred F. Schnepp, S.M., *To God Through Marriage* (Milwaukee: Bruce, 1957), pp. 108–109.

[2] *Ibid.*, p. 9.

[3] "The Real Secret of Successful Marriage," K. C. pamphlet, St. Louis 8, Mo., pp. 25–26.

[4] *Ibid.*

[5] Rev. Henry V. Sattler, C.SS.R., "Marriage Is a Three-Ring Circus," *Our Sunday Visitor,* Oct. 13, 1957.

NOTES — CHAPTER III

[1] Very Rev. Msgr. George A. Kelly, "Parents and Their Children's Marriages," *Our Sunday Visitor,* June 5, 1960.

[2] Rt. Rev. Msgr. Francis W. Carney, S.T.D., "Help Your Children to Happy Marriages," *Columbia,* June, 1960, p. 18.

[3] *Ibid.*

[4] Edward V. Stanford, O.S.A., *Preparing for Marriage* (Chicago: Mentzer, Bush & Co.), p. 39.

[5] Ernest F. Miller, "Teen-agers and Dating," *The Liguorian,* Liguori, Mo., April, 1955.

[6] Alan Beck, "What Is a Boy?" Courtesy New England Mutual Life Insurance Company, 501 Boylston Street, Boston 17, Massachusetts.

[7] Alan Beck, "What Is a Girl?" Courtesy New England Mutual Life Insurance Company, 501 Boylston Street, Boston 17, Massachusetts.

[8] Paul H. Landis, *Your Dating Days* (New York: McGraw-Hill Book Co., 1954), p. 11.

[9] John J. O'Connor, S.J., *Preparation for Marriage and Family Life* (New York: The Paulist Press, 1947), p. 19 (out of print).

[10] *Ibid.*, pp. 21–22.

[11] Dr. Michael P. Penetar, "The Importance of Dating," *Our Sunday Visitor,* November 13, 1960.

[12] Philip Mooney, S.J., "Dating in Charity," *Today,* reprint.

[13] Roma Rudd Turkel, "The 'Going Steady' Crisis," *Information,* March, 1957.

[14] Stanford, *op. cit.,* pp. 43–44.

[15] Capt. J. L. Abbot, Jr., U.S.N., Assistant to the Commandant of Midshipmen, United States Naval Academy, "The Navy vs 'Going Steady,'" *Saturday Evening Post,* Vol. 230 (March, 1958), p. 36.

[16] See Joseph T. McGloin, S.J., *You Should Be Going Steady* (St. Louis: The Queen's Work, 1957).

[17] Stanford, *op. cit.,* p. 42.

[18] Rt. Rev. Msgr. Thomas J. Cawley, *Unwed Mother Speaks to Teen Girls* (Techny, Ill.: Divine Word Publications), pp. 7–16.

[19] Ed Willock, *Dating: a Guide for Parents* (Notre Dame, Ind.: Ave Maria Press, November, 1960).

214

NOTES — CHAPTER IV

[1] Dr. Michael P. Penetar, "The Meaning of Courtship," *Our Sunday Visitor,* December 11, 1960.

[2] Edward V. Stanford, *Preparing for Marriage* (Chicago: Mentzer, Bush & Co., 1958), p. 52.

[3] Clement S. Mihanovich, "Whom Should I Marry?" *Ave Maria,* June 11, 1960, p. 12.

[4] *Ibid.,* p. 13.

[5] Rev. Henry V. Sattler, C.SS.R., "Soundness of Body," *Our Sunday Visitor,* November, 1957.

[6] Mihanovich, *op. cit.,* p. 13.

[7] Rosalind Russell, "I'm Glad I Didn't Marry Young," *Reader's Digest,* February, 1959, p. 75.

[8] Charles Hugo Doyle, *Blame No One but Yourself* (Tarrytown, N. Y.: The Nugent Press, 1955), pp. 211–213.

[9] *Ibid.,* pp. 203–209.

[10] Msgr. J. D. Conway, *What They Ask About Marriage* (Chicago: Fides, 1955), pp. 4–6.

[11] Paul Popenoe, *Modern Marriage* (New York: The Macmillan Co., 1925), p. 12.

[12] John A. O'Brien, *Strategy in Courtship* (Notre Dame, Ind.: Ave Maria Press, 1954), pamphlet.

[13] Stanford, *op. cit.,* p. 82.

[14] Marjorie C. Cosgrove and Mary I. Josey, *About You* (Chicago: Science Research Associates, 1952), p. 67.

[15] Richard L. Rooney, "Out on a Date," *The Queen's Work,* April, 1954.

[16] Paul Popenoe, *Building Sex Into Your Life* (Los Angeles: A.I.F.R., 1930).

[17] Donald F. Miller, C.SS.R., "Privileges of the Engaged," *The Liguorian,* August, 1958.

[18] Popenoe, *Modern Marriage, op. cit.,* p. 113.

[19] Henry V. Sattler, C.SS.R., "Getting Ready for Marriage," *Our Sunday Visitor,* December 18, 1960.

[20] *Ibid.*

NOTES — CHAPTER V

[1] Harry S. Smith, C.SS.R., "Here Comes the Bride!" *The Liguorian,* June, 1958, p. 18.

[2] Edward V. Stanford, O.S.A., *Preparing for Marriage* (Chicago: Mentzer, Bush & Company, 1958), pp. 100–101.

[3] Msgr. James A. Magner, *A Check List for Your Wedding* (Notre Dame, Ind.: Ave Maria Press, 1959), pp. 11–12.

[4] Gerard Breitenbeck, C.SS.R., *How to Arrange for Your Wedding* (Liguori, Mo.: The Liguorian Press, 1957), pp. 17–18.

[5] *Ibid.,* p. 19.

[6] Magner, *op. cit.,* pp. 17–18.

[7] Stanford, *op. cit.,* pp. 108–109.

[8] Gerald Ellard, S.J., and Sister M. Anne Burns, O.S.B., *Service* (Chicago: Loyola University Press, 1951), pp. 37–39.

[9] Copyright by St. Anthony's Guild, Paterson, N. J. — Permission granted.

[10] Stanford, *op. cit.,* p. 110.

NOTES — CHAPTER VI

[1] Dorothy Dix, *Philadelphia Evening Ledger,* December 1, 1936.

[2] *America,* August 1, 1931, p. 394.

[3] Alice Case, "I Refused to Risk an Inter-Faith Marriage," *The Family Digest,* March, 1960, pp. 25–28.

[4] Helen Wayne, "Marriage, Mixed or Unmixed," *Our Sunday Visitor,* October 2, 1960.

[5] Edward V. Stanford, *Preparing for Marriage* (Chicago: Mentzer, Bush & Co., 1958), p. 72.

NOTES — CHAPTER VII

[1] Germain Flammand, "The Mystery of Love," *Our Sunday Visitor,* Huntington, Ind., February 3, 1957, p. 4.

[2] Edgar Schmiedeler, O.S.B., *Looking Toward Marriage* (Washington, D. C.: N.C.W.C. Family Life Bureau), p. 22.

[3] Fulton J. Sheen, *Three to Get Married* (New York: Appleton-Century-Croft, Inc.), pp. 151–152.

[4] Alphonse Clemens, *Marriage and the Family* (Englewood Cliffs, N. J.: Prentice-Hall, Inc., 1957), pp. 155–156.

[5] Clifford R. Adams, "Making Marriage Work," *Ladies Home Journal,* September, 1960. p. 34.

[6] Edward V. Stanford, *Preparing for Marriage* (Chicago: Mentzer, Bush & Co., 1960), p. 126.

[7] Rev. James J. Killgallon, "The Church and Sex," *Ave Maria,* February 21, 1959 (Notre Dame, Ind.: The Ave Maria Press).

[8] Pope Pius XII, "Apostolate of the Midwife," 1951, *Papal Pronouncements on Marriage and the Family,* Alvin Werth and Clement S. Mihanovich (Milwaukee: The Bruce Publishing Co., 1955), p. 65.

[9] Killgallon, *op. cit.*

[10] Stanford, *op. cit.,* p. 128.

[11] Henry V. Sattler, C.SS.R., "Two in One Flesh," *Our Sunday Visitor,* November 22, 1959.

[12] Mae M. Bookmiller, R.N., and George L. Bowem, M.D., *Textbook of Obstetrics and Obstetric Nursing* (Philadelphia: W. B. Saunders Co., 1954), pp. 81–133.

[13] *Ibid.,* pp. 44–46.

[14] G. O. Nabors, M.D., "The Rh Factor Reconsidered," *Marriage,* September, 1960, Vol. 42, No. 9, pp. 13–15; Courtesy of the Metropolitan Life Insurance Company.

[15] G. O. Nabors, M.D., "Save the Mother . . . and the Baby," *Marriage,* February, 1961, Vol. 43, No. 2, pp. 53–54.

[16] Joseph A. Owens, "Frontier in Catholic Adoption," *Voice of St. Jude,* October, 1960, p. 10.

[17] Joseph H. Reed, "Let's Stop Giving Babies Away," *Family Weekly,* May 1, 1960, pp. 8–9.

[18] Rev. Walter Imbiorski, ed., *The New Cana Manual* (Oak Park, Ill.: Delaney Publications, 1957), p. 120.

[19] Joseph B. McAllister, *Ethics* (Philadelphia: W. B. Saunders Co., 1955), p. 351.

[20] Pius XII, address to the Fourth International Congress of Catholic Doctors, September 29, 1949, quoted by Thomas J. O'Donnell, S.J., *Morals in Medicine* (Westminster, Md.: The Newman Press, 1959), p. 304.

[21] Pius XII, address to Second World Congress on Fertility and Sterility, *The Pope Speaks,* Vol. 3, Autumn, 1956, pp. 193–194.

NOTES — CHAPTER VIII

[1] Alfred M. Rehwinkel, *Planned Parenthood and Birth Control in the Light of Christian Ethics* (St. Louis, Mo.: Concordia Publishing House, 1959), p. 16.

[2] Philip Goldstein, *Genetics Is Easy* (New York: Lantern Press, 1956), p. 222 ff.

[3] Pope Pius XI, *On Christian Marriage* (New York: The Paulist Press, 1931), p. 18.

[4] "The New Fertility Test and Rhythm," a *Marriage* pamphlet, St. Meinrad, Ind., p. 12.

[5] Gerald Kelly, S.J., distinguishes between obligation and ideal in this matter, *Grail,* March, 1955, p. 17.

[6] "The New Fertility Test and Rhythm," *ibid.,* pp. 13–14.

[7] John R. Cavanagh, M.D., "The Psychological Effects of Birth Prevention," *Marriage,* St. Meinrad's, Ind., September, 1960, p. 9.

[8] "Abortion Facts Reported," *Science News Letter,* Vol. 78, August 6, 1960, p. 86.

[9] Alfred M. Rehwinkel, *op. cit.,* p. 39.

[10] *Moral Aspects of Birth Control,* New York, 1938, issued by the Committee on Marriage and the Home of the Federal Council of Churches of Christ in America, p. 5.

[11] Rehwinkel, *op. cit.,* pp. 41–42.

[12] Pius XI, *op. cit.,* p. 17.

NOTES — CHAPTER IX

[1] John J. Kane, "Why Marriages Fail," *Voice of St. Jude,* September, 1960, p. 34.

[2] Judson C. Landis and Mary G. Landis, *Personal Adjustment, Marriage and Family Living* (Englewood, N. J.: Prentice-Hall, Inc., 1955), p. 267.

[3] Howard Whitman, "Divorce Granted," *Reader's Digest,* October, 1954.

[4] Jim Collison, "America's Divorce Scandal," *Ave Maria,* July 2, 1960, pp. 5–7.

[5] L. H. Terman, *Psychological Factors in Marital Happiness* (New York: McGraw-Hill Book Co., 1938).

[6] *Detailed Statistics on Divorces and Annulments,* 1955, Vol. 46, No. 4, p. 95 published by The National Office of Vital Statistics, U. S. Department of Health, Education and Welfare, April 9, 1957, indicate that 50.2 per cent of divorces occur in marriages where there are no children and an additional 22.8 per cent occur in marriages with only one child.

[7] Howard Whitman, *op. cit.*

[8] Msgr. George A. Kelly, "Seven Danger Signals in Marriage," *The Sign,* April, 1961, pp. 12–14.

[9] Edward V. Stanford, O.S.A., *Preparing for Marriage* (Chicago: Mentzer, Bush & Co., 1960), pp. 172–173.

[10] *Ibid.,* pp. 174–175.

NOTES — CHAPTER X

[1] Rev. George A. Kelly, *The Catholic Family Handbook* (New York: Random House, 1959), p. 18.

[2] Edward V. Stanford, *Preparing for Marriage* (Chicago: Mentzer, Bush & Co., 1960), p. 184.

[3] Kelly, *op. cit.,* p. 19.

[4] *The American Weekly,* August 4, 1957, p. 4.

[5] Msgr. George A. Kelly, *The Catholic Marriage Manual* (New York: Random House, 1958), pp. 183–184.

[6] Stanford, *op. cit.,* p. 189.

[7] Robert P. Odenwald, M.D., "Teaching Responsibility to Your Child," *Ave Maria,* March 26, 1960, p. 7.

[8] *Ibid.,* p. 6.

[9] Stanford, *op. cit.,* p. 191.

[10] Rev. John L. Thomas, S.J., *Catholic Laymen in the Crisis of the Modern American Family,* NCCM reprint, p. 7.

[11] Stanford, *op. cit.,* pp. 192–193.

[12] Kelly, *The Catholic Marriage Manual, op. cit.,* p. 6.

[13] *Together in Christ,* Washington, D. C., National Catholic Welfare Conference Family Life Bureau, "Of Cabbages and Things," p. 7.

[14] Pope Pius XI, *On Christian Marriage* (New York: Paulist Press, 1930), pp. 38–39.

[15] Timothy Reilley, O.Praem., "The Family Allowance Plan," *Our Sunday Visitor,* June 30, 1957.

[16] Selig Greenberg, "The Later Years," *Grail,* December, 1958, St. Meinrad Abbey, St. Meinrad, Ind.

INDEX

gluttony, 171 f; evil of, 171; Federal Council of Churches on, 169 f; intrinsically evil, 171 f; Lutherans on, 170; in mixed marriage, 125 f; 1930 Lambeth Conference on, 169; by pills, 162; Pius XI on, 170 f; Sanger, Margaret, on, 168 f

Costs, in first year of marriage, 145

Courtship, chaste, 86; importance of, 72; infatuation in, 73; meaning of, 73 f; Pius XI on, 72, 82; prayer during, 82; prelude to, 65; questions that should be asked, 85

Dating, beginning of, 58; definition of, 58; and drinking, 70; Fleege, Urban, on, 61; group, 70; importance of, 60 f; Kelly, Gerald, on, 61; and parking, 70; prayer before, 71; qualities in a partner, 69 f; rules, 70; sensible, 68 f; serious, 60; social, 59; ultimate purpose of, 61

Death, certificate required in desertion, 185; infant rate, 151; maternal rate, 151

Desertion, definition of, 185

Dissolution of marriage, 50 f; nonconsummated marriage, 51; Pauline Privilege, 51; Privilege of the Faith, 51

Divorce, 174 ff; among childless couples, 177, 188; breeds divorce, 179; calamity for children involved in, 178 f; causes of, 44 f, 177; Church's teaching on, 179 f; definition of, 174, 184; involving teens, ix; number of, 174; number of children affected, 177 f; partial, 185; rate of, in mixed marriage, 122 f; reasons for, 175 f; St. John Chrysostom on, 182; St. Mark on, 45; St. Matthew on, 43; Scripture and Tradition on, 179 f

Education, begins at home, 194; of children, 194; qualification for life mate, 77; responsibility of parents, 192 ff; sex, 195 f

Elopement, definition of, 49

Engagement, breaking off, 94 f; definition of, 90; formal or solemn, 90 ff; informal, 90; length of, 92 f; liberties in, 92; marks of affection in, 92; Paul Popenoe on, 93; prayer during, 93 f; reasons for breaking off, 95; retreat during, 94; ring, 91

Family, frictions, 189 f; large, 189; responsibility of, 193 f; source of happiness in marriage, 188

Family Allowance Plan, 199

Family planning, 157 ff; Church's teaching on, 157 ff; see also Rhythm

Fatherhood, 198

Feeblemindedness, causes of, 160; and eugenic sterilization, 159 ff

Fertilization, 150

Finances in marriage, see Budget

Going steady, 61 ff; adults and, 63; allowed, 65; definition of, 62; high school opposition to, 66; how many marry, 65; moral problem of, 64 f; and pregnancy, 66 ff; reasons for, 62; sinful situation, 65; social harm of, 62 f; U. S. Navy on, 63 f

Groom, prayer of, 118 f; responsibilities of, 104 f

Health, qualification for lifemate, 77

Home, education begins at, 194; environment in mixed marriage, 124 f; religious attitudes in, 194 f

Honeymoon, 138 f; at home, 138 f; sexual adjustment in, 138

Impediments to marriage, invalidating, 48 ff; prohibitive, 47 f

Impotency, definition of, 48; impediment to valid marriage, 48

Income, in first year of marriage, 144 f

Indissolubility, 43 ff, 50

Infanticide, 159

Infatuation, 83; compared to love, 84; Conway, Msgr. J. D., on, 84; in courtship, 73

Interfaith marriages, see Mixed marriage

Interracial marriage, 135 f; laws on, 107

Interviews, see Careers

Invalid marriage, 50

Invitations, for marriage, 103; when to send, 103

Kidnapping, as impediment to marriage, 49

Kissing, 86 ff; boy's attitude toward,

who enter into, 127; religious disputes in, 124 ff
Mixed religion, as impediment, 48
Money, in marriage, 144 f; *see also* Budget
Monogamy, 43
Moral character, qualifications for a lifemate, 78 f
Moral restraint, in marriage, Thomas Malthus on, 168; *see also* Continence
Motherhood, 198

Natural birth control, 158; Pius XI on, 163 f; *see also* Rhythm
Natural childbirth, 155 f; Grantly Dick-Read on, 156
Natural law, contraception perverts, 171
Non-Catholic, concessions in mixed marriage, 122 f; on contraception, 169 ff; instructions in mixed marriage, 99
Nonconsummated marriage, dissolution of, 51
Nuptial blessing, 115 f; forbidden in Lent and Advent, 101, 116 f; forbidden in mixed marriage, 116; forbidden to widows, 116
Nuptial Mass, 103 f; Epistle of, 113 f; Gospel of, 114; souvenir booklet of, 113

Old age, 199 f
Onanism, 162; St. Augustine on, 162
Overpopulation, Malthus, Thomas, on, 168; problem of, 172 f; solutions to, 172 f

Parental love, 54
Parenthood, 148 ff
Parents, administering punishment, 193; Kelly, Msgr. George A., on, 191 f; objections to childrens' behavior, 190; obligations toward children, 191 f; overprotective, 191; overrestrictive, 191; perfectionist, 192; Thomas, John L., on, 196; today's challenge for, 196
Partial divorce, *see* Separation
Pastor, consultation with, 97
Pauline Privilege, 51; *see also* Dissolution of marriage
Personality, 137; meaning of, 74; Ter-

man, Lewis T., on, 74 f; traits to look for in a man, 75; traits to look for in a woman, 74 f
Petting and necking, 87, 92
Photographer, professional, at wedding, 102
Planned parenthood, 158; *see also* Contraception
Planned Parenthood Federation of America, number of clinics in U. S., 169
Planning a wedding, duties of bride and bride's family, 104; groom's responsibilities, 104 f; professional photographer allowed, 102; *see also* Premarital instructions
Polygamy, 43; elimination of, 173
Prayer, throughout marriage, 200
Pre-Cana instructions, during engagement, 94; need of, x
Pregnancy, before marriage, 66 ff; in marriage, 150 f
Premarital instructions, 98; given by, 100; questionnaire, 99 f; special requests, 101; supplying necessary documents, 98 f; time of, 98
Prenuptial promises, by the Catholic, 134; in mixed marriage, 132 ff; by the non-Catholic, 133 f
Priestly or religious life, as impediment to marriage, 49; *see also* Religious and priestly state
Primary purpose of marriage, 41 f
Privilege of the Faith, 51; *see also* Dissolution of marriage
Punishment, of children, 192 f; by sterilization, 160 f

Religious and priestly state, the brotherhoods, 17 f; diocesan clergy, 14; impediments to, 11 f; Kempel, Ida Mae, on, 21 ff; kinds of Brothers, 18; kinds of Sisters, 19 f; knowledge of, 5; mental fitness of candidate, 9; moral fitness, 7 ff; need of Brothers, 19; need of Sisters, 20 f; neglecting the call, 12; physical fitness, 10; religious orders and congregations, 14 f; right intention, 10 f; St. Francis of Assisi on, 13; St. Thomas on, 6; seminary routine, 15 f; signs of, 6 ff; the Sisterhoods, 19; testing the call, 12 f; what is a nun?, 22 f